Education for the Embodied Human

Global Education in the 21st Century Series

The titles published in this series are listed at *brill.com/gecs*

Education for
the Embodied Human

*A Contemporary Understanding on Human Nature
for Holistic Education*

By

Akhil K. Singh

BRILL

LEIDEN | BOSTON

Cover illustration: iStock.com/lolloj

All chapters in this book have undergone peer review.

The Library of Congress Cataloging-in-Publication Data is available online at https://catalog.loc.gov

Typeface for the Latin, Greek, and Cyrillic scripts: "Brill". See and download: brill.com/brill-typeface.

ISSN 2542-9728
ISBN 978-90-04-72435-8 (paperback)
ISBN 978-90-04-72436-5 (hardback)
ISBN 978-90-04-72437-2 (e-book)
DOI 10.1163/9789004724372

Contents

Preface

This book investigates the intricate relationship between understanding of human nature and education. It questions the dominant dualistic notion in modern mainstream education—that the mind-body and human-world are distinct. This divisive notion not only alienates students from their surroundings, but it also encourages an exam-centric, achievement-driven system that undermines critical thinking and an exploratory mind-set. At the very core of this problem is a fundamental misunderstanding about human nature. Because educational procedures are invariably impacted by underlying assumptions about human nature, this misunderstanding permeates our educational endeavours as well. Thus, revisiting our assumptions about human nature becomes vital in educational design and reform.

Further, even a cursory examination of classical notions regarding human nature reveals that they often arise from philosophical speculation with dualistic tendencies. However, recent empirical study in cognitive science paints a different picture. According to contemporary research, humans are profoundly embodied and inextricably linked to their physical and social environments. This embodiment is the result of a dynamic integration of mind, body, and environment, which challenges the old divisive perspective. But, despite the growing body of research supporting the embodied characteristics of humans, this dualistic notion is frequently neglected in everyday life and educational discourse, owing to a variety of psychological, neurological, and social reasons.

Therefore, to address the issue, we need to employ a dual-structured approach: outer and inner curricula. The outer curriculum employs an "outside-in" technique, developing pedagogies that are consistent with embodied concepts. However, simply modifying pedagogies externally will be inadequate without an internal realisation of our embodied identities. An inner curriculum that fosters transformation from the "inside-out" can help to cultivate this realisation. Mindfulness meditation techniques are vital to this inner curriculum, as they increase self-awareness of our thoughts and sensations, building a stronger connection with our embodied nature and the world around us.

This integrated approach to education, which emphasises both the exterior and inner curricula, aims to foster a more democratic and collaborative learning approaches. This work, in turns, is in line with the visions of prominent educational thinkers of twentieth century, with the goal of developing a more engaged and holistic educational environment.

Acknowledgements

This book, which has evolved from my PhD work, owes its existence to the support and guidance of numerous individuals. Foremost, I extend my deepest gratitude to my research advisor Dr. V. Hari Narayanan, whose mentorship was instrumental in shaping both the original research and its adaptation into this book. His commitment to rigorous inquiry and critical thinking has profoundly influenced my academic journey.

I also owe a significant debt of gratitude to the members of my research committee and the external reviewers. Their insightful feedback and thoughtful critiques were pivotal in refining my work and provided the encouragement needed to pursue its transformation into this publication.

I would also like to express my appreciation to my friends, colleagues and the broader academic community at IIT Jodhpur. Their diverse perspectives and ongoing support have been invaluable in broadening my understanding of the complex issues addressed in this work.

Finally, I am immensely grateful to my family—my parents, siblings, and in-laws—whose unwavering support and motivation have been the bedrock of my success. To my wife, whose love, understanding, and companionship have been my guiding light, I offer my heartfelt thanks.

Figures

Abbreviations

DST	Dynamical System Theory
EEG	Electro Encephalography
FA	Focused Attention
FMRI	Functional Magnetic Resonance Imaging
L1	First/Native Language
L2	Second Language
LOT	Language of Thought
OM	Open Monitoring
SESI	Social Service Ministry
TLSR	Translational Learning Sciences Research
TMS	Trans-cranial Magnetic Stimulation

CHAPTER 1

Introduction

All educational practice implies a theoretical stance on the educator's part. This stance in turn implies—sometimes more, sometimes less explicitly—interpretation of man and the world.
    PAULO FREIRE (1970a, p. 5)

• • •

Whatever we do in teaching depends upon what we think people
are like.
    ARTHUR COMBS (1962, p. 1)

• •
•

These two quotations encapsulate the central impetus behind the present
work. They underscore a fundamental premise: *the need to understand human
nature as an essential foundation for effective educational discourse.* Our beliefs
about human learning, motivation, and intrinsic tendencies directly shape the
educational approaches and methodologies we adopt. If we believe that learners are passive and require external coercion to engage in learning, this belief
may lead us to favour authoritarian teaching methods, emphasizing control
and compliance. Conversely, if we view learners as inherently curious and self-
driven, we may adopt student-centred pedagogies that prioritize autonomy,
creativity, and exploration. Similarly, if we assume that abilities are fixed, educational practices may lean towards rote memorization and standardized testing, rather than fostering critical thinking and growth. Thus, reflecting on our
assumptions about human nature is crucial to developing a more nuanced and
effective approach to education.

For centuries, human nature has been a subject of deep inquiry among
philosophers, theologians, and scientists. Traditionally defined as the shared
characteristics that distinguish humans from other species, human nature
encompasses the fundamental dispositions, ways of thinking, feeling, and acting that are considered intrinsic to the human condition (Duignan, 2016). Disciplines such as biology, sociology, psychology, anthropology, and philosophy

have each explored the concept of human nature, offering varied perspectives shaped by their unique methodologies and assumptions. Yet, despite these extensive inquiries, a single, definitive understanding of human nature remains elusive. Each discipline provides insights that are, at best, partial and context-specific, resulting in explanations that are often fragmented and discipline-bound.

Historically, human nature has often been understood through a dualistic lens, especially within Western philosophical traditions, which posit a fundamental separation between the physical body and the non-physical mind. This dualistic worldview has profoundly influenced educational systems, many of which continue to operate under the assumption that the mind and body are distinct and separate entities. Even today, as Manuela Macedonia (2019) observes, this dualistic perspective remains deeply embedded in modern mainstream education, shaping not only pedagogical practices but also broader educational objectives. Rooted in the philosophical tradition of mind-body dualism, this paradigm has significantly influenced educational practices, particularly in Western education systems and countries influenced by Western ideologies. At the core of this approach, the mind is often regarded as the seat of reason, intelligence, and consciousness, while the body is seen merely as a vessel, secondary to the cognitive functions of the mind. This view can be traced back to thinkers like René Descartes, who famously declared, "Cogito, ergo sum" ("I think, therefore I am"), emphasizing the primacy of thought over the physical body. Moreover, this view is so intensely ingrained in our thinking that, despite numerous pedagogical advancements, the mentalistic emphasis remains prevalent, perpetuating a limited view of human potential and development.

However, recent years have seen a significant shift in how human nature is understood, largely driven by advancements in cognitive science and empirical research. Contemporary scientific theories, particularly those informed by the theory of evolution and embodied cognition, challenge the long-standing dominance of dualistic thought. These theories propose that humans are inherently embodied beings—creatures whose cognitive, emotional, and behavioural capacities are deeply intertwined with their physical and social environments. This embodied perspective marks a departure from traditional mentalistic approaches, emphasizing the integral role of the body in shaping human cognition, emotion, and behaviour. This perspective holds profound implications for education. If humans are indeed embodied beings, then educational practices must account for the body's essential role in learning and development. Education, in this view, should not only address cognitive skills but also foster physical, emotional, and social growth, recognizing these dimensions as inseparable components of the human experience.

Yet, despite compelling evidence supporting the embodied nature of human beings, dualistic conceptions of mind and body continue to exert a powerful influence on educational discourse and practice. This persistent dualism raises critical questions: Why does this outdated perspective remain so deeply entrenched in our educational systems? What barriers prevent the adoption of a more holistic, embodied approach to education? These questions are not merely academic; they strike at the very core of how we conceive of education's role in human development. To move beyond the limitations of dualistic thinking, it is necessary to redesign educational systems with a clear recognition of the embodied nature of human beings. This requires a paradigm shift that integrates the latest insights from cognitive science and acknowledges the diverse cultural, social, and economic contexts in which education takes place.

It is also important to recognize that education must be understood as a dynamic process deeply influenced by the specificities of time and place, rather than a one-size-fits-all model imposed uniformly across different regions and cultures. Although this book primarily discusses what it means to be human and, consequently, how we educate, human nature cannot be universally defined without considering the various forces that shape human identity and behaviour. Social, cultural, economic, and political factors all contribute to our understanding of human nature, making it a concept that is far from a simple, universal, fixed idea. As such, mainstream education should not be viewed as a monolithic entity, nor should the concept of human nature be detached from its contextual underpinnings. Effective educational practices must be responsive to these diverse influences, offering a more comprehensive and contextually informed approach to human development.

Furthermore, it is important to note that the claim of dualism is understood as universal, applying to all human beings across cultures. Similarly, if embodiment is true, it too is universal. Although embodiment may manifest in different ways, the underlying principle can be considered universal due to its biological basis. This is akin to how different metaphors can be used to understand the same abstract concept, but the fact that abstract concepts are understood metaphorically is a universal phenomenon. Additionally, if metaphors are absent, understanding becomes vacuous—an implication that may hold universally. In the same way, educational practices may vary widely, yet there can still be an underlying common factor if they presuppose dualism or embodiment.

For this reason, the present work does not claim to provide a unified and ultimate answer but sets the stage for a deeper exploration of how an embodied understanding of human nature can reshape educational practices in ways that better align with the realities of human experience. By critically examining the assumptions underlying mainstream education and challenging the persistent dualistic notion that has shaped it, this work aims to contribute to the development of a more holistic and inclusive educational paradigm.

We are in the age of scientific exploration, and humans are now considered to be embodied beings rather than primarily mental ones. Current empirical evidence supports the view that humans are inherently embodied. This shift has been largely influenced by advancements in cognitive science, which highlight the interconnectedness of the body and mind. The embodied perspective acknowledges the importance of the body in shaping human cognition, emotion, and behaviour, asserting that the body is central to understanding what it means to be human. This new perspective has significant implications for education. If humans are primarily embodied, education must consider the crucial role the body plays in cognition, emotion, and behaviour. It must also recognize the significance of embodiment in human growth and provide opportunities for students to develop their physical, emotional, and social abilities. Additionally, despite evidence supporting the embodied nature of humans, it is essential to question why the dualistic concept continues to prevail in our daily lives and educational practices. Addressing this dualistic dominance is crucial for redesigning educational systems to better reflect the embodied nature of humans.

Building on these foundations, this work addresses the following four key questions:

1. How does a particular assumption about human nature impact the conception of education?
2. How can we formulate a comprehensive theory of human nature based on available evidence?
3. How does embodied cognition theory offer a compelling explanation of human nature?
4. In what ways can we restructure our educational practices based on an evidence-based (embodied) theory of human nature?

These questions are intended to help us understand our inherent, embodied nature and its impact on education. They explore the relationship between our self-awareness and educational practices, suggesting ways to align pedagogy with the latest theories on human nature. Through embodied education, students are expected to form stronger connections with their environment, gain a deeper understanding of themselves and their inner experiences, and interact with the physical world in a healthier way. Ultimately, this awareness may lead students to recognize that they are not isolated from nature but rather an integral part of it. At its core, this book seeks to contribute an additional step towards designing a holistic learning environment, one that recognizes and values learners as complete, subjective, and embodied individuals.

1   Overview of the Chapters

The present work is structured into seven chapters, each designed to build upon the core themes of understanding human nature, developing the concept of embodied human nature, and exploring its implications for education. The chapters progress from theoretical understanding of human nature to applying the understanding in educational context, offering a comprehensive analysis that bridges philosophical discourse with actionable educational strategies.

   Chapter 1: Introduction, sets the stage for the entire work, outlining the fundamental assumptions and objectives of the study. It highlights the central premise that our views on human nature profoundly influence educational practices. By framing the study within the broader context of educational philosophy, it establishes the groundwork for subsequent discussions on embodied human nature and its relevance to contemporary education.

   Chapter 2: The Interplay between Education and Human Nature, delves into the connection between education and human nature, presenting a broad overview of education as a social institution and its role in shaping human behaviour. This chapter posits that educational practices are deeply rooted in underlying beliefs about human nature. To investigate this hypothesis, the chapter focuses on three influential educators from distinct cultural backgrounds: John Dewey, Paulo Freire, and Jiddu Krishnamurti. Each thinker's perspective on human nature and education is examined in three dimensions: their views on human nature, their educational philosophy, and the connection between the two. This analysis aims to reveal how these educators' philosophical frameworks reflect their conceptions of human nature and influence their educational practices. By triangulating their viewpoints, the chapter seeks to validate the claim that a nuanced understanding of human nature is crucial for developing effective educational methods.

   Chapter 3: Understanding Human Nature: Theories and Debates, provides an in-depth exploration of human nature, beginning with a historical overview of major theories. It covers classical philosophical and religious perspectives, as well as modern scientific and evolutionary theories. This chapter identifies two primary debates within the discourse on human nature: the mind-body relationship and the nature versus nurture debate. It argues that a synthesis of these perspectives, through the lens of embodiment, offers a more comprehensive understanding of human nature. The emerging framework of embodiment is discussed as a way to reconcile the dualistic views of mind and body, suggesting that human cognition, emotion, and behaviour are deeply intertwined with our physical existence. This chapter lays the theoretical foundation for subsequent discussions on embodied human nature.

Chapter 4: Foundations of Embodied Human Nature, shifts focus to embodied cognition, a theory that challenges traditional cognitive science perspectives. The chapter begins by examining the motivations behind the emergence of embodied cognition and its critique of symbolic computation theories. It explores the phenomenological roots of embodied cognition and presents empirical evidence supporting this approach. By highlighting studies that demonstrate how mental properties emerge from bodily interactions with the environment, this chapter builds a compelling case for the embodied nature of humans. The objective is to illustrate that traditional cognitive theories, which separate mental processes from physical experiences, are insufficient for a complete understanding of human nature. This chapter thus serves as a pivotal point in transitioning from theoretical discussions related to human nature to practical implications in education.

Chapter 5: Rethinking Education through Embodied Approach, translates the concept of embodied human nature to educational theory. It critiques the dualistic paradigm prevalent in mainstream education, which often prioritizes mentalistic approaches and relegates the body to a secondary role. This chapter investigates the origins of these biases, tracing them to philosophical, psychological, socioeconomic, and political factors. It also examines how the brain's hemispheric division contributes to dualistic thinking. The chapter proposes two key strategies for integrating an embodied perspective into education: an "outside-in" approach that aligns educational practices with embodied theory, and an "inside-out" approach that fosters self-awareness of our embodied nature. This chapter sets the stage for the practical applications of embodied education discussed in the following chapter.

Chapter 6: Embodied Education in Practice: Designing Holistic Learning Environments, serves as a critical transition from the theoretical discussions presented in the previous chapters to the real-world application of embodied principles in educational settings. This chapter is dedicated to exploring how the concept of embodied human nature can be effectively integrated into teaching practices, curriculum design, and the broader educational environment. It argues that recognizing and leveraging the embodied nature of human cognition can lead to more holistic, engaging, and effective educational experiences. The chapter is structured into two main sections: Designing an Embodied Pedagogy and Realizing Our Embodied Nature. The first section focuses on the practical design and implementation of educational practices that align with the principles of embodied cognition. It begins by challenging the traditional view of learning as a purely cognitive process, isolated from the body and environment. Instead, it presents a compelling case for understanding learning as an inherently embodied activity, where cognition is deeply intertwined with sensory-motor experiences and physical interactions with the world. For example, gestures, which are used implicitly in any kind of learning process, demonstrate this. I also provide examples of two subjects, English and mathematics, to show that linguistic and mathematical learning is embodied in nature, even though these subjects are typically considered abstract and mental.

The second section of the chapter addresses the more complex and introspective aspect of embodied education—helping students and educators become more aware of their embodied nature. It argues that beyond designing an embodied pedagogy, there is a need to cultivate self-awareness of our physical and emotional selves as integral to the learning process. This section is closely related to what the chapter terms the "inner curriculum." The chapter also highlights the importance of mindfulness practices and its potential outcomes such as improved mental health, greater social and emotional skills, enhanced creativity, and a stronger sense of connection to oneself and others. The chapter concludes by envisioning a future where education fully embraces the embodied nature of human beings, leading to more compassionate, inclusive, and effective learning environments.

Chapter 7: Conclusion: A Path Forward, summarizes the key findings and contributions of the study. It reflects on how the exploration of human nature and embodied education has informed the development of educational practices. The chapter also acknowledges the study's limitations and suggests areas for future research. By synthesizing the insights gained throughout the work, this chapter aims to offer a comprehensive conclusion that reinforces the importance of integrating an embodied perspective into education.

CHAPTER 2

The Interplay between Education and Human Nature

Education is an essential component of any functioning society. Education helps in developing knowledge, skills, values, and attitudes, which are crucial for the overall progress of humans and society at large. Education has a long history, and the concept of education can be traced back to early civilizations in one form or another. This is done to ensure that the population is well-informed, disciplined, and well-prepared for the challenging political, social, and economic environments. Education is also used as a tool to create, maintain, enhance, and transmit social values, beliefs and culture. The institutionalized transfer of knowledge and learning is what makes us different from animals in this aspect. However, formal educational set-up tends to be less common in primitive societies since people lived in small groups. But as society gradually developed into bigger groups, it attached more importance to formal set-ups of education.

Education is the result of conscious effort that directly or indirectly affects every human being across the globe. Moreover, it is an important human activity that is performed to influence our behaviours, relations and choices. That means education plays an important role in defining our role as humans and specifying our actions in the world. Therefore, it is very important to understand the very target of the whole educational activity i.e., human beings. Undoubtedly, a deliberate effort for knowledge transfer can only be designed with the help of some conceptions about human beings, their fundamental nature, capacities, and limitations. Therefore, it is vital to understand human beings first before discussing education. This chapter is dedicated to illuminate the connection between human nature and education. I explore the initial hypothesis that "a particular conception about human nature influences the educational discourse." I shall begin the discussion by outlining the role and nature of education in human society. Then in the second section, I shall discuss how a particular assumption about human nature influences educational practices. Based on these discussions, I shall argue that the philosophy of human nature is a precursor to the philosophy of education. To validate this hypothesis, I shall review three prominent educationists from different parts of the globe. The discussion shows that there is a close interrelation between a particular assumption about human nature and education. This chapter will pave the way for our in-depth discussion about human nature in the next chapter.

© AKHIL K. SINGH, 2025 | DOI:10.1163/9789004724372_002

1   The Role of Education in Human Society

Passing on experiences and knowledge to the next generation is one of human-kind's most ancient practices. This process involves the transfer of all those experiences of parents and society that will help offspring to produce changes in their behaviour as well as modifications of surroundings. Humans are the only organism that has created such large societal structures in the whole evolutionary history. Moreover, unlike other animals, human progress is the result of more collective and cooperative activities through social institutions. Also, these social institutions are the result of human imagination and mutual trust among all members. But, as these institutions are the result of human's unique imagination capabilities and knowledge acquisition, they cannot be transferred to the next generation through genetic means immediately. Therefore, it becomes necessary to make a system through which society's laws, customs, knowledge, and procedures can be transferred to the future generation. Hence conscious effort is required to ensure the existence of the social structures even after one generation. Although the form of this deliberate transfer usually varies in respect of region, culture, and time, it is assumed to be present in almost every complex society. Every generation, at the minimum, holds this responsibility of understanding nature and transferring existing knowledge to next generation for enhanced control over the environment in expectation of better survival conditions. In short, education can be thought of as the institution for transmission of the values and accumulated knowledge of society (Naka et al., 2022). Moreover, education is also essential for other social institutions as a means for cultural transmission.

It is also important to point out that cultural beliefs, customs, ideas, and practices are dynamic elements of society. That means these elements are not limited to one generation of the constituent members of a social group. Each individual or unit who is the carrier of these elements will surely pass away in time, but the culture continues to exist and grow through its elements. At the same time, every new constituent member of a particular social group is born immature, and they must learn the necessary knowledge and customs of the group so that they can represent the future generation and replace the out-going members of the group. In this process, constituent members of a social group come and go, but the group and its culture continue to exist. Therefore, it is also essential to produce and compile the proper knowledge database or content for transmission. The content should be created according to the needs and aims of the social group so that immature members can be trained for real-world challenges. This database should also be updated frequently and enhanced according to the needs of fast-changing societies. Hence, to sum up, we can say that education is an instrument to conserve, renew, and transmit culture in its broadest sense.

Education is not only a result of growing human civilization, but it is a process in itself too. Education is an important social institution resulting from a dynamic process of continuous interaction between humans with other species and the environment. It is still growing and constantly developing on the basis of the interaction of a person with their socio-cultural situations and the physical environment in any given particular time period. At the same time, it is a means of transmission for various social thoughts, feelings, habits, and skills from the older generation. Education is expected to help not only in developing social and cultural understanding but also in understanding the world and one's own self. Further, it is expected to develop critical thinking, thereby realizing one's original capacities, which is vital to contribute efficiently in a social group and enhance, preserve, and transmitting the socio-cultural features of a group to future generations.

As a result, education as a social institution has dual aspects of product and process, which go hand in hand. It works like a closely connected loop in which education as a "process" tries to enhance the established information, customs, skills, and practices, and in result (as a "product"), a new set of information, customs, skills, and practices get ready for transmission to the next generation. Education as a process continuously changes its shape and size in terms of quality and quantity of delivered content according to the problems, needs and aims at a particular time. In this whole paradigm, members are born and die, but this system continues to exist due to its entangling nature with society or, in John Dewey's words, "constant reweaving of the social fabric" (Dewey, 1916, p. 4).

1.1   *Education as a Deliberate Practice*

Learning is a natural process and can be found in almost all organisms. Every organism needs to learn some basic skills and behaviours in order to survive in a fast-changing environment. Each biological organism, including humans, interact with its surrounding and gain experiences. Even a unicellular amoeba learns to adapt according to the different surroundings based upon stimuli and responses. The learning process may occur in different forms, such as a result of habituation, classical conditioning, operant conditioning, or even more complex activities such as play (Zosh et al., 2017). These experiences form a building block for further learning to understand the world and change behaviour accordingly. Not only through self-experience but, most animals acquire various skills and necessary information from other members of their clan. Imitation plays a significant role in this process.

New immature members learn and adapt by observing and imitating elders' behaviours of their group. But learning through this process is limited to the essential skills required for survival. For example, through observation and imitation, a baby elephant learns to break a branch from a tree to eat or make a specific noise in case of danger. A human child learns in a similar fashion, at least in its initial phase of life. However, learning through this method is limited to basic necessary biological and physiological skills only and which majorly help in biological survival and advancement. Since human life is not limited to biological and physiological functions, a child needs to be trained in social and cultural aspects to become an active and responsible member of a social group. A child must learn the norms and values of the group to become an accepted and important member of the group (Rao, 2014). Therefore, unlike other animals, in humans, a child needs to be inculcated with society's socio-cultural norms and necessary knowledge and skills for survival and advancement.

There are many ways through which children can get experiences and, in turn, learn to prepare themselves for future life. A child continuously learns through their parents, family, neighbourhood and other members of society. This is a natural way of learning which is incidental, informal, unregulated, and automatic. Hence, this method cannot guarantee that all the knowledge gained by a child is sufficient, correct and worthy to cater for the needs of a particular time and place. Therefore, in order to create every child an effective member of society, there should be a defined mechanism for mass transmission of some necessary common knowledge as well as to help in the development of a variety of skills, values, social and emotional capacities in them. Thus, education becomes a tool to create, maintain, enhance, and transmit social values, beliefs, and culture. Unlike the previously discussed natural learning, this is a deliberate and intentional process. Therefore, the formalization of educational activities became necessary with the evolution and advancement of human societies.

1.2   *Education as a Formal Institutional Setup*

The institutionalized transfer of knowledge and learning is what makes humans different from animals in this aspect. However, formal teaching in the form of institutionalized knowledge transfer tends to be less common in primitive human societies because people lived in small groups in which they supported each other's learning in a variety of ways without a formal setup (Boyette & Hewlett, 2018). As societies gradually developed into bigger groups, they attached more importance to formal setups of education. It also tried to formulate the overall objectives, content, organization, and strategies for education. When societies became gradually more complex, the amount of knowledge to be passed on from one generation to another also increased, which required a proper means of transmission, and the outcome was a formal education system. As a result, various agencies such as schools, colleges, and common curriculum came into existence. The task of transmission has been delegated to a set of specially trained persons known as teachers. Finally, education became institutionalized.

Education fundamentally includes three major activities—learning, teaching, and creating a knowledge base to be taught. Other auxiliary activities include creating places for tutoring, such as schools, developing methodologies for teaching-learning (pedagogies), developing learning tools and technologies etc. Education as an institution is primarily formed to transform human behaviour and make them socially cultured. It facilitates learning in humans to make them acquainted with various necessary skills which help them to grow into a more cultured and responsible member of society. More specifically, learning is "a process that leads to change in behaviour, which occurs as a result of experience and increases the potential for improved performance and future learning" (Ambrose et al., 2010, p. 3). Similarly, teaching is one of the primary activities through which humans impart information, knowledge, skills, and culture to individuals. It is a cooperative activity with the main aim of making children able to grasp the available knowledge easily, as well as preparing them for self-directed learning in the future. A crucial fundamental task of a teacher is to communicate with the learners actively and try to make students to become self-directed learners in future. To conclude, it can be said that education involves ongoing, active processes of inquiry, engagement, and participation in the world around us (Bransford et al., 2000).

Education normally involves an active interaction among different stakeholders. Whether they are students or teachers, both gain new experiences in the process of education. These newly acquired experiences not only make them modify their own behaviour in order to deal effectively with real-world problems, but they also try to impart this new knowledge to other members of society. This process continues generation after generation and thereby updating and improving educational practices. Today we understand education in the sense of actualizing our potentialities, learning or cultivating various skills through proper methods, curriculum and more such ways. But, the purpose of education was not the same always and everywhere. It varies according to the immediate and future needs of a particular society. Social institutions, including education, are man-made institutions with an aim of efficient functioning of the society. The education which we look at today is the result of combining and implementing different ideas.

1.3 *Education as a Means to Fulfil Societal Purpose*

The content of education has always been purpose-driven, and the need of a particular society regulates that. For instance, initial civilizations such as India, Egypt or China had a tremendous focus on religion and spirituality because these aspects were prominent in these civilizations. At the same time, training in various vocational skills was also important for the continuous day-to-day functioning of society. Similarly, training in agricultural skills in agrarian societies and hunting in primitive nomadic societies had central importance. This is also important to note that education was not always connected to "bread-earning education" or what we call today 'career-oriented education' only. For example, in the Indian context, during the Vedic period, we find the gurukul system, where the knowledge of Vedas was given with the purpose of realizing one's true self and attaining liberation. Similarly, in ancient Greek society music, dance, and poetry were essential aspects of formal education for the purpose of appreciating harmony and rhythm (Beck, 1964).

Various phases in the history of civilization greatly influence the content of education and steer its practices. The history of civilizations, phases of invasion, expansion of power, industrialization, renaissance, freedom movements, democracy, socialism, capitalism, globalization etc., are important factors that cannot be overlooked in the process of understanding education and how it has evolved as a social institution. The way educational institutions have been operating in today's world, their seeds can be traced back in history, and we must see that it is mainly dependent upon the structure of society of each era. For example, gender sensitization is an important aspect of our present education system because we now understand and accept the concept of equality. But that was not always the case. For example, in ancient Greek society, females and slaves were not preferred for formal education because they were thought inferior to the other members of the society (Downey, 1957).

Similarly, in ancient India, education was predominantly accessible to the Brahmins, the highest social class, indicative of a system that was not democratic in its approach. This class segregation reflected the societal norms of that time, which were hierarchal and exclusionary in nature. In contrast, contemporary society has evolved to recognize the importance of equality across genders and social classes, promoting a more democratic ethos in education that appreciates the unity and equality of humankind. Nonetheless, the transition has not been solely structural; it has also affected the content and objectives of education. Currently, the focus has largely shifted towards career-oriented education, a development that carries its own set of advantages and disadvantages.

These issues are significant to mention because education as a social institution has seen many changes from its evolution to its current form. Moreover, the idea of universal education emerged in recent times only after protracted demand and struggle for the same. Hence, it needs to be illuminated that societal structures had a significant influence over education, and they still influence our patterns, methods and ways of education. Today, many educationalists talk about the democratic foundation of education in the form of providing freedom and open space to children, but some centuries back, that wasn't a prominent idea in society. At the same time, education has become primarily tool to fulfil societal purpose in terms of material progress and increased control over nature.

Therefore, to summarize, we can say that the historical processes go hand in hand with the development of education in each part of the world at a specific time period. It is also clear from the discussion that education majorly works upon an individual to develop her capacities by enhancing their skills so that they can be a better version of themselves. Therefore, the initial focus of discussion for all human activities, especially in education, should be human beings themselves. Humans have certain common features and dispositions that need to be understood to enhance and honed through education. Moreover, as Meenakshi Thapan notes, students always "remain central" to any educational activity (Thapan, 2014, p. 11). Therefore, without understanding the core of the educational process—the human beings, their capacities, characteristics, and limitations—we cannot design an appropriate system or carry out effective educational activities.

2   Transforming Human Nature through Education

2.1   *Need to Study Human Nature*
A person's personal beliefs and dispositions are the prime drivers for her activities and behaviour towards others. Humans are social species, and most of their activities occur in their relationships with other human beings and their environment. Humans have similar or different beliefs and assumptions about their nature, which are reflected in their behaviour and affect almost all aspects of social life. Education is no exception. But, before explaining human activities, it is vital to explain human beings themselves. Conceiving a simple definition of human beings is hard to make because each human being can have a very different conception about their own nature. Moreover, every human being has their own personal subjective experiences which lead to diverse range of understandings about their own nature. Therefore, it becomes necessary to enquire for an objective theory of human nature and articulate

some of the common features shared by all human beings before designing an appropriate system of education.

The concept of human nature is, by and large, itself one of the most prolific topics in philosophy. A common understanding of human nature can be the set of characteristics shared by all human beings. According to an encyclopaedic definition, it is the "fundamental dispositions and traits of humans" (Duignan, 2016). The word 'human nature' in its fundamental sense can be referred to as intrinsic and essential qualities of humans, which differentiate us from other species. The concept of human nature can also be explained as 'fundamental dispositions and characteristics'—including ways of thinking, feeling and acting—that humans are said to have naturally. Although various disciplines in sciences and social sciences, such as biology, sociology, psychology, anthropology, philosophy, etc., try to explain 'human nature,' there is no single discipline that can claim the exact explanation. Sciences try to theorize humans in terms of common physiologies, whereas social sciences explain human nature in terms of shared human behaviours. Similarly, some disciplines such as philosophy try to explain human nature in terms of metaphysical aspects. However, we arguably cannot say that these different approaches are completely right or wrong, we can only say that they do not provide a complete picture of human nature. Every theory is bounded by its own discipline-specific assumptions and methodologies; hence, the explanations are also discipline-specific. Not only this, as discussed in the previous section, each theory or philosophy about a particular thing is time, place, and society dependent.

Etienne Gilson (1950, pp. 303–304) aptly put this point as:

> Any philosophy can be explained by its time, its birthplace and its historical setting. Any philosophy can be accounted for by the collective representations that prevailed in the social group in which it was conceived. And any philosophy can as successfully be traced back to the economic structure of the nation in which the philosopher himself was born.

2.2   *Influence of Philosophy of Human Nature upon Education*

Education is an important social institution of modern society that directly or indirectly affects every human being across the globe. This is an important human activity that is performed in this world and influences our behaviour, relations, and choices. Being human also means how to acknowledge our place in the world along with other species. Education plays an important role in defining our role as humans and specifying our actions in the world. In general, educational activities primarily aim to transform humans and their behaviour. Whether it is training to curb undesirables or honing the desirables, both practices act upon human beings. And, without understanding the actual nature of this locus of all educational activity, we will not be able to succeed in transforming human lives as desired. Without having some conception about human nature, it is impractical to develop theories that are focused on humans. Moreover, various conceptions about the nature of humans get reflected in educational activities—both in theory and practice. Hence, the nature of human should be explored first before studying actions and activities such as education. That is why most educationists initiate their discussion with humans and their nature in order to theorize on educational activity.

Undoubtedly, educational activities are considered necessary to shape children's minds as per society's needs, as well as to equip them with the necessary skills and values to become active members of society. Moreover, a child can be trained in any manner depending upon a particular educational system. That is why the minds of students, specifically children, have often been compared to the potter's clay. The teacher is compared to the potter and the wheel to the conditions in which the student's mind is trained and skills honed. This is to imply that during the school years, the minds of students are extremely impressionable, and the influences they are subjected to can decide the direction of their future. Just as the potter's skill and the wheel's efficiency are necessary, it is also prudent to understand the quality of the soil for the pot to turn out beautifully.

The importance of understanding the psyche and nature of young minds then becomes vitally important when it comes to deciding the kind of knowledge that is to be imparted upon them. More than that, understanding the inherent nature and how the mind works are also crucial to design an appropriate method of imparting education. In all these complex situations of educational practices, it is important to step back and look at the bigger picture, i.e. to understand the nature of humans. Moreover, human nature isn't static, similar to education. It continually evolves and develops through external influences. Therefore, understanding this constant evolution is also necessary to further establish the scope of our educational discourse. The basic question of 'Who am I?' is a constant in philosophy. Although the answer to this question keeps changing as we change as well as our understanding of us changes. But this issue indeed becomes the major driving force behind finding the answer to 'what can I be?.' In simpler words, a particular philosophy of human nature may remain implicit in the philosophy of education.

The discussion so far suggests that understanding human nature is a crucial part of understanding and practicing education. Human nature, as a concept, has been explored by many educators and philosophers, who have attempted to define what it means to be human and how this definition influences educational practices. However, these explorations often present partial views, shaped by the core philosophies and assumptions of the thinkers themselves. While each theory or explanation contributes to uncovering the mystery of human nature, no single perspective can claim to present a complete picture. This is because the lens through which these theories are developed is often colored by the personal, cultural, and historical contexts of the philosophers. Consequently, educational practices are influenced by these varying and sometimes conflicting assumptions about human nature.

Nevertheless, a survey of major educational philosophies reveals a clear pattern: *underlying assumptions about human nature profoundly shape the design and implementation of educational practices.* Therefore, before moving to understand humans comprehensively and formulate an objective theory of human nature, it is imperative to delve deeper into this hypothesis and appreciate its crucial implications. While an exhaustive review of all educational philosophers is beyond the scope of this work, a focused analysis of three prominent educationists will serve to illuminate the intricate relationship between their conceptions of human nature and their educational philosophies.

3   Insights from Global Perspectives: A Tri-Continental View

The selection of John Dewey, Paulo Freire, and Jiddu Krishnamurti as key figures in this discussion is both intentional and essential for a comprehensive understanding of the relationship between human nature and educational practices. A closer examination reveals that Dewey, Freire, and Krishnamurti provide a valuable insight for understanding the close connection between human nature and education on a global scale. For instance, John Dewey, an American philosopher, brings a perspective rooted in Western pragmatism, emphasizing the social and interactive nature of human beings. Dewey's concept of education as a process of growth, grounded in experiential learning, provides a framework for understanding how education can align with the natural, embodied capacities of human beings. His focus on learning as an active, ongoing process of engagement with the environment highlights the importance of creating educational practices that are responsive to the social and embodied nature of learners. Dewey's influence on progressive education, his critique of traditional schooling, and his advocacy for democratic learning environments make him a foundational figure in understanding how education can be designed to reflect the complex, interactive nature of human beings.

Similarly, Paulo Freire, hailing from Latin America, offers a perspective deeply concerned with the social and political dimensions of human nature. His critical pedagogy is informed by his experiences in Brazil and other parts of Latin America, where he witnessed the effects of oppression and marginalization. Freire's understanding of human nature as inherently capable of critical reflection and social change adds a crucial dimension to the discussion of embodied education in later chapters. His emphasis on dialogue, the co-construction of knowledge, and the importance of consciousness-raising aligns with the view that education should engage learners as active participants in shaping their world. Freire's focus on liberation, social justice, and the emancipatory power of education provides a necessary counterbalance to Dewey's more pragmatic approach, ensuring that the social and ethical dimensions of education are integral to the concept of education for the embodied human.

Whereas, Jiddu Krishnamurti, representing Eastern philosophical traditions from India, introduces a perspective that focuses on the inner, spiritual dimensions of human nature. Krishnamurti argues that education should be a process of self-discovery, helping individuals transcend societal conditioning and realize their true nature. His emphasis on mindfulness, self-awareness, and inner freedom complements the more socially-oriented approaches of Dewey and Freire, providing a holistic view of education that addresses both the outer and inner dimensions of human existence. Krishnamurti's insights into the role of inner transformation in education are particularly relevant to the concept of embodied education, which seeks to integrate the mind, body, and environment in a harmonious and balanced way. His critique of traditional educational systems, which he saw as stifling creativity and perpetuating psychological conformity, adds a dimension of introspective and spiritual inquiry to the educational process, essential for cultivating a deep sense of self-awareness and holistic learning.

Having said that, the decision to focus on thinkers from three different continents—North America, South America, and Asia—is not arbitrary but reflects the intention to cover a broad spectrum of human experience and educational philosophy. By examining the perspectives of Dewey, Freire, and Krishnamurti, the intention is to highlight how different cultural, social, and philosophical contexts influence educational thought. Dewey's pragmatism, Freire's critical theory, and Krishnamurti's spiritual humanism represent distinct but interrelated approaches to education, each grounded in a different aspect of what it means to be human. This tri-continental view allows for a more comprehensive exploration of human nature, ensuring that the analysis is not limited by any single cultural or philosophical tradition. It also demonstrates how the concept of embodied education transcends geographic boundaries, offering a universally relevant framework for understanding and improving educational practices.

The decision to focus on John Dewey, Paulo Freire, and Jiddu Krishnamurti, rather than others, is also driven by their unique capacity to illuminate a contemporary, global approach to holistic and embodied education. This section aims to validate the initial hypothesis that a particular philosophy of human nature significantly influences educational philosophy. To achieve this, the thoughts of these three influential thinkers will be explored and analysed. The analysis will proceed in four parts for each thinker: a brief overview of their biographies, an examination of their views on human nature, a discussion of their educational philosophies, and finally, an exploration of the interconnections between their conceptions of human nature and their approaches to education.

3.1   *John Dewey (1859–1952)*
3.1.1   Brief Biography

John Dewey was an American philosopher, psychologist, educationalist, political thinker and a leading proponent as well as co-founder of the philosophical school known as pragmatism along with Charles Sanders Peirce (1839–1914) and William James (1842–1910). Pragmatism is a theory which claims that an ideology or proposition is true when it works satisfactorily or is found to be practically applied. It tries to build a link between knowledge and practice. Talking about his early life, he was born on October 20th 1859, in Vermont, America. He graduated from the University of Vermont and received a doctorate in philosophy from Johns Hopkins University. After that, Dewey accepted a teaching post at the University of Michigan. He was influenced by Hegelian thoughts in his early years (J. Campbell, 1995). However, his thoughts got shifted from Hegel's idealism to empirically based knowledge during the time when he was at the University of Chicago. His interest in child psychology prompted him to develop a philosophy of education that would meet the needs of a change in a new democratic society. He founded a laboratory school in Chicago, where he used to apply and experiment with his own novel pedagogical methods. He spent the majority of his career at Columbia University, where he came in close contact with many philosophers. His major work includes 'Democracy and education,' 'Experience and education,' 'How we think,' 'Experience and nature,' 'Human nature and conduct,' and many more.

3.1.2   Thoughts on Human Nature

John Dewey's philosophical ideas were radical. He opposed the old philosophies and put forth his views that reality is not completely given or a fixed system but rather it is continuously changing, growing and developing things.

In Dewey's view, old philosophies neglected the elements of human desire and purpose, which tend to create virtual isolation between humans and the rest of nature. In contrast, Dewey advocated for a humanistic naturalism position in which humans are considered part of the natural world (Lamont, 1961). This view related to humans can be found as an underlying position in his further developed thoughts, such as education. Moreover, Dewey's philosophy of human nature also seems to be partially influenced by Charles Darwin's theory of evolution. Specifically, Dewey was interested in the idea of replacing the established assumption of the superiority of 'the fixed and final' by the notions of change, growth, process, and evolution (J. Campbell, 1995, p. 28). Dewey argues for a continuity among living creatures, and recognized that humans are changeable social creatures despite having some common traits.

Dewey considers the world as well as human nature, to have both changing and constant features. He forwards this idea with the concepts of Precariousness and Stability. He argues that reality is a mixture of precariousness and stability. The stability part indicates the finished and completeness, and at the same time, precariousness indicates the unfinished nature, and thus progress and evolution. According to him, every existing thing has some unfinished traits and thus always evolving. Simultaneously, it has some constant traits which are unaffected by the situation or the temporal changes. He clearly notes:

> We live in a world which is an impressive and irresistible mixture of sufficiencies, tight completenesses, order, recurrences which make possible prediction and control, and singularities, ambiguities, uncertain possibilities, processes going on to consequences as yet indeterminate. They are mixed not mechanically but vitally like wheat and tares of the parable. We may recognise them separately but we cannot divide them, for unlike wheat and tares they grow from the same root. (Dewey, 1929, p. 47)

Dewey characterizes humans as physical-biological beings (fixed) and social-practical beings (changeable). According to him, human beings have some constant physiological features commonly available to all. But on the psychological front, they are subject to change through their active experience in the natural world. In the essay "Does human nature change?" (Dewey, 2021), Dewey proposes that human nature 'does' and 'does not' change. He argues that there are some unchangeable elements of human nature—'innate needs' like food, drink, and so on, which we cannot stop under any circumstances. It can also include some tendencies which are an integral part of human existence. However, there are some changeable elements in human nature that are based on culture. One must understand that not everything in us is natural, but the development and transformation of human beings is due to human culture. In this way, Dewey sees human beings as creatures who are by nature inextricably bound up in the culture. That means there is no changeless nature of human beings, and they are continuous with the world through their culture.

On similar lines, Dewey also argues for continuity of mind and cognitive activities (Hildebrand, 2021). He conceives the mind as an activity instead of a substance (as dualists conceive). He criticizes the dominant scientific psychology for conceiving of mind and body as separate, which eventually creates a dualism between mind and practice because practice is usually linked with the body (Dewey, 1980). On the contrary, Dewey stresses that mind is a dynamic process of interaction between an organism and the world, rather than an independent entity. He argues that this kind of psychophysical dualism emerges from considering a world 'out there' and a mind 'in here.' But according to Dewey, a cognitive activity or an experience emerges due to complex interactions between subject and object (Dewey, 1929).

3.1.3 Thoughts on Education

The educational ideas of John Dewey are very much aligned with his overall philosophy. He notes: "If we are willing to conceive education as the process of forming fundamental dispositions, intellectual and emotional, toward nature and fellow-men, philosophy may even be defined as the general theory of education" (Dewey, 1916, p. 354). In the process of developing his thoughts on education, he not only gave theories concerning the true meaning of education, but he also put them into practice. He established a laboratory school in Chicago where he practiced and experimented with his ideas on education. Additionally, Dewey was a pro-believer in democratic values, and laboratory school was like an experimental site for applying his educational theories as well as democratic values (Hildebrand, 2021). He constantly emphasized over creating democratic learning environments in schools since schools are important social institutions that can bring positive change in society. These are core commitments of John Dewey's educational philosophy, and a general overview of the literature suggests that 'education through experience' and 'democracy through education' are two major strands in the philosophy of John Dewey.

As stated previously, Dewey was a pragmatist philosopher, which means he was more concerned and inclined towards practical knowledge rather than mere theoretical knowledge. As a pragmatist, he gave importance to the successful application of any theory. He criticized the traditional dominant theory of education, which presupposes that there are some proven and tested values that should be passed onto future generations, and hence young minds should get training on those values. Rather he believes that students must look for right and wrong conceptions by themselves based on their own past experiences and not what is told by the traditional system. He considers the traditional way of education to be motivated by conservative thoughts that largely give importance to order, discipline, and a one-way teacher-centric direct instructions. In contrast with this, Dewey stresses that "we never educate directly, but indirectly by means of the environment" (Dewey, 1916, p. 20). Therefore, a school should be an interactive place where training for critical and reflective thinking is practiced. That is why he considered 'training' to be more appropriately aligned with schooling purposes instead of 'educative teaching.'

John Dewey emphasizes upon interaction and dialogue for the knowledge exchange process in schools. These ideas emerged against the traditional approach of the one-way process of education, which was teacher-centric and authoritarian in nature. Apart from this, he also emphasizes experiential learning or what we can call 'learning by doing.' So apart from curriculum, students can be engaged in some activity. Through such opportunities to take part in their own learning, students also learn various virtues. Teamwork and cooperation can be learned by taking part in various activities. In this way, children learn rules and regulations, and accept them voluntarily rather than as an external force by the teacher. This 'learning while doing' allows a child to flow naturally into the system. One of the roles of teacher is to understand the general nature of human learning and the processes through which one learns. The schooling setups should also be reshaped accordingly, then only, it will help children to grow and to bring social change. The curriculum should also be presented to the students in such a way that they can establish a connection by relating it with past experience to acquire new knowledge. Experiential education is beneficial in the sense that it can inculcate the virtue of cooperation in learners. It also makes possible effective knowledge exchange through dialogues and interactions, which eventually inculcates democratic values among children. Here, it is important to clarify that for Dewey, democracy means more than a form of government. It involves not only shared common interests in social control, but it also encourages for freer interaction between social groups. Implying to it, Dewey emphasizes a balanced approach in educational setup that gives proper justice to individual interests to ensure social changes without introducing disorder.

3.1.4   Connection between Thoughts on Education and Human Nature

Based on the above discussions, a clear close connection can be seen between Dewey's view on human nature and his ideas of education, both theoretically and practically. In fact, it can be said that Dewey's thoughts on education are derived from his philosophy of human nature and the world. He largely tries to provide a middle path between the two extremes. While talking about human nature, he neither rejects the notion of innate and essential tendencies nor rules out the cultural and social role in cultivating the intrinsic qualities of human beings. Similarly, in education, we find how he synthesizes conservative and progressive ideas in education. The 'experience' aspect is very crucial in Dewey's overall thought, and that can be related to his views on human nature and education. The core of Dewey's philosophy of human nature is the recognition of changeable and unchangeable aspects of humans, and the implication of it in education can be seen in two forms.

Firstly, John Dewey believes that students are not "tabula rasa" or "empty slate." Therefore, he says that students should get an environment in which they get engaged in some activities of their interest. Teachers too should understand the natural tendencies of children and accordingly direct them—this shows an unchangeable aspect of human nature. This is to appreciate the innate aspects of human nature. Basically, here it is presumed that we have some natural tendencies according to which we work, act, or perform. Secondly, he also gives importance to the changeable factor, which is due to culture. Culture shapes our personality, thinking, and behaviour, and ultimately shows the way to live life. Being an advocate of democracy, for John Dewey, the societal aspect becomes important. Therefore, he emphasizes the role of interdisciplinary curriculum and teachers in imparting knowledge. An interdisciplinary curriculum provides wide scope to pursue one's own interests and to acquire as well as apply knowledge. In this process, the role of the teacher is to observe the natural flow of interest of the child. Dewey not only talks about the role of the teacher but also how much knowledge and what skills must be there. In this way, teachers act as an active facilitator in creation of an environment that is suitable to the natural tendencies of children. This is possible by applying the principle of "learning by doing" and through engaging in dialogues. Human beings cannot get away with culture, but we can change the culture. Culture impacts our personality heavily; therefore, I believe Dewey wants to make society more democratic by changing the educational setup. He focuses on the roots, basics, and foundations of education by talking about experience and learning in accordance with the natural flow.

To conclude, I would like to put forward that from Dewey's overall thought, it is clear that the study of human nature and psychology is a must for educational practices. The reason why we are trying to establish a connection between ideas of human nature with education is that education is the foundation upon which the whole life can be reshaped. Moreover, if we understand the basic nature of a child or human beings in general, then collectively we can move towards a better society by designing the apt learning environment for the members of society.

3.2   *Paulo Freire (1921–1997)*

3.2.1   Brief Biography

Paulo Freire was one of the prominent educational thinkers of the 20th century who worked for liberation pedagogy and social change. His ideas were the result of the socio-political scenario of previously colonized Brazil at that time and his personal experiences of prolonged hunger and poverty. During the late 1940s, Freire was actively involved in the literacy projects and became Director in the Division of Education and Culture at the Social Service Ministry (SESI) of Pernambuco state in Brazil. SESI gave Freire a platform to engage with the working class and to understand the roots of the problem from the inside. He started to experiment with an alternative literacy program specialized for the working class. Later Freire was appointed as the city's Secretary of Education in 1989, where he instituted various reforms related to curricula, teacher training, community involvement and promotion of interdisciplinary studies in nearly 600 schools. He resigned in 1991 but continued to write and teach at the local university, consult with local and international grassroots organizations, and attend international presentations and conferences. Freire was influenced by existentialism, phenomenology, Marxism, Christianity etc. Notable thinkers such as G. W. F. Hegel, Karl Marx, John Dewey, Anísio Teixeira and Erich Fromm contributed towards Freire's development of thought (Dale & Hyslop-Margison, 2010). On top of that, among many thinkers, Hegel and Marx have a special place in the maturation of Freire's theories and practice. He produced some of his notable works such as 'Pedagogy of the Oppressed,' 'Pedagogy of Indignation,' 'Pedagogy of Hope: Reliving Pedagogy of the Oppressed,' 'Letters to Cristina: Reflections on My Life and Work,' 'Pedagogy of the Heart, and Pedagogy of Freedom: Ethics, Democracy, and Civic Courage,' etc.

3.2.2   Thoughts on Human Nature

Freire's general philosophy is a direct result of his concrete experiences as an educational activist and critical reflection on the socio-economic condition of his homeland people (Schugurensky, 2011). Freire was very influenced by Hegel's metaphysics, social ethics, phenomenology, and the process of dialectic, which can be seen in his overall philosophy. Specifically, Freire's views related to humans and their fundamental nature also seem to be influenced by Erich Kahler's writings, in which Kahler differentiated human beings from other non-human beings (Harris, 2011). Similarly, Freire differentiated between human beings and non-human beings, and placed humans above non-human beings since the former have some extra capabilities through which they can transform their reality, unlike the mere adaptive activities of the latter. He argues that humans can act as subjective beings who interact with the world, unlike non-human beings (animals), which do not have a clear subjective outlook towards the world. He also acknowledges that human's orientation in the world is neither purely subjective nor purely objective, but unison of objectivity and subjectivity is the key to understanding our true nature.

According to Freire, humans are inherently unfinished, a condition that renders us open beings devoid of a predetermined purpose or horizon. This 'unfinished' quality is a form of freedom, a state towards which we ought to consciously orient ourselves. In the absence of a pre-established goal, it becomes imperative for humans to create objectives and work towards them, a process Freire refers to as 'humanization' (Freire, 1970b). The philosophical underpinnings of Freire's concept of humanization bear notable resemblance to the Hegelian dialectical process, particularly Hegel's notions of 'being,' 'nothingness,' and 'becoming.'

In Hegel's dialectical framework, 'being' and 'nothingness' are antithetical perspectives from which arises 'becoming,' a transformative process that reconciles the contradictions between the two (Gray Carlson, 2007). Freire adopts this dialectical lens in his explanation of humanization and its opposite, dehumanization. He employs the term 'praxis' to refer to this dialectical process, asserting that 'praxis' is an attribute unique to humans due to their awareness of their activity and the world around them (Freire, 1970b, p. 71).

Freire presents idea of praxis in terms of reflection and action. It includes a combination of involvement in worldly action as well as distancing oneself from the world through developing consciousness. This means human beings change the world through action. At the same time, they get knowledge by having a dialogue with the world by distancing themselves from it. Here, an obvious confusion emerges that whether Freire's views of man and the world are ultimately idealist or materialist. Here, Freire tried to mediate between the two and weave the objective world around subjective human beings. According to Freire, human nature has both discernment and transcendent qualities. Discernment means separation from the world to have an objective outlook and to respect subjectiveness with respect to the world (object). At the same time, the transcendent quality of human nature enables them to grow beyond their physical capacity (consciousness).

Freire draws these thoughts mainly from Erich Kahler's views on the nature of human beings (Harris, 2011). Kahler recognizes two elements that differentiate humans from other animals: objective conditions as limits (discernment) and the ability to overcome those limits (transcendent). Moreover, Kahler observes that the combination and unity of these two features is the essence of human nature. On similar lines, Freire characterizes human nature as a process of going beyond their immediate moment to become more. Freire argues that men and women are capable of transforming the world, unlike other animals, through the process of conscious action or praxis, which is the combination of discernment and transcendence. That is why Freire gives much importance to the process of praxis to come out from the illusion and understand reality. According to Freire, the realization that humans are men of praxis is a basic step in the development of their critical consciousness.

The central thesis of Freirean humanism is the belief that people should realize their ability to change reality and become active subjects instead of remaining passive objects. He constantly made clear that in the current social environment, humans are devoid of their true nature and perceived as mere worldly objects. For instance, he once showed concern over a boy's killing by a group of teenagers. He comments that the boy has been burned as if it is just a thing, something useless like a worthless piece of rag. He analyses the whole episode as an act of dehumanizing (Freire, 2015, p. 46). Therefore, Freire emphasizes over developing subjective consciousness for making sense of one's own contexts so that one can try to change it through transforming their environment. Thus, an educational process is needed to respect the subject-hood and to develop the consciousness of their true human nature. This is called 'critical pedagogy' by Paulo Freire.

Freire formulated his ideas of humanization, critical pedagogy, dialog-ics, and the process of conscientização in his best-known work 'Pedagogy of oppressed.' To understand Freire's educational philosophy holistically, it is nec-essary to understand the nature of man and their relationship with the world. In terms of actual educational philosophy, he is known for his critical peda-gogy, which we will see next.

3.2.3   Thoughts on Education

Freire is best known for his attack on the traditional way of education, what he called the 'banking' concept of education. In the banking model, students are viewed as empty deposit boxes to be filled by the knowledge of the teacher. He argues that "it transforms students into receiving objects. It attempts to control thinking and action, leads women and men to adjust to the world, and inhibits their creative power" (Freire, 1970b, p. 50). This kind of process makes humans distant from their true subjective nature and dehumanizes them. However, this critique was not entirely new. Rousseau's conception of the child as an active learner was already a step ahead of John Locke's tabula rasa (which is techni-cally like the 'banking concept'). Additionally, we have already seen how John

Dewey too described education as a tool for social change. Freire's explanation, however, updated the concept in the light of his surroundings and placed it in context with contemporary theories and practices of education, which laid the foundation for critical pedagogy.

Freire's critique focused on the banking model of education, which positions teachers as expert knowledge sources, and students as passive recipients who need to be filled with knowledge. In this model, teachers possess all the power, authority, and knowledge, while students are viewed as "empty vessels" without any prior knowledge or experience. Consequently, students are perceived as mere "collectors" or "cataloguers," expected to learn solely through the direct transfer of knowledge from teachers, without engaging in any critical inquiry or exploration. Freire argues that the banking system of education promotes passivity in learners by disregarding the spirit of inquiry and critical thinking. In this system, the teacher is the sole possessor of knowledge, and their primary responsibility is to develop lessons on the subject matter, which are then transmitted to students as static information. Students are expected to record and memorize this information without questioning its validity. As a result, the banking model of education restricts the scope of action to receiving, filing, and storing information, with success measured solely by a student's ability to repeat the particular narrative about the world that they have been given.

In banking education, there is an absolute dichotomy between the teacher and the student. The teachers are considered as persons who always have knowledge, and students are devoid of knowledge. The teacher must present himself as the complete opposite in front of their students. That means, a teacher justifies his own existence by ignoring the humane aspect of students. Freire compares students with slaves in the form of the Hegelian dialectic. A teacher has complete and absolute control over the knowledge and students. Therefore, a teacher becomes not just a subject-authority but the authority of social control. The teacher, in this environment, becomes an absolute authority to choose what is to be learned, thereby, imposing himself on students. In short, a teacher becomes the person who is available not with the students but for the students.

Likewise, students are treated as mere passive listeners who receive the content that teachers narrate. Students are expected to collect and catalogue information, memorize it, and mechanically repeat it. Additionally, knowledge in this model become a gift that is bestowed upon ignorant children by knowledgeable teachers. This projection of ignorance onto students is in fact an oppressive ideology. In such oppressive scenarios, even the students internalize their ignorance and accept their subservience to the teacher, unaware that they are integral to the process of knowledge creation.

Freire argues that knowledge emerges through the process of invention and reinvention. It is a process of active inquiry by human beings with the world and with each other. It is the result of the reconciliation of two poles of contradiction between teacher and students. Knowledge emerges through the dialectic process between teacher and student. It is not like a one-way channel, but both parties are actively involved in the construction of knowledge. Each of them has a dialectical relationship with the other.

Freire also views the banking model of education as a tool for domination, whereby students are indoctrinated and conditioned to accept and adapt to oppressive systems without questioning them. The education system serves to transmit the culture and beliefs of the oppressors, rather than fostering critical inquiry and the possibility of change. The structure of this education model reinforces the dichotomy between oppressors and oppressed, with educators positioned as those who possess knowledge and students positioned as those who lack it. Thus, students are alienated from their own reality, resulting in a false understanding that students are mere objects. This leads to the dehumanization of students and a necrophilous mindset, where active and critical thinking of the students is killed. Students are transformed into passive objects instead, active thinking agents. Overall, Freire argues that the banking model of education perpetuates oppressive power structures and fails to encourage critical thinking and reflection. Instead, he advocates for an approach to education that fosters active, critical inquiry, and empowers students to take action to change oppressive systems.

Freire proposed the use of dialogue as a means to address the oppressive nature of the banking model of education. He believes that the word is a crucial component of dialogue as it contains both action and reflection, or praxis, which is integral to human nature. Without praxis, the word and the human being are negated. Therefore, the right to speak the word is not a privilege of a few but a right of every person. The authentic word acknowledges the power of praxis in others to transform the world. Dialogue, according to Freire, is an encounter between individuals mediated by the world in order to name the world (Freire, 1970b, p. 61). However, this dialogue is impossible when one party wants to name the world while the other party does not believe in it. The latter party is the one who engages in the depositing process, which is an anti-dialogue approach rather than a true dialogue.

According to Paulo Freire, the efficacy of education is contingent upon dialogical encounters rather than the traditional 'banking model,' where knowledge is 'deposited' into students by an authoritarian figure. In his view, dialogue functions as an act of collective transformation, an action-reflection praxis that serves to humanize both the individual and the collective (Freire,

1970b). Authentic dialogue presumes a fundamental equality among its partic-ipants, allowing for the fusion of learning and action aimed at societal trans-formation. Freire criticizes the banking model, particularly for the way it stifles the development of critical thinking among the dominated or oppressed. But crucially, this is not just a problem for the oppressed. The oppressors in the banking model are also rendered incapable of critical dialogue, a nuance that Freire posits as essential for understanding the comprehensive failure of such an educational system to foster critical pedagogy.

In the problem-posing educational model Freire advocates, both students and teachers are co-creators of knowledge. This pedagogical approach disman-tles the traditional superior-inferior dynamics, thereby disrupting the bank-ing model's monopoly on educational authority. The problem-posing method encourages students to engage with issues critically, recognizing the complex-ity inherent in many social and academic questions. This not only develops the students' critical faculties but also serves to undermine the fallacy of the teacher as the sole fount of wisdom.

In this way, we find a contrast between the banking model of education and critical pedagogy. As he opposes the system in which facts are deposited into the mind of passive students, he gives importance to curiosity and critical thinking. Freire's ideas are democratic and radical in nature, which is the result of his own experiences as a teacher and interactions with his students. His ideas are mainly about education, but there is also an appeal to be aware of social and political circumstances.

3.2.4 Connection between Thoughts on Human Nature and Education

Freire was very certain that any educational practice must imply a theoretical stance related to interpretation of man and the world (Freire, 1970a). That is why the relationship of humans with the world is a central topic of discussion in his educational thought. Freire clearly differentiates between humans and non-humans where humans are subjective beings who can transform their reality. At the same time, Freire's idea of human nature shows that although by nature we are incomplete, we can work towards our own development, which is possible through education. Hence, understanding ourselves and our relationship with the world should be the starting point before embark-ing on our journey to liberation from oppressive environment. Moreover, through his experiences in society, he concludes that the existing banking model of education is not the right way to achieve that. He believes that undermining the subjective nature of human beings eventually leads to a de-humanizing and oppressive behaviour in society. While he recognizes that relations among human beings are often oppressive, he also sees human relations as the key to collective liberation. In education, this kind of oppressive human relation is taken as the relationship between teacher and students. On the contrary, critical pedagogy proposed by Freire criticizes the existing established relationships where some people have power or knowledge, and some do not; and where some people give orders, and others obey without question.

Freire's analysis of the dual aspect of human nature, i.e., Discerning and Transcending human beings, has been reflected in his pedagogical thoughts. He emphasizes over developing contextual curricula to help in developing critical consciousness among the masses in order to proceed towards humanization. Freire argues that curriculum should not be prepared by the educator beforehand, but it must be evolved through the process of participation and interaction with the students (Horton & Freire, 1990, p. 155). This stance, clearly, is an implication of the idea of praxis and the process of discerning and transcending. Moreover, he also emphasizes that content should not be fixed, but it must be updated and recreated according to the region, time, context, and audience. He argues that when a teacher prepares content *apriori*, then it necessarily leads to the transferring of information directly to the minds of children without scrutinizing or having a critical dialogue.

The banking model, which is rightly pointed out by Freire, is problematic for individuals as well as society. Even today, most of the existing pedagogies have become a tool for controlling students. Teachers are reduced to the status of technicians, and hence critical thinking, reflection, imagination, creativity etc., have no scope in education. We also find that in the initial shaping years of students, there is a lack of sympathy, empathy, and acceptance towards other people's opinions. Openness, carefulness, humility, tolerance, equality, and freedom can only be the result of a democratic way of imparting education. In this sense, the ideas of Paulo Freire are not only limited to a particular location and period, but they have global implications. Based on the above discussions, we can say that his ideas on education are broad enough which take into consideration the basic human nature, individual freedom, and equality among teachers, students, and others for the transformation of society. Hence, for such an oppressed system where there is no space for individuality, freedom and equality, Freire introduces problem-posing education. The notions of freedom, equality, and dialogue are significant because if human by nature is incomplete, then there is a need to have an equal connection with other humans to grow at the personal level as well as collective levels.

Freire considers dialogue based on the 'word' as a form of praxis. If praxis is part of the nature of the human being, then the word is also an inseparable part of human nature. In praxis, both action and reflection are required to transform the world. Similarly, a word is an essential part of critical dialogue for people. Dialogue is an act of love, humility, faith, trust, critical thinking, and hope. Dialogue is an act that makes real education possible and, as a result, overcoming banking contradictions. Moreover, Dialogue functions in a horizontal relationship among humans. Therefore, it eliminates the vertical hierarchal relationships of banking education and provides a new dimension to education i.e., education for freedom.

To sum, Freire's educational philosophy is anchored upon his belief in the human capacity for freedom, growth, and effective social action. While all persons (and societies) are conditioned by the past, they are never fully determined but are permanently 'unfinished' and 'incomplete.' Therefore, Freire tirelessly voiced for more humanization of people through critical dialogues and the process of questioning. Moreover, the question of human nature lies at the centre of his educational thought.

3.3   Jiddu Krishnamurti (1895–1986)

3.3.1   Brief Biography

Jiddu Krishnamurti was one of the original and revolutionary thinkers of the contemporary era. He was born in 1895 in a small town called Madanapalli, India. He was initially associated with the 'Theosophical Society' but later left it as he realized that to find truth one need not necessarily require a defined path which is generally shown by a particular religion or sect. According to him, no organization, dogma, creed, ritual, philosophical knowledge can lead one to the truth. He stresses that one must find it through the mirror of relationship, through the understanding of the contents of mind, and through observation. Krishnamurti travelled all over the world to give talks and engage in dialogues with common people as well as scholars, teachers, and students. In general, Krishnamurti criticized modern educational institutions as they cultivate competitiveness and fear in children through discipline, authority, and conformity. On the other hand, he advocated for right kind of education which should be based upon freedom and self-knowledge for inner transformation of the human beings, as well as liberation from the societal conditioning. He emphasized that central goal of education is to understand life and us. With these aims he established many schools in India and abroad to provide an environment for wholistic development of children. Krishnamurti was not a formal academician that is why most of the literature related to his ideas are the collection of his public talks and dialogues. Some notable collections include 'Freedom from the known,' 'The book of life,' 'The first and the last freedom,' 'The awakening of intelligence,' etc. Until his death in 1986, Krishnamurti continued to focus upon finding the true meaning of life.

3.3.2   Thoughts on Human Nature

Krishnamurti was not an established academic philosopher, at least in terms of modern academic parameters. Most of his primary works are the collection of his teachings, and we can clearly witness the vastness and frequent diversion of thoughts from one topic to another. Although finding a clear philosophy or specific views about 'human nature' from his teachings is a herculean task, a common thread can be extracted from his diverse range of thoughts which majorly revolves around 'to become absolutely and unconditionally free.'

Krishnamurti observed human life in totality. He argues that an individual entity is liable to be conditioned, frustrated, aggressive, jealous, or miserable. But a human being is also capable to elevate above all these little negativities. Through human beings, he talks about the whole mankind, and that is why he stressed that individual transformation is essential for larger social transformation. That is why he emphasizes over close integration between man and their society, culture, and the environment as a whole. He puts is as "One has to understand ... as an actual fact—that we are the world and the world is us" (Krishnamurti, 1973, p. 75). Krishnamurti further argues that we are prone to societal conditioning through ideologies, religions, and education. This conditioning results into creation of a false image of ourselves which eventually distant us from the world. Therefore, to remove this conditioning and become completely free, one needs to understand our relationship with the world. But, in the process of doing it, one needs to understand herself first because the human being is centre for all of our actions and thoughts.

To understand oneself, Krishnamurti suggests looking in totality and not in fragmentation. This understanding should be at the deeper levels of our beings and not at just superficial levels of mind. In this process, Krishnamurti invokes the idea of 'observer' and 'observed.' He questions that how can an observer be different from what he observes? He asserts that an observer is the accumulation of all the past experiences and cultural influences (Krishnamurti, 1969). Everything an observer observes is based upon his past knowledge. He further argues that when we look at the observer, we look at ourselves, which is made of memories and experiences. It is like observing our own inner thing. For example, when an observer who is afraid look into his fear, he is not different than the fear itself. That means any effort to get rid of the fear assumes that both (fear and observer) are separate but, in actual they are not. Krishnamurti argues that "when you see that you are a part of fear, not separate from it—that you are fear—then you cannot do anything about it; then fear comes totally to an end" (ibid., p. 46). Therefore, Krishnamurti asserts that there should not be a differentiation between the observer and the observed. He further claims that this division leads to the identification of things in terms of 'I' and 'not I,' which leads to conditioning. In Krishnamurti's terms, the observer is our conditioned mind, and that is the main concern. He claims that a conditioned mind (observer) identifies the division of the observer and the observed (Krishnamurti, 1973). Thus, he suggests, to remove this conditioning we need to break this division of observer and observed, and that will be the state of absolute freedom.

Here, although not clearly expressed, we can infer about Krishnamurti's overall understanding of the inherent nature of human beings. It can be said that he looked at human beings as the bundle of various fundamental dispositions and characteristics which is accumulated over a period. He argues that our consciousness becomes conditioned from the moment we are born. Our consciousness is the result of all the experiences we get intentionally or unintentionally. Therefore, he concludes: "What are you? You are all that conditioning" (ibid., p. 389). A human is the result of all the experiences in the form of conditioning, and we cannot separate her consciousness from the experiences. Here, it can be interpreted from the above discussion that Krishnamurti does not see any major difference between man and the world since the world is created by a conditioned man. Hence, to change the world the man has to change first. It is also clear from the above discussion that Krishnamurti sees human beings as the result of various kinds of conditioning, and that is the main cause of problems. This is because, until we are free from all the conditioning, we cannot see things very clearly, whether it is our own personality or anything outside. This conditioning gives the sense of differentiation of observer-observed but, there is no fragmentation as such.

As per Krishnamurti, the human mind is by nature deeply conditioned and contaminated by thoughts. From the very childhood, all experiences get imprinted in our minds, which get reflected in our actions. These experiences are mixture of many emotions and thoughts, which are mainly of the nature of violence and peace. Not only from birth, but he also even sees these experiences as the result of long evolutionary history of mankind (Krishnamurti, 1969, p. 5). He argues that past experiences are responsible for our actions (positive or negative) in life because every action, positively or negatively, can be traced back to our habits and behaviour. He also argues that these experiences form layers to our true nature, and in that sense, we are conditioned. And since these are external conditioning, we are capable of removing them.

Krishnamurti suggests the practice of meditation in the form of awareness to overcome conditioning. Awareness, for Krishnamurti, is a means to know ourselves and our relationship with the world, including ideas, people, and things (Krishnamurti, 1954). He emphasized equally upon awareness of external stimuli as well as our own sensations. To begin with, he suggests for being aware of our pleasure and pain without being attached to it. Therefore, he gives immense importance to 'choiceless awareness.' He explains choiceless awareness as: "to be aware from moment to moment without accumulating the experience which awareness brings; because, the moment you accumulate, you are aware only according to that accumulation, according to that pattern, according to that experience" (ibid., p. 110). He also clarifies that we should not confuse awareness with introspection. We do introspection by examining ourselves in order to change or modify. In this process a desire for the end result is always attached. In that case, we are again get caught into the process of accumulation where 'I' examine something, which leads to a process of frustration. Hence, Krishnamurti emphasizes over choiceless awareness, which brings understanding without any attachment or accumulation of new thoughts. He sees choiceless awareness as constant observation of every thought, feeling and action arising within oneself.

To sum, in order to become free, first step is to look at things in totality and accept that we are not free. We need to realize that we are conditioned and controlled by the various dimension of life. Therefore, Krishnamurti suggests to analyse ourselves and our relationships carefully. And in the process, we increase our awareness towards our true nature and our bond with the world. In order to achieve this state of fully aware and free, Krishnamurti suggests to start with the observation of everything, including our own thoughts, actions, feelings etc., for which he calls choiceless awareness. His main motive was to cultivate this choiceless awareness in children because if one is aware of their conditioning, thoughts, dispositions, fears etc., then only further effort of undoing it could be possible. In Krishnamurti's view, choiceless awareness is key for reverting back to our true nature, which is free from all bonding.

3.3.3   Thoughts on Education

Krishnamurti criticized traditional education throughout his writings. He was highly critical of the traditional methods of teaching and the values being infused in the children. In his view, the traditional educational system focuses on imparting knowledge rather than making students learn through various methods and activities in which they have space for themselves. It encourages comparison and competition in a child, which leads to frustration, fear, and envy, as well as becomes an impediment to the natural process of learning (Krishnamurti, 1963). Moreover, Krishnamurti argues that any educational method that emphasizes upon the differences in children encourages division in society. On the contrary, education, in a true sense, should help a child to become mature and free, and to develop an integrated outlook toward life and the world (Krishnamurti, 1953). But the traditional system tries to shape children according to some idealistic pattern, which is problematic. It focuses on how to conform children to an existing societal structure. They try to shape a child to abide by the rules of a pre-existing system. Education today has remained only about technologies, skills, and institutions, and only produce specialists in all fields. Krishnamurti was totally against it as he wanted to make humans free from all kinds of 'conditioning.'

Krishnamurti also shed light on what should be a 'right education.' In his view, the right education is that which eliminates fear from the children. Fear generally emerges as the result of negative activities such as competition and comparison. These fear-producing activities gradually make the mind dull and cripple our thinking. Therefore, Krishnamurti argues that the right education should work to remove various kinds of fear from our life, such as fear from parents, teachers, and opinions as well as from marks, grading, comparison, etc. (Krishnamurti, 1963). Krishnamurti contends that education is not a mere accumulation of information and correlating them, but it should focus on understanding the significance of life. In addition to that, the right education is entirely different from merely learning certain facts and passing a few examinations to get a job, but it should prepare one for whole life. That is why he opposes the overemphasis on vocational training at an early age. It creates a society in which people are not balanced and happy with their chosen fields. They are not able to understand their true potential and hence, are unable to find a profession that will satisfy their talents and interests. Therefore, He insists that education should prepare children to understand the problems of life and help them to know their own selves. Without knowing oneself, one cannot progress much in terms of decision-making or problem-solving (Krishnamurti, 1953).

Krishnamurti opposes the traditional education system because, in his view, it focuses on 'what one should become.' The whole business is directed towards some future goal which creates the sense that the person is not complete in his present moment. He emphasizes that the right education should make people understand 'what they are' rather than 'what should become.' He argues that only that mind which is trained to think, analyse, and adjust in the present moment will be able to adjust according to future challenges. Therefore, educational institutions should focus on developing the qualities of sensitivity, awareness, and critical thinking. He urges students to become thoughtful and fully aware of their surrounding as this practice leads to becoming more sensitive about us and everything related to ourselves (Krishnamurti, 1970).

Krishnamurti emphasizes the cultivation of awareness in children. He sees education as a means for the all-around development of the human, not just training of a mind to fit in the norms of a particular society. Awareness, in

Krishnamurti view, is a tool that enables us to understand ourselves, our situations, and our capacities, thereby ultimately becoming a good human being.
It is also important to note that he doesn't mean awareness as looking within
oneself process only, but he gives ample importance to be aware of our surroundings and nature equally. He urges that children should have exposure
to nature and art too. It creates a sense of beauty and deteriorates a sense of
attachment and egoism. This helps a person to have a good understanding of
his relationship with others as well as with nature. Education should create
an intelligent mind with love and compassion in students. For that, spirituality is a key factor. Here spirituality, in Krishnamurti's view, is not something
religious, but to be spiritual is to have a mind which is absolutely and unconditionally free.

These are some of the core ideas of Krishnamurti related to education and
learning. Now, let us analyse how his general philosophy of humans is related
to his thoughts on education.

3.3.4   Connection between Thoughts on Human Nature and Education

It can be seen very clearly from the above discussion that the purpose of education and the general philosophy of Krishnamurti goes along similar lines.
In simple words, it can be summarized that by emptying the mind, one can
perceive truth. So, education should be such that it teaches students the nature
and limitations of thought and helps them to get rid of all conditioning and
go beyond all limitations such as confusion, fears, conflicts, etc. According to
Krishnamurti, learning can only happen when we become aware and observe
things. Total awareness, which is the outcome of not having impressions of
any things on our mind, is the key to learning. Krishnamurti, from an educational perspective, proclaims that parents and teachers shouldn't force their
ideas and thoughts upon children. Children are not a psychological extension
of their parents. A true teacher is one who 'directs' the students to live life
truly. Again, to clarify here, directing doesn't mean forcing ideas or thoughts
on children.

For Krishnamurti, factor of becoming free from every conditioning and getting away from all kinds of influences is a major concern in his general idea of
the philosophy of human nature as well as in education. He wants such education which emphasizes upon a child's own ideas, thoughts, and teachers should
provide ways in order to achieve freedom from all kinds of conditioning. His
basic philosophy contends that problems, sufferings, and sorrows in life are
due to our own conditioning. We build different identities given by society,
religion, culture, status, tradition, qualifications, etc. that lead to divisions in
society. These identities can be removed by the process of un-conditioning.

And education is an important medium for this. The basic human nature of negative psychological tendencies like greed, and selfishness, along with the psychological impact on us from environment, causes problems. Total freedom from such problems is only possible by being aware of things. Educational activities which allow creative thinking, contact with nature, learning without choosing, and engaging in arts lead a child to see things objectively, to observe things, and to become aware of them without having prejudices in their mind.

Krishnamurti established such schools in which this kind of education is provided. The appointment of a teacher is also made by considering these factors. Krishnamurti's dialogues and public talks on topics of education, silence, the purpose of education, awareness, and many more are relatable and practically applied in these schools. The schools are usually found in an open natural environment. Here, students are not pressured by educators; instead, they are involved in any activities or subjects of their interests. Activities like art, gardening, sculpture making, reading, writing, etc. are promoted, which bring overall transformation in a child's life. Apart from tangible skills, these natural environments provide the avenue for the development of good virtues like humility, selflessness, and compassion. Through regular practice of pure observation of the surroundings and of one own self, slowly and gradually, the mind becomes prejudice-free, which makes a man free in the truest sense.

To conclude, I would say that Krishnamurti's views on education stems from his views related to nature of human beings. He emphasises upon understanding of human psyche to make transformation in the education as well as society. He argues that any fundamental changes in society require a change in human understanding, and education should be designed in such way to facilitate these changes.

4   Conclusion

We have seen how humans deliberately practice education to change and modify the behaviour of a particular person. At the same time, education works as a tool that equips us to understand ourselves and our relationship with the world. Therefore, it will not be fallacious to say that we are as much influenced by education as we influence educational practices. Unlike other animals, education plays a crucial role in human lives. It not only helps to transfer knowledge to the next generation, but it also gives us the ability to understand ourselves and our relationship with the world. Thereby, the ability to change and transform the world according to our needs. It is also evident that the forms and structure of educational practices were not always the same. Education is dependent upon the requirements of a particular society in a particular time and space. But, in all those different scenarios, one underlined assumption is common throughout, i.e., 'education transforms humans.' That is why we try to establish a link between humans and their practices. Until we have some idea about the nature of humans, we cannot design a system to transform them. Hence, it is very much essential to understand the fundamental nature of humans. There are various efforts made throughout history to understand the fundamental nature of humans, but they see humans from a particular perspective, mostly emerging out of various socio-political and personal biases. That is why we try to formulate an evidence-based theory of human nature that can be made a reference point to design the new educational system or calibrate our existing systems.

In examining the philosophies of John Dewey, Paulo Freire, and Jiddu Krishnamurti, one finds that their views on education are deeply rooted in their conceptions of human nature. However, a comparative analysis reveals significant divergences that offer distinct pathways for educational philosophy. Freire, for example, is preoccupied with socio-political structures that create a dichotomy between oppressors and the oppressed, leading to his critique of the 'banking model' of education. In contrast, Krishnamurti posits that human suffering stems from internal psychological conditioning, effectively de-emphasizing socio-political structures as the primary source of educational challenges.

The two diverge fundamentally on whether obstacles to meaningful education are external or internal, a distinction that has profound implications for educational practice. Meanwhile, Dewey, with his focus on experiential learning and democratic schooling, offers yet another lens, suggesting that human nature is fundamentally social and must be nurtured through interactive and communal educational experiences. Dewey's analysis also opens another avenue for discussion, particularly concerning the cultivation of empathy and sympathy as integral to a democratic educational model. This contrasts with Freire's model, which may implicitly accommodate empathy and sympathy but primarily through a lens of social justice.

The objective here is not to affirm the veracity of these philosophers' views but to explore the complex relationships between their foundational assumptions about human nature and their theories of education. The insights gleaned from such a comparative analysis demonstrate the interrelatedness of their philosophies of human nature and education, albeit in distinctly different directions.

To conclude, we can firmly say that a particular assumption about human nature gives rise to different conceptions about education. Hence, it becomes of utmost importance to understand human beings first before discussing education. Thus, in the next chapter, we will try to formulate an objective evidence-based theory of human nature. Understanding the nature of human beings is an age-long question that almost every philosopher has pondered over. However, most of them were the result of speculation or shared understanding about humans and the world. But now, we are much more capable of doing objective research due to the advancement of technology and empirical methods in cognitive science. The upcoming chapter will outline some of the historical efforts in understanding human nature, followed by modern understanding based on recent empirical evidence in cognitive sciences.

CHAPTER 3

Understanding Human Nature

Theories and Debates

Throughout intellectual history across the world, people have been trying to understand the world and humankind. Any person with an enquiring mindset tries to formulate at least some opinions about the fundamental nature of humankind. Defining human nature is a complex undertaking due to the diverse characteristics, cultural backgrounds, and historical contexts that humans possess. Grant Ramsey (2023) notes that, universal generalizations about what is essential to all humans are difficult to pinpoint, as they risk being either overly broad or excessively trivial. Moreover, defining human nature also depends upon the background and beliefs of the enquirer. A lawyer, a biologist, or an economist, for instance, might give completely different opinions. Therefore, to formulate a consistent and objective theory of human nature, we need to consider the discussions from various fields of sciences and social sciences like—Biology, Sociology, Anthropology, Philosophy, Psychology, and many more. Whatever activities related to human beings we do, more or less, depend upon what theory of human nature we accept. Therefore, any activity related to humans, including education, should begin with understanding their basic nature, capacities, and limitations.

A common everyday understanding of human nature refers to something which can be called essential to humans. In other words, we can say that it is intrinsic to humans, differentiating us from other species. But this generalized view too has problems which we will see in the later part of this chapter. There are diverse range of debate concerning whether there are some inherent traits that all humans possess, or if we are just result of environmental influence. Another significant point of discussion is whether there is something beyond the physical body of humans or not. These different stances try to uncover some elements, if not all, of human nature. These different stances or beliefs lead to different views about what we are, what we can do, and what we ought to do.

Almost every philosophical view presupposes one or another concept of human nature within it. Some try to emphasize physical aspects, and some focus more on the psychological aspects of human nature, which give rise to various points of debate among philosophers. Indeed, there are numerous theories about the fundamental nature of human beings, but collectively, most such theories are the result of armchair thinking. But now, with the advent of empirical

© AKHIL K. SINGH, 2025 | DOI:10.1163/9789004724372_003

methods, we are no longer handicapped by mere speculation or armchair thinking, and now we are much more capable of articulating a comprehensive empirically grounded theory of human nature. But, before discussing recent theories based on empirical evidence, let us have a brief historical excursus.

In the following paragraphs, a brief survey of various conceptions about human nature has been outlined. Subsequently, I shall outline two major issues that emerge from the discussion of various theories related to human nature. These issues are the mind-body problem and the nature vs. nurture debate. Then in the last section, I shall discuss how contemporary empirical studies challenge the existing viewpoints and provide a convincing solution to the age-old debates. The objective of this chapter is to establish that contemporary studies provide a middle ground among the opposing viewpoints about the nature of humans and how they paint the picture of humans as embodied persons.

1   Historical Survey of Theories of Human Nature

This section provides a brief overview of major theories of human nature across traditions. I have mostly drawn from the book 'Thirteen theories of human nature' (Stevenson et al., 2018) for the purpose of reviewing major theories.

1.1   *Early Greek Views*
1.1.1   Plato
Plato dates back around two and half millennia, but his thoughts have been influential among many thinkers down the line and are still relevant. Plato's core ideas are reflected in his metaphysical theory of forms. 'Forms' are unchangeable and indestructible immaterial aspects of reality that have their own place of existence. Everything else on earth are the shadows of forms. Plato exercises a similar dualist notion for the explanation of human beings. According to that, human beings consist of two parts: a soul (or mind) with non-material and eternal nature; and a body of material nature. He emphasizes that the human soul exists apart from the body, and it is eternal as it exists before birth as well as after death.

Further, Plato explains three tendencies of the human mind, which are famously called Plato's tripartite theory. These three tendencies are Appetite (physical urges such as hunger or sexual desires), Reason, and Spirit (emotions of anger, jealousy, etc.). He argues that all three tendencies are present in every human; however, the degree of all three might differ.

Another vital point of Plato's understanding of human nature is that Plato considered humans as social beings. He explains that an individual is not self-sufficient, and each of us has many needs that we cannot fulfil alone. We need help and co-operation from other individuals. That means different individuals have different aptitudes and interests. Therefore, we see diversity of experiences and occupations in the world. Here we can see that despite making the human soul eternal and unchangeable, he accepts the changeable nature of human beings due to the three aspects of the personality in varying degrees. Following this philosophy, Plato's views on education stress appropriate education to produce well-balanced and just people.

1.1.2 Aristotle

Aristotle was a pupil of Plato, but despite being influenced by Plato's ideas, he criticized him on several issues. Also, Aristotle's writings were more inclined toward empirical scientific methods due to his medical family background. Plato's theory of Forms influenced Aristotle, but he criticized the idea of the total separation of Forms and Matter. He argues that there are some properties common to all, but their existence is not separate from the things that have them. He rejected the idea of another intelligible world beyond the world of perceptible material things. Implying this, he accepts the existence of the soul as the Form of humans but not in Platonic terms. According to Aristotle, the soul is the Form of living beings that makes something the fundamental 'sort of thing.' It is not something that exists outside in some other world apart from the material body, but it is something that is the very essence of things. Hence, the soul or human mind is not a thing or substance which can exist separately from human beings.

According to Aristotle, the human mind or soul has the property of various reasoning faculties, such as thought and Intellect. He conceived these properties as a formal cause for the existence of a thing. Also, these properties are commonly present in similar kinds of things in a group. He also emphasizes the understanding of categories that classify various groups of things. For example, all humans will have some things or substances categorically different from plants or other animals. Therefore, to conclude, we can say that Aristotle draws from the platonic view of human nature, but he opposes the independent existence of the soul/mind apart from the human body and puts it back to the very existence of a thing. According to Aristotle mind/soul is the inseparable property of the human.

1.2 *Religious Views*

1.2.1 Christianity

According to the Old Testament (Hebrew version), God created humans to occupy a special position in the universe and have dominion over the rest of animals, plants, or anything on the earth (Towner, 2005). It establishes the theory of creation in which the human race is considered unique and different from other creatures. At the same time, humans are seen as continuous with nature as they are made from dust to which they return. Moreover, a human being is made in the image of God. Hence, humans are creatures that have rationality and the personhood of God, which makes us unique and different from all creatures. Human beings also have self-consciousness, freedom of choice, and the ability to love freely. Here we do not find any differentiation of material-nonmaterial (body and soul) aspects of humans. Also, the Old Testament is silent on the afterlife.

But, after the coming of Jesus, we can witness some differentiation of human beings in terms of Spirit and Flesh (Romans 8: 1–12). This does not mean our usual understanding of Spirit and Flesh in terms of incorporeal soul and physical body. Instead, it is the progression from living in our old nature (biological needs and desires) to the new spiritual nature (spirituality and peace). One important development in the New Testament was the doctrine of the incarnation. A human life is possible after death through resurrection. That means they have some underlying beliefs of some kind of immortal and eternal aspect as part of humans.

Stevenson et al. point out that the notion of freedom given to humans is the most critical point in terms of understanding human nature. Humans are supposed to be free to choose between good and evil. But, we tend to choose evil (as Adam did), and therefore, God punishes our disobedience by sending pain and suffering. Furthermore, to restore our relationship with God, we should do our duties and incline towards good. Then, we can get salvation through the mercy of God. Hence, it can be implied that humans are by nature sinful, but that might be transformed through our actions. This emphasizes nurturing good qualities to transform one's old innate nature.

1.2.2 Confucianism

Confucius (551–479 BCE) has the most significant influence over Chinese thought and civilization. Most of the Confucian philosophy is based upon a text known as 'Lun Yu,' translated in English usually as 'The Analects.' Confucius gave much emphasis on the discourse of humans rather than metaphysics. He cared more about human conditions and activities than explaining grand theories of the universe or metaphysical entities like God, spirit etc. Confucius was optimistic about human potential and their accomplishments. He was convinced that every person has the potential to become a sage. He conceived all human beings as fundamentally equal with the same potentiality for growth. He mentions that men are "in nature close to one another, in practice far apart" (B. Watson, 2007, p. 120). From the above statement, we can infer that he pointed toward divergence in behaviour through our actions in the world. We can argue that for Confucius, all human beings are by nature the same, but they become different due to their nurture. He seems to be suggesting that our surrounding greatly influence our personality.

However, Confucius originally did not claim that humans are fundamentally flawed nature which needs to be improved, or they are with good character and it got maligned due to our course of actions. It gave rise to various views and opinions in the Confucius tradition later on. For instance, Mencius (371–289 BCE) contended that human nature is originally good. Whereas, Hsün Tzu (310–220 BCE) argued that human nature is originally evil. The core takeaway of both thinkers is that they both considered fundamental human nature as innate. On one side, Mencius argued that humans are by birth good and compassionate but they become evil when they lose their original nature due to their desires. Contrary to it, Hsün Tzu says that Man's original nature is evil and goodness results from conscious activity. Although both philosophers have very opposites views over the original nature of humans in theory, they both emphasized the importance of culture. Hence, they believed in proper education and training to transform human beings into sages.

1.2.3   Hinduism (Vedic) Views

Summarising the philosophical thoughts of the whole Vedic tradition is a herculean task, as there is no single authoritative text and no definite beginning. Vedic philosophy is present mainly in the collection of texts known as the *Upaniṣad*, which are more than a hundred in number. Nevertheless, Principal *Upaniṣad* (ten in number) are usually considered base texts. A general overview of Vedic philosophy can be traced to *Bṛhadāraṇyaka Upaniṣad*. It is one of the oldest and largest texts in the group of *Upaniṣad*. It mainly lays down the fundamental principles concerning the creation of the universe. The central tenet is that universe is ultimately interconnected in the form of an ontological unity. It is denoted as Brahman, which is the ultimate reality. Other multiplicities in the world which we usually experience are mere illusions, and therefore they are not ontologically different from the Brahman. Similarly, regarding humans, Vedic philosophy believes in the existence of an eternal and immaterial aspect of humans which is denoted as *Ātman* or Soul. It considers Brahman to be the only reality, and other things are a mere representation of it, so in a way, the only real ultimate reality is Brahman. At the same time, every human has *Ātman*, which is a small fraction of *Brahman*. Hence, every human might have a different soul, but logically, every soul is identical to the Super soul or Brahman. This can be understood from the examples of a centre and the various nodes connected to the exact centre. *Bṛhadāraṇyaka Upaniṣad* explain this concept with the help of the metaphor of the moon and its multiple reflections. They consider the moon as the Brahman, and multiple reflections in the pond can be equated as different *Ātman*. If we analyse, it is evident that the only real thing is the moon (*Brahman*), and others are mere reflections (*Ātman*). That is why the *Upaniṣads* argue that every human derives the same qualities as Brahman.

Regarding the theory of human nature, *Upaniṣads* recognize human beings as interconnected to other creatures as every creature has an *Ātman*, and each *Ātman* reflects the same Brahman. The Brahman has the character of truth-consciousness-bliss or *Sat-cit-ānanda*. But, this individual self, when attached to a body, develops the level of ego (*Ahaṁkāra*). This ego-attached self is the self that we generally recognize and experience. Therefore, we cannot identify the true nature of the self. It becomes conditioned and finite and masks our true selves. Moreover, Atman is the subject—a true witness of all of our activities. Therefore, according to the *Upaniṣads, Ātman* cannot be an object, and we cannot know about it. We can only remove these additional from it, and it will reveal its true nature automatically.

If we analyse the above-generalized views, it can be implied that human is born with all the good qualities essentially. Still, due to our course of action in the world, multiple layers (aspects of personality) get attached. Also, as *Ātman* is identical to Brahman, it is immortal and eternal. Here we can find complete differentiation between material bodies and immaterial soul aspects of humans. It implies that educational practices evolved in Hinduism focused on removing extra worldly layers (e.g., ego, etc.) of conditioning so that we can realize our true selves.

1.2.4 Buddhist Views

Buddhism as a tradition emerged during the 5th–6th BCE in the northern part of India. It includes a variety of philosophical thoughts and conceptions about human life based on Gautama Buddha's teachings. Buddha's main focus was to help people come out of their misery. Soon, his teachings spread across many parts of Asia and took the shape of religion. In the initial phase, Buddha used to give verbal lectures, but when the size of the sangha started to enlarge, the codification of his teachings became necessary, which led to the compilation of three different texts known as Pali canons (*Tripiṭaka*). Buddhism mainly focuses on understanding oneself and the world to become free from misery. Metaphysical issues such as God, Soul, etc., have been largely avoided from the discussion. However, Gautama Buddha himself avoided the metaphysical questions, but various inferences are drawn from his preaching later on.

Moreover, as Buddha was silent on some of the metaphysical questions, his pupils tried to interpret his teachings in different ways, which created divisions in Buddhism in the later period. However, the core principles of Buddhism are unanimously accepted by all sects.

The core philosophy of Buddhism is the theory of existence which have three central pillars. These are the Theory of impermanence (*anicca*), No-self theory (anatta), and un-satisfactoriness (*duḥkha*). Buddha holds that nothing in this world is permanent or has independent existence. With the help of the theory of dependent origination (*pratītyasamutpāda*), he explains the conditional nature of things which is why nothing is permanent, and one product may become the cause of another product. The same theory applies to our mental aspects too. All thoughts are linked with other thoughts or experiences. Even our senses, mind, body, consciousness, etc., have dependent origination and hence are not permanent in nature. But, due to our ignorance of noble truths and the real nature of things, we tend to suffer. Therefore, Buddha suggests that breaking this chain is necessary for achieving liberation.

A more detailed explanation of humans and their nature of existence is found in the later-developed text *Milinda Pañha* which is the transcription of a conversation between one King, Milinda, and a wise Buddhist sage Nagasena. The conclusion of the encounter is the establishment of the theory of aggregates. Nagasena sees no basis to believe in the claim (prevailing at that time) that a person consists of a permanent, unchanging, autonomous self. He gave an example of a chariot to make Milinda understand. A chariot comprises various parts like axles, wheels, seats, structure, etc. But separately, these constituents cannot be called chariots. However, when we aggregate all the components, the concept of the chariot becomes a reality. At the same time, any particular constituents of the chariot are not the chariot itself. A similar case is with humans. We have different constituents, and when all constituents are combined, we call it a living being. Nagasena argues for five components or aggregates of living beings called *Skandhas*.

Buddhists emphasize that as there is no chariot separate from its components, likewise, there is no 'person' apart from these five Skandhas. These five components (*Skandhas*) are 'form' (*rūpa*)—the body including sense organs, 'sensations' (*vedanā*)—a physiological process resulting from the interaction of sense organs with their subjects, 'perception' (*saṃjñā*)—object recognition due to sensations, 'mental formations' (*saṃskāra*)—our predispositions, impulses, attitudes, etc. which make our unique personality, and 'consciousness' (*vijñāna*)—awareness of one's own living moments. These *Skandhas*, like everything, have a dependent origin, and they can be considered neither independent nor permanent. This view makes a shift from the common understanding of a central permanent entity which we denote as self or soul. However, Buddhism does not deny the sense of self-reference, individuality, or continuity of memory. Owing to these experiences of passing moments, we tend to believe in a central permanent entity, but this is merely an illusion. We constantly have experiences, creating new memories and continuous state of flux. That means a human 'being' is more of a human 'becoming.' This explanation removes the requirement of a permanent and eternal soul, eliminating the idea of one's permanent individuality.

Therefore, to conclude, it is clear from the above discussion that all of our mental activities, including the sense of individuality and continuity, arise out of the chain of events that ultimately starts from our body and sense organs. Therefore, Buddhism proposes the idea of embodied human beings, which eliminates the necessity of an eternal and fixed entity such as the soul, since human is no more than an aggregate of five *Skandhas*.

1.2.5 Islamic Views

Islam is a monotheistic religion that has historical roots in Christianity and Judaism. It arose in the seventh century in Arabia when the prophet Muhammad had a series of direct revelations from God. These direct revelations were codified in the form of the Quran, which is the central text of Islam. As Quran is a religious text, it mainly contains ethical and directive narrations. Later it is interpreted by many followers as peeking into the nature of human beings. Although the Islamic theory of genesis proceeds on similar lines to the Biblical account, the Quran and *Ḥadīth* (record of words and actions of Prophet Muhammad) revisit Adam-Eve's tale with some new and revised interpretations. According to Quran, Adam and Eve were tempted together by *satan* in the garden, but Adam repented, and Allah forgave him. Thus, unlike Christianity, in which sin becomes the inherited property of humankind due to Adam's fall, forgiveness becomes fundamental property for repented Adam in Islam. Later commentaries in Islamic tradition pairs Adam with Muhammad as the alpha and omega in the history of prophecy. Moreover, Islamic tradition believes that God communicates with humankind through selected representatives (prophets) to help humans for leading righteous life. To sum up, Islamic tradition believes that God is full of mercy and forgiveness. Furthermore, all of humanity inherits this nature of 'repent' instead of 'original sin.'

In Quran and other later works of literature in Islam discuss two aspects of humans: *nafs* and *ruh*. *Nafs* is literally translated into English as 'self' and *ruh* as 'breath' or 'wind,' which indicates the divine quality. Some commentaries use both terms interchangeably, but collectively, *nafs* (soul) is an innate aspect of humankind that desires good things in the world. However, it is inclined towards evil (Quran 12:53). Therefore, God's mercy becomes necessary to save a human soul from falling into evil. From the above explanation, it can be surmised that human beings do not inherit the 'Evil' quality. Still, it is the consequence developed through the actions taken to seek particular desires. That is why Quran prescribes to restrain from these desires (Quran 79:40). Apart from *nafs*, the Quran also refers the existence of a *fitra*—inner nature in humans, which is an inclination towards God.

To sum up, in Islamic philosophy, there is not much discussion specifically about the human mind but have some references to the inherent nature of human beings. It suggests that human beings have something innate other than their body. Also, the role of the environment in shaping this inner nature has also been taken into account.

1.3 *Early Modern Western Views (Age of Scientific Methods)*

In the medieval era, western philosophy was dominated by Christian philosophers due to the control of the Church upon society. During that period, most of the views were influenced by Biblical beliefs about humans and the world. But, from the beginning of the sixteenth-century modern physical sciences started to rise. Many metaphysical and natural conceptions were being explained with the help of experimental methods and systematic mathematical calculations. Galileo Galilei (1564–1642 CE) and Isaac Newton (1642–1727 CE) were the initial torchbearers, inspiring many pathbreaking theories related to the universe and the physical world. This led to a question: how far can the scientific method be applied to human beings? This raised diverse opinions among philosophers and consequently resulted in many rival theories, such as Materialism and Dualism. The central issue was whether human beings are entirely composed of the same kind of matter which makes up the rest of the universe. Or are we a combination of material and something immaterial, which is different from the universe? I shall now discuss some major views concerning human nature which are influenced by new-age scientific methods:

1.3.1 Thomas Hobbes

Thomas Hobbes was primarily a political philosopher, but his ideas seem to be derived from his views related to the nature of an individual. Hobbes explicitly opposed dualism and Aristotelianism. He argued that the notion of the soul as an incorporeal substance is self-contradictory. Hobbes emphasized using the methods of physical sciences to explain human nature and society. He claimed that humans, by their intrinsic nature, are selfish, and everyone's desires are responsible for their survival and reproduction. To escape this state of nature, Hobbes argued that individuals must give up some of their rights and freedoms to a strong government, who would then enforce laws and maintain order. He notes that without a government people's life would be "solitary, poor, nasty, brutish, and short" (Hobbes, 1651).

1.3.2   Jean-Jacques Rousseau

Jean-Jacques Rousseau (1712–1778) was a French philosopher and had a very different view of human nature. He believed that human beings are inherently good but are corrupted by society and civilization. He saw modern society as being artificial and inauthentic, and believed that it was responsible for many of the problems people face, such as poverty, inequality, and conflict. Rousseau argued that human beings in their natural state were happy and fulfilled. But as society developed, people became more selfish, competitive, and isolated from one another. He believed that people in society are driven by their passions and desires, and that they have lost touch with their innate sense of morality and compassion. That is why Rousseau insists that institutions should aim to foster children's innate nature.

1.3.3   Descartes, Spinoza, and Rationalism

Rationalism is a philosophical and epistemological theory that asserts that reason is the primary source of knowledge. According to this theory, knowledge and certainty can be achieved through the use of reason and intuition, independent of experience and observation. French philosopher Rene Descartes (1596–1650) was a central figure of the scientific revolution and torch bearer of the rationalist tradition. He developed the dualist account of human nature; according to it, humans consist of an independent body and a mind or soul. Descartes conceived that body and mind are two distinct substances that exist independently; however, they interact together. He argued that the human body is just a physical entity without any thinking properties and is subject to laws of physical nature. Whereas the mind is the central thinking entity and does not occupy space, thereby cannot be studied by the methods of physical sciences. He even claimed that the soul is immortal and can survive after bodily death. This sharp distinction goes very deep as our complete knowledge, rationality, thinking, feeling, and consciousness become innate and designated to the soul.

Baruch Spinoza (1632–1677) further advocated this dual aspect of human nature with slight modification. For Spinoza, mind and matter are two aspects of one underlying reality. That means there are no two distinct substances but two attributes of one substance. Descartes is considered a pioneer of dualism in the West, which has had great influence over many philosophers and even on modern scientific developments. We will revisit the dualistic position in detail in further sections.

1.3.4   Locke, Hume, and Empiricism

John Locke (1632–1704) gave counterviews to rationalism and argued that all ideas originate from experiences. Though he retained the dualistic views, he asserted that all knowledge about the world must be based on experiences, unlike the existence of innate ideas according to rationalism. George Berkeley (1685–1753) and David Hume (1711–1776) further developed empiricism in the eighteenth century. Hume went one step ahead and argued that all ideas are derived from impressions, either of the 'senses' or 'reflection.' Hume even discarded the notion of a soul or mental substance since we are aware of nothing but a succession of mental states. He asserts that we are simply a bundle of perceptions. Therefore Empiricism explains consciousness as the stream of a continuous succession of various events in our life. This is opposite to the notion of a fixed human nature and advocates the significance of nurture aspect in humans.

1.3.5   Immanuel Kant

Immanuel Kant (1724–1804) was one of the most influential thinkers in modern history and is generally recognized as on par with Plato and Aristotle. He started his philosophical journey with the German rationalist tradition and was influenced by Gottfried Wilhelm Leibniz. But, he later inclined toward Hume's radical empiricism and developed a synthesis of rationalism and empiricism. In the book "Critique of pure reason," he sets out his fundamental epistemological views. He argues that we perceive everything through two forms (space and time), twelve categories (a priori concepts like substance and causation), and certain synthetic a priori propositions related to applying the categories. So, according to Kant, we have three kinds of knowledge: first, the majority are posteriori knowledge, justified by an experience like science, geography, etc. Secondly, a small amount of analytical knowledge, provable by pure reasoning like logic and languages; and thirdly, some amount of synthetic a priori knowledge like geometry.

On the metaphysical front, Kant suggests the existence of an independently existing material world. But, our perception of the external world depends on how our cognitive faculties process the inputs from our sensory organs. This means that whatever knowledge we get is a representation of the information captured by sensory organs. And this information cannot be considered absolutely correct since sensory organs process differently in different humans as well other organisms. This implies that we know the world as it appears to us, not as it is. This is also an important conclusion drawn by Kant that we are the centre of our own reality structured by us. Further, he suggests that maybe only God, endowed with "intellectual intuition" beyond sensory capacities, can perceive things as they are. In the second part of Critique of Pure Reason, he argues that human reason tries to go beyond the limits of its legitimate use by equating the presentation of things with actual things. Hence, according to him, we can neither prove nor disprove them by reason nor even acquire empirical pieces of evidence for or against them. Therefore, he famously declared that theological claims are a matter of faith rather than knowledge.

Kant's views concerning human nature can be seen as a direct fallout of his reconciliation of rationalism and empiricism. He declared that our perceptual knowledge depends upon the interaction of two factors: sensory states caused by physical objects and our internal mental activity in organizing these data according to different conceptual structures and finally making a judgment. Humans have both capacities (sensibility and understanding), unlike other non-human animals who lack the conceptual structures to think or something like language. Therefore, they are driven mainly by their sensory desires. This distinction puts humans above non-human animals in terms of our actions. It implies that we are not merely perceiving beings, but we are agents—we do things and affect the world through our actions. However, other non-human animals also act in the world but cannot regulate their actions because they cannot think (reason) about what they are doing.

Kant was a firm believer in human freedom. Since humans can think, individuals can behave differently according to their reasoning and freedom of will. Therefore, moral responsibility becomes essential for humans. But, the real question is whether the reasoning ability makes humans dualists or we are merely material. Kant leaves this question open and irresolvable as we cannot know either of them because we cannot know what we are 'in ourselves.' For our biological bodies, we are determined as other things in the physical world (in a sensing material). Since we are rational beings, we have control over our actions (non-material). Although Kant has not taken any clear position regarding this, it is evident through his arguments that he rejects "a soul-less materialism" (Stevenson et al., 2018, p. 177).

1.3.6 Evolutionary Views

Today biological evolution is accepted as a fact by everyone beyond any reasonable doubt due to its empirical basis. Although Charles Darwin (1809–1882) is accepted as the central figure of the evolutionary theory, there were voices before Darwin that started to question the Biblical stories. For example, in 1755, Kant propounded the nebular hypothesis that the solar system had evolved through a gradual process, unlike the creation theory. Moreover, scientists before Darwin also discovered fossils of creatures that no longer existed, although they could not explain much. That means predecessors of Darwin at least realized that there is some mechanism for existence, but what Darwin did exceptionally was to show how it all happened. He learned that there is a causal mechanism of natural selection for evolution and existence.

He concluded his findings with four basic principles:
1.   There is variation in the traits of individuals of a given species.
2.   Traits of parents tend to be passed on to their offspring.
3.   Species are intrinsically capable of a geometric rate of population increase.
4.   The environment's resources typically cannot support such an increase.

Above four promises build Darwin's theory of natural selection. Darwin showed through empirical evidence that there is competition for survival and breeding in every species. Humans are no different. That means it was a complete turnaround and challenged the creation theories that prevailed during his time. However, Darwin did not explicitly mention that humans evolved from apes or have some other ancestor from different species. At the end of the book "The Origin of Species," he writes: "light will be thrown on man's origin and history (Darwin, 1909, p. 414)." But, later, in 1871, he published the book "The Descent of Man," in which he vouched for human evolution through various anatomical, embryological, and behavioural evidence. It is now considered to be a fact like any other scientific phenomenon, such as gravity or the solar system.

Darwin propounded that humans are evolved from lower life forms like any other species. Darwin also suggested that not only is our body developed, but our intelligence, language, emotions, and morality are evolved gradually since these traits can be seen continuous with other life forms. However, at that time, he was speculating only by extending the evolutionary theory to the human mind and behaviours along with their bodies.

However, starting from the twentieth-century evolutionary theory was explored in greater depth. It provided further support and evidence for a biological basis of human nature through different domains and empirical research. And nowadays, many scientists try to represent the complete picture of the human through empirical studies without going into the extremities of biological and environmental factors. I shall discuss these contemporary views in depth in the forthcoming sections as they paint an empirically convincing picture of the overall nature of humans.

2   Challenges in Defining What It Means to Be Human

In the preceding section, I have briefly presented different ideas concerning one central question: 'What is to be a human being?' It is pretty evident through the discussions in the previous section that the pursuit of understanding the fundamental nature of human beings is not an easy task. It is complex not only because human beings have different facets of their existence but also because they constantly grow in terms of knowledge and understanding about themselves and their surroundings. It fuels us to revisit our current knowledge and enhance it by changing it through challenging and/or further exploration. Some theories like Dualism are built upon existing beliefs, whereas some other theories like Darwinism challenge the commonly held notions. Different approaches touch on various aspects of human beings, but if we want to analyse holistically and try to formulate a theory that is empirically grounded and adequate, we have to consider similarities as well as differences among them. So, my foremost task will be to find a common thread from all (most of them) theories that can help us bind the various aspects of human nature together and provide a holistic picture.

A cursory review of these theories shows that two common aspects of human beings are assumed. Almost every philosopher or tradition considered human beings as having dual characteristics, i.e., material and non-material. Moreover, the influence of the external environment on human beings is also given due respect in most theories. Some theories acknowledge it clearly and provide a significant effort to explain it. On the other hand, we can find consideration of external influence as a subtle underlying feature in many other. Additionally, Human beings have a trait of self-reflective awareness which means they can think and reflect on their own mental processes (Henriques, 2011). This ability might be a reason to acknowledge that we all have some inner subjective life that is different from other material objects. This gives rise to an obvious adoption of a dualistic approach and, consequently, division of material-immaterial or physical-mental aspects of human beings. Moreover, various thinkers highlight different aspects of human mind while following same dualistic approach. This whole discussion is an age-long debate and can be labelled as a 'mind-body problem.'

Apart from the discussion about mind-body, another major theme present explicitly or implicitly is related to how the environment influences the nature of human beings. Some thinkers believe that environmental influences don't make many differences in what we are and how we behave. At the same time, some thinkers firmly accept that human nature is not fixed and that external stimulants constantly shape us. This indicates that both sides believe that humans have a set of some fixed and some changeable aspects. Although the degree of environmental influence is a matter of debate, this very assumption of the changeable nature of human beings is accepted by most thinkers. This issue has been labelled as the 'Nature versus Nurture' debate.

These two debates are crucial in the process of understanding human beings and their nature. For example, most religious traditions associate reasoning with our immaterial aspects, often denoted as the soul. Souls are often identified as some higher transcendental entity related to God. In that case, all the reasoning, consciousness, and intellect are the characteristics of the soul, which are distinct from our body. Not only in religious traditions but in the majority of modern western philosophy, understanding of the nature of humans is concerned with knowledge of the immaterial aspects of human beings, which are termed as the mind or psyche. Usually, the mind is considered a separate entity from the body in human beings. If this is the case, then every human being is assumed to be knowledgeable by birth, and the education system should provide an environment only in which they can realize their abilities and unravel the absolute knowledge which is already present in their mind.

On the contrary, according to recent views, human beings are considered as just any other biological species, and all of their features are defined in the context of biology and the environment. This leads to the view that all knowledge and skills should be imparted upon them from outside. Therefore, a particular view about the nature of human beings shapes how we design and operate the education system. Nevertheless, these are extreme positions, and recent empirical research shows that we are not on any of the edges. Contemporary scientists do definitive studies to find a middle ground of explanations that are validated from different disciplines. Hence, first, it is essential to discuss these two issues concerning human nature, namely, the 'mind-body relationship' and 'nature versus nurture,' as they directly affect education. Then I will show how contemporary research from cognitive sciences tries to solve these fundamental issues and provide a plausible account of human nature supported by empirical studies. Once we get a convincing idea about the fundamental nature of human beings from different disciplines, then we can look into educational activities around it.

2.1   *Relationship between Mind and Body*

The relationship between mind and body has been debated since ancient times. As Stevenson et al. (2018) observe, mind-body dualism is a traditional metaphysical doctrine about human nature. Dualism holds that both mental and physical properties are real and have an independent existence, and human beings are uniquely endowed with a mind. Physical properties are attributed to the world and share features with specific worldly physical objects. Contrary to it, mental properties are private and available only to the subjects. Physical properties are public and tangible and might be observed by other persons to some degree. But mental properties are available to the possessor only. For example, "I may be able to tell that you are in pain by your behaviour, but only you can feel it directly" (Robinson, 2020). Owing to the fundamental difference in the experience of both properties, dualist views have been prominent in most philosophical discussions in the past, and it is still present in contemporary discussions in some or other forms. Moreover, there are multiple versions developed in due course of time concerning the ontology of mental and physical properties, as well as on the basis of the nature of the interaction between the two. Anyways, the dualistic paradigm, in general, holds that mental and physical properties are real and have a separate independent existence.

The genesis of dualist perspectives on the mind and body can be traced back to Plato's dialogues, particularly 'Phaedo.' In it, Plato posits that the true substances are not the ephemeral physical bodies, but the eternal 'Forms,' which serve as imperfect prototypes for physical manifestations. These forms not only make the world possible but also render it intelligible by functioning as universals. This dualist view was subsequently refined and elaborated upon by philosophers like Rene Descartes in the seventeenth century. Philosophers with dualist views generally agree that both the mind and body are crucial components of human existence. However, they diverge on whether these are independent substances or merely different properties of a single substance.

Descartes, for his part, firmly believed that the mind and body are separate substances. He placed greater emphasis on the mind, asserting that one could conceive of oneself without a body but not without a mind. Such a stance becomes evident in his seminal declaration, 'I think, therefore I exist' (Descartes, 2006). This statement illuminates Descartes' clear prioritization of thought, positioning the mind as a 'thinking thing' that takes precedence over the body. The notion of the 'self' in Descartes' philosophy is thereby construed as an innate idea, immediately and irrevocably known to the mind.

In Indian philosophical traditions, the dualism between material and non-material aspects of human nature is articulated distinctly. The *Sāṅkhya* school delineates two independent entities: *puruṣa* and *prakṛti*, representing consciousness and matter, respectively (Dasgupta, 1922). Unlike Western dualism that positions mind and matter as separate entities, *Sāṅkhya* philosophy places the mind (*manas*) within the realm of matter as an evolute of *prakṛti*. This form of dualism is not strictly about mind and matter but emphasizes the differentiation between consciousness and matter. The allied school of Yoga complements this by introducing the notion of union and mindfulness, thereby coming close to the central discourse of the present study.

Contrastingly, Buddhist philosophy questions the dualistic separation between mind and body. It tries to dismantle the idea of mind-body as two independent entities and stresses the dependent existence of mental and physical states through the theory of *Pratītyasamutpāda* (Sharma, 2000). However, it would be more accurate to mention the theory of *Anātmavāda*, which asserts that there is no "self" in the sense of a permanent, integral, autonomous being within an individual existence. It holds that the concept of a permanent self is an erroneous mental model. All things are interdependent and constantly changing. Buddhists believe that there isn't a separate self that is conscious of the experiences or thoughts one has. Instead, it is the thoughts themselves that constitute the thinker, and the experiences themselves that constitute the experiencer (G. Dreyfus & Thompson, 2007). These different perspectives enrich our understanding of mind-body relationship by offering an alternative to the dualistic frameworks prevalent in Western and Indian philosophies.

Matthias Forstmann and Pascal Burgmer (2015) argue that dualist accounts of the mind can be considered as a 'default belief' that all humans rudimentarily share from early on in their lives. These are primarily based on our intuition or the way things appear to us, which ascribes all mental activities to an entity that is different from the body. This paints a dichotomized version of human nature in which reason or mental activities are cut off from nature and the material world, including our own bodies, since the body is usually experienced as a perishable and destructible object like any other thing in the world. Apart from the ontological issue—the origin and nature of mental states and physical states, there is another prominent issue of debate in the course of the mind-body problem. It is a causal problem, which means do physical states influence mental states? Or vice versa, and if so, then how and which is the primary cause? This again gave rise to various conceptions such as Interactionism, Parallelism, Epiphenomenalism, etc.

The core problem in almost every version of dualism is that if both are distinct substances with entirely different natures, then how can they both interact with each other? Descartes tried to solve this issue by bringing forth the hypothesis of the pineal gland. He argued that the pineal gland is the principal seat of the soul and the place in which all our thoughts are formed. It is also essential to consider that dichotomized approach toward mind-body generally emerged in the domain of religious traditions, and the notion of supremacy of mind was part of the religious beliefs. Paul M. Churchland (1999) sees the dualist approach as deeply entrenched in most of the world's prevalent religions. Many dualist philosophers, including Descartes, bring the intervention of God to solve the problem of interaction between mind and body. However, we also have to keep in mind that these various historical views arise based on the mere contemplation of the thinkers. Those were primarily apriori judgments given upon observation of multiple human behaviours, and there is no scientific backing for these arguments. But, as neuroscientific research advances, it is evident and widely validated that we humans do not have something transcendental related to our minds.

Having a dualistic outlook in our day-to-day life seems obvious to us because it is validated by our common sense understanding of folk psychology. For example, we differentiate between the mental and physical realms because of our exclusive subjective experiences and thinking. Moreover, our shared experience is that our psychological (mental) states change our physical states and vice versa. For instance, when we feel fear or anger, then our heartbeat goes fast; similarly, our extreme bodily fatigue makes us mentally tired too. Although we experience mental and physical states differently, it doesn't mean that both are ontologically separate. In this regard, neuroscientist Antonio Damasio (1994) argues that reason is unlikely to begin in a rarefied cognitive domain, but rather it originates from the biological activity of an organism intended to survive.

Of late, there have been various empirical studies shedding light on the age-old questions regarding the nature of the mind, the way knowledge is acquired, etc. They try to present a more holistic picture of humans, which is continuous with nature. The embodied approach is one such interdisciplinary domain of exploration that tries to bridge the rift of mind-body as well as subject-object. We will discuss it in detail in the next chapter.

2.2   *Nature vs. Nurture Debate*

The nature versus nurture debate is centred around whether a particular aspect of human behaviour is the product of an innate factors or acquired through environmental influences. Nature is what we think of as our innate features, often explained in genetic terms nowadays. In contrast, nurture is generally taken as the acquired qualities through the influence of environmental factors. It is indisputable that we get knowledge of the external world through our sensory organs, but to what extent are we dependent on our sensory organs to acquire knowledge? Historically, philosophical discussions over this question gave rise to two streams of thought, namely, rationalism and empiricism. Rationalists claim that knowledge is innate, and therefore knowledge is independent of any experience. Whereas empiricists claim that sensory experience is the ultimate source of our knowledge and concepts (Markie & Folescu, 2021). Empiricists focus more on gaining knowledge through experience, whereas rationalists are inclined towards hidden power in oneself. Modern rationalists such as Descartes argued that humans have innate ideas in their minds. Followers of this standpoint believe that most, if not all, behaviours, characteristics, and knowledge are the results of inheritance (Kurt, 2021). Whereas empiricist philosopher John Locke advocated the idea of a 'blank slate' in which he argued that humans acquire almost all of their traits through 'nurture' (Uzgalis, 2022). It means that all behavioural traits and knowledge in a human result from experiences gained and environmental conditioning. However, later on, Kant tried to reconcile these two extreme viewpoints of rationalism and empiricism.

The nature vs. nurture debate often invites two opposing perspectives that can be analysed in the light of how we as human beings, are generally predisposed to act. The central issue is whether the reason for our behaviour is genetic or it is the outcome of sociocultural and environmental impacts. Moreover, in case our genetics causes our behaviour, then what precisely is our nature? Many thinkers address this issue from the perspective of moral philosophy and ethics. For example, Thomas Hobbes argued that humans are by nature selfish and evil. Therefore, he advocated for coercive political authority for the overall good of humanity. At the same time, Jean Jacques Rousseau believed that humans are good by nature but get corrupted by society. However, they both did not deny the influence of society on the traits of humans. Apart from the ethical point of view, there can be various strands of discussion in the whole nature vs. nurture debate. For instance, one strand of arguments enquires that is there one common human nature or are there multiple human natures? Anyway, there can be many aspects to studying and theorizing about the nature of human beings, and therefore, the focus of inquiry gets shifted according to the domain of application. Thus, for the scope and context of the discussion, we will limit ourselves to the most common and existing historical disputes.

Jesse J. Prinz analyses that there are three significant disputes which are most influential in shaping contemporary debates of nature vs. nurture (Prinz, 2014, p. 8). First, the issue is related to knowledge. The core question is, do we have innate knowledge or ideas? The inherent notion means knowledge without the need for instruction or learning. According to this view, humans by birth are equipped with the concepts of reasoning, love, morality, etc. Second, the issue is related to the origin of individual and group differences. We find many behavioural differences among humans, and sometimes these differences correspond to the group. For example, generally, women are more emotionally expressive than men (Kring & Gordon, 1998). Although empirical studies show that these kinds of differences can be the result of both biological (Graham et al., 2018) and socio-cultural factors (Jansz, 2000), at least this opens up the debate about what are inheritable traits and what are just socio-culturally induced, restricted to one's lifetime. And the third most crucial issue is related to evolutionary theory. This claim is based upon Darwin's theory of natural selection, and it argues that most of the observable traits are developed through the process of natural selection and are liable to change due to genetic mutations. It further proposes that many human traits are selected and transmitted into the next generation based on their usability for survival.

These issues, along with some other significant disputes, created a rift between the two positions. Even nowadays, many thinkers adapt an extreme position. For example, supporters of the 'nature' position, called nativists, have the basic assumption that the characteristics of the human species are the product of our evolutionary history and that individual differences occur due to the unique genetic codes of each person. Noam Chomsky, for instance, based on this assumption, proposed that language is gained through the use of an innate language acquisition device that is unique to humans. Similarly, Freud proposes aggression as being an innate drive (Mcleod, 2024). On the other side, there are supporters of the extreme nurture position who have a basic assumption that during the birth of the human, the mind is a blank slate, and it is gradually filled through the experiences gained in the world. They argue that psychological characteristics and behavioural differences that emerge through childhood result from learning in the world. This applies to most psychological behaviours; for example, according to Bandura's social learning theory, aggression is learned from the environment through observation and imitation (Bandura & Walters, 1977).

However, in contemporary discourse, positions on nature versus nurture have become less extreme, with most theorists accepting that both 'nature' and 'nurture' are essential in overall human development (Ridley, 2003). With the advent of empirical studies in psychology, biology, and allied disciplines, the divide between nature and nurture has become blurred. Many researchers in the 21st century are trying to reconcile both positions with just varying degrees of emphasis. Several empirical pieces of evidence show the importance of both nature and nurture (genetic and environmental) in forming a complete human being (N. R. Carlson et al., 2005; Richerson & Boyd, 2008; Ridley, 2003; E. O. Wilson, 2004). We will now discuss some contemporary views, which show that human beings cannot be fitted into two distinct compartments. Instead, there is an 'embodied person' who is the result of her biological history, at the same time, continuously shaped by their environmental surrounding.

3   Modern Approaches to Understand Human Nature

Historically, as we have seen, discussion about human nature was often polarized. Whether it is mind-body or the nature-nurture aspects of human beings, taking extreme positions was primary in both issues. But, contemporary researchers are now more concerned with the relative contributions. They try to reconcile both extreme ends and provide a holistic view of human nature. It is also important to note that contemporary research is mostly inspired by evolutionary theory. Now, human beings are not considered fundamentally very different from other animals and are seen as continuous with others in the process of evolution. Therefore, discussions about humans in relation to other animals also become a prominent concern in understanding human beings. Therefore, it is vital to dig deeper into our evolutionary history from the perspective of biology.

3.1   *Evolution Is the Key*

Even before Charles Darwin challenged the existing Biblical notion of the theory of creation, many thinkers started to question ancient gospels. They began to find scientific explanations for universal laws and objects. Particularly, the theory of creation was already challenged in eighteenth century by discovering fossils and other geological evidence. Starting from the 19th-century, scientists began to provide scientific explanations related to biological species. Even the term 'biology' first appeared in the 19th century, and Jean-Baptiste Lamarck was one of the first to use it. Lamarck was a French naturalist who gave the theory of inheritance of acquired characteristics. Although, the discovery of genetics has discarded Lamarck's theory later, these efforts collectively made researchers to accept the possibility that there can be some natural law in the world that can be applied to every kind of organism (Coleman & Coleman, 1977). However, Darwin's significant contribution lies in articulating a causal mechanism for gradual adaptive species change through natural selection.

Darwin compiled all the pieces of evidence and proposed the theory of natural selection in his book 'The Origin of Species,' published in 1859. He presented various pieces of evidence to support the idea of survival of the fittest through natural and sexual selection. Although he did not explicitly say much about human evolution in the origin of species, at least he laid the foundation. Later, in 1871, he published 'The Descent of Man' to address the issue of human evolution. In the descent of man, he put humans as one evolute of the common descent and gave various shreds of evidence to support the evolution of humans from lower forms of life. The major paradigm shift was that Darwin gave evidence to link human development from lower forms and mapped not only physical characteristics but mental and behavioural characteristics of humans to the lower forms of life (Darwin, 2004).

Although Darwin suggested that there are variations between different individuals and that these variations are inherited, he did not know the mechanism of it. This mechanism was discovered later by George Mendel in his theory of inheritance. Mendel figured out that the parents pass genes to the offspring through which various traits get transmitted. We also know that sometimes mutation happens in the genes, which again validates the theory of natural selection by Darwin. The theory of evolution is now considered a fact, and it has been continuously validated in recent times (Lenski, 2000). It is deemed to be revolutionary as it paved the way for further scientific research. Consequently, is further developed, criticized, refined, and validated by many new scientific discoveries in the twentieth century. For instance, James Watson and Francis Crick (1953) built upon these ideas and discovered the biochemical basis of gene copying which is DNA. The critical point here is that we can see how these discoveries validate Darwin's theory of biological evolution. These fundamental elements, such as genes or DNA, can be found in every organism, and there is a similarity in the structures of these in any particular species. Genetics as a domain continuously tries to map almost all of our behaviours and bodily features to the genes. For instance, a prominent sociobiologist of our times, Edward O. Wilson, takes an example of the genetic basis for eye colour and argues that the same logic can be applied to all human social behaviours (E. O. Wilson, 2013).

However, the extreme view of the biological basis for all of our physical-social properties is challenged by many and argues for the influence of the environment and cultures. For instance, B. F. Skinner emphasizes that environmental causes can explain human behaviour. Furthermore, Darwin's theory sometimes being held responsible for racism and sexism too because it implies that there are innate differences between individuals. This led to justification for slavery and colonialism by the Western world in the name of 'racial supremacy.' However, these judgments are mere sociological rather than biological because even now, we cannot mark any gene as bad or good. This further led to a reaction against the biological basis for explaining human evolution and over emphasis on behavioural aspects of humans. The early twentieth century in the west was dominated by thinkers who argues that environmental causes can explain all behaviours. For example, B. F. Skinner stresses that environmental causes can explain human behaviour. He argues that the environment selects behaviour (rather than biology) by rewarding organisms or eliminating any particular behaviour by punishing them (conditioning). However, there are flaws in this kind of extreme position too. This is evident in the case of twins who share identical genomes and are reared apart—revealing the strong influence of biological reasons compared to the environment (Campos et al., 2019). Thus, Evolutionary theory provides a plausible middle ground for the nature vs. nurture and the mind-body debate by reconciling both extreme ends.

3.2 *Solution Is in Reconciliation*

It is pretty evident from the previous discussion that there is strong support for genetic basis (nature), as well as environmental influences for the fundamental nature of human beings. Indeed, the genes of a human play an important role in their physical properties, but we cannot overlook the environmental factors which help in the development and expression of those genes. Although we do not control genetic selection, our behaviours exerted by genetic expressions greatly depend upon our lifestyle. For instance, in the case of identifying colour, it is more of an innate ability and depends upon our genes. But, in the case of, say, soccer player, the player has the innate ability to run or walk, but the behaviour required for playing the game is an acquired and learned trait.

Similarly, the trait of anger is innate and developed in almost every organism because it is an automatic response to fight-or-flight situations. Still, the way anger is expressed is more culture-induced, and it can vary in different socio-cultural setups. Therefore, it is reasonable to say that genes and socio-cultural influences both contribute to what we are and how we act in the world. It is also notable that many scholars claim that our learned behaviours, beliefs, practices, and ideas also get transferred to the next generation apart from biological traits. For instance, Richard Dawkins posits that culture transmission occur through memes in addition to biology. via memes (Dawkins, 1976). Meme acts as a unit for cultural beliefs, ideas, customs, or practices that can be transmitted from person to person through imitation. He put memes analogous to genes as it is also liable to self-replicate, mutate and respond to evolutionary challenges. Although there is no firm scientific support for memes, Dawkins's proposal puts cultural evolution on the same level as biological evolution. It provides a new perspective that cultural transmission is also as important as biological transmission in evolution.

Recently, contemporary research in genomics has shown the role of external influences upon inheritable permanent modifications in our genes. Studies exhibit that environmental factors heavily influence genetic expressions through epigenetic modifications (Sah et al., 2018). Epigenetics is the study of heritable changes in gene expressions without any change in the respective DNA sequence. It tries to understand the difference in phenotype without any change in genotype. Epigenetic mechanisms regulate the structure and expression of genes through non-genetic reasons such as environmental influences. Various kinds of research in epigenetics now show that biological processes are controlled by the expression of inherited genes and environmental conditions together. This implies that even though most of the traits are transferred through genes, their expression is based on environmental factors. Hence, empirical scientific research validates that we are not simply a result of either nature or nurture but rather a combination of both.

In terms of mind-body relationship, we have seen that most religious traditions consider both as two distinct entities. This dichotomy between mind-body was a prominent basis for most research until the early 20th century. But the emergence of cognitive science as a research domain in the 1950s gave substantial challenges to the religious conception of the superiority of mind over body and even the Cartesian legacy by breaking the mind-body dichotomy. Cognitive science is the interdisciplinary research area that aims to study the mind and intelligence, converging various domains such as philosophy, psychology, artificial intelligence, neuroscience, linguistics, anthropology, etc. (Thagard, 2023). However, in the initial years of cognitive science, it was assumed that mental processes could best be understood in terms of representational structures or abstract models. But subsequently, mere abstract information processing models were no longer accepted as satisfactory accounts of the human mind. Many researchers nowadays give attention to the question of interactions between the material human body and beyond body surroundings and to how such interactions shape the mind.

Proponents of this view argue for an embodied approach and are convinced that it will ultimately dissolve the dichotomy between the immaterial mind and material body (e.g., Damasio 1994; Gallagher 2005). It is further claimed that the mind and body are not only interdependent, but they move one step ahead and claim that mental properties arise out of our enaction in the world (Varela et al., 1991). In the words of Phenomenologist Maurice Merleau-Ponty explicitly says, "I cannot understand the function of the living body except by enacting it myself" (Merleau-Ponty, 1962, p. 87). Contemporary researchers working in cognitive science now have agreed that human mental properties are not exclusive but arise from bodily activities. It draws a continuity between human beings and their surroundings too, which puts more support to the fact that human beings are inherently embodied and embedded in the world. Although the embodied thesis is a recent development, some roots can be traced in Aristotelian views. Aristotle countered Plato's mind-body dualism and put the mind back into the body. He tried to present a more holistic picture of human beings.

Moreover, if we look back upon the evolutionary theory, human beings certainly evolved in and through the environment. Survival and reproduction are the main driving force behind evolution, and for that, every organism starts acting in the world just after they are born. Therefore, to understand the mental phenomenon too, one needs to understand the bodily actions and sensory-motor interaction with the world. This is a more plausible explanation about human beings, and therefore, human activities, such as education, should be aligned with it. It is also important to note that arguments for the 'embodiment of mind' thesis are not based upon merely apriori philosophical speculations, but recent research in cognitive science validates it in multiple ways. There are empirical studies in various domains, such as visual consciousness, concepts, memory, the understanding of other minds, and moral cognition which substantiate the theoretical framework of embodied cognition (Wilson and Foglia 2017).

Thus, to sum, it is now an almost accepted fact that humans do not have something immaterial-transcendental-sacred powers, but they are merely a product of long evolutionary history. It is also the accepted fact that various traits or features of human beings can be mapped with the other ancestors, and we are different in degree rather than kind. These all outcomes lead to the realisation that human does not possess two ontologically different mind-body entities. Instead, such differences can be reconciled in the light of embodied approach towards human beings.

3.3   *Humans Are Embodied Persons*

It is clear from the above discussion that the recent development of experimental research in cognitive science converges toward the integrated view of humankind. We come to realize that the solution is in the reconciliation of the mental and physical as well as biological and environmental. We have also seen that embodied theory is the way out to bridge two extreme ends. Embodied theory, in general, challenges dichotomized views and presents a holistic and integrated line of thinking. Therefore, following the embodied theory, a holistic picture of human beings would be more conducive in which human beings are inherently embodied and embedded in the world. Humans should not be seen as separate creations; instead, they should be identified as continuous with the world. Similarly, the fundamental characteristics of humans should not be identified as distinct from the body that they inevitably possess. Instead, these characteristics are inseparable aspects from the existence of humans. There is nothing like a human, which possesses some kind of nature that independently exists, but it is more like characteristics developed in humans due to intertwining with the world. On a similar line, there is nothing like some exclusive mental properties which we acquire or inherit, but mental properties emerge due to human's enaction in the world. Therefore, a better way to define human nature can be in terms of an embodied person. An embodied person is the integration of material as well as immaterial aspects without making any rigid separation between a biological organism and its environment. The embodied person will also mean that human enaction is the primary, and all the immaterial conceptions are the result of it. Therefore, it would be more conducive to understanding human beings as embodied persons that are thinking and acting agents in the world.

The embodiment theory also provides a holistic, integrated picture of a person which is closely interwoven with the world. Therefore, it is vital to understand the embodied approach in depth to unravel the various aspects of humans. We will see embodied theory in detail as it also gives alternative explanations to most of our conceptions and activities, including education. It shifts our shared understanding of separative tendencies to more grounded in the world.

4   Conclusion

It is evident from the discussion that almost every philosophical tradition tries to decode the fundamental nature of human beings. Religious traditions are no exceptions. In general, human nature refers to the essential features of human beings upon which an objective picture of humans can be drawn. Moreover, understanding the fundamental nature of human beings becomes necessary in designing and understanding any human-led activity such as education. We have also seen that various conceptions about human nature emerged in different time frames. At the same time, these conceptions are culture-dependent too. Although any theory cannot be considered complete, they at least uncover some aspects of human nature. It is clear from the historical excursion that some ideas of human nature presuppose a particular view on the problem related to mind-body relationship and nature versus nurture aspects of humans. In general, most of the views conceived human nature on dichotomized line. However, collectively, these historical efforts are a priori judgments in nature. There is no empirical backing for these views. But, with the rise of scientific theories, specifically the theory of evolution, the whole paradigm changed.

The theory of evolution challenges the view that humans have something over and above physical existence (something like an independent and permanent soul). Additionally, it also counters the biblical notion of the theory of creation and puts human beings in continuity with other animals in the process of evolution. Contemporary research in evolutionary biology validate that human beings are just biological organisms like any other organism in the world. Moreover, various findings from genetics validate that many aspects of humans are based on biology, not completely alienated from the environment. Now, results from multiple domains are converging toward the fact that humans are inherently embodied and embedded in the world. The current embodied theory allows us to reconcile the two opposite standpoints, such as mind-body and nature-nurture. The embodiment theory provides a holistic, integrated picture of a person which is closely interwoven with the world.

Hence, it would be more appropriate to think of the human as an embodied person. An embodied person is the amalgamation of mental as well as bodily features, at the same time not dissociated from its surrounding. Implying it, we can argue that an embodied person does not live in the world but lives with the world. Sensory motor enaction in the world is the main activity that makes humans what they are. On a similar line, it is also conducive to say that mental properties are linked with our enaction in the world instead of separate exclusive existence. The embodied approach holds that mental properties emerge out of bodily interaction in the world. This is the complete reverse of what we have seen in most of the historical viewpoints. Therefore, before starting our discussion about the most significant human activity, that is, education, we need to delve deeper into this new paradigm to appreciate the embodied stance of humans. In the next chapter, I shall discuss embodied cognition theory. I shall present the theoretical basis of this theory and argue for the embodied person with the help of recent empirical evidence for validation. Once we are able to appreciate the embodied nature of ourselves, then we shall see how most of the conceptions about humans and their activities, such as education, get changed.

CHAPTER 4

Foundations of Embodied Human Nature

In the previous chapter, we have discussed that recent developments in cognitive science suggest a continuity between mind and body, challenging the traditional Cartesian view of separate substances. This is supported by studies in evolutionary biology indicating humans' continuity with other animals and questioning the transcendent status of the mind. Recent developments in cognitive science propose the idea of embodied human beings, where the boundary between mind and body has been blurred. Moreover, the body has a primary influence on mental properties. Further, some theories even suggest that the mind is not confined to the body and that the environment plays a vital role in shaping it. These diverse perspectives require a clear definition of embodiment, which is more than just the integration of mind and body. It is basically a framework that takes into account the role of both body and environment in shaping mental processes. Embodiment as an approach challenges traditional cognitive science, which views mental processes as purely computational. Embodied researchers argue that mental processes are not just computational but also involve the body and environment.

Although the embodied theory was once a fringe movement, it is now a prominent theory due to empirical validation from various fields such as psychology, neuroscience, and linguistics, as well as its successful applications in AI, robotics, and education (Shapiro & Spaulding, 2021). While there are multiple variants of embodied theory, they all fundamentally reject substance dualism and the idea of a rigid divide between mental and physical realms. Embodied theories consider the brain as one aspect of the body responsible for cognition, along with other sensory organs, and recognize the constitutive role of motor organs in cognition, which was ignored in traditional cognitive science.

Now, before discussing the application of embodied theory in education, a detailed examination of embodied theory is necessary. The primary objective of this chapter is to understand embodied theory both as a stance and as a research program. As a stance, embodiment refers to the idea that humans are embodied beings.

This raises questions about how we acquire and create knowledge. By exploring embodied theory as a research program, we can delve deeper and consider the possibility of rethinking and re-designing our educational practices. Therefore, a thorough investigation of embodied cognition is essential to truly appreciate both our nature and practices.

I shall initiate the discussion by outlining the motivations behind the emergence of the embodied approach in cognitive science. I shall examine how the embodied approach challenges traditional cognitive science, which was primarily based on computationalism and symbolic representationalism. Then, in the next section, I shall outline the key themes of embodied theory and provide an overview of how it offers a comprehensive account of human nature through various empirical studies. The aim of this chapter is to demonstrate that traditional understandings of the human mind and cognition are based on incomplete or incorrect theories and need to be re-evaluated in light of embodied cognition. This chapter will focus solely on the embodied approach, while the following chapter will explore the larger impact of this theory on our understanding of education.

1   Inspirations for Embodied Cognition

1.1   *Emergence of Cognitivism*
The growth of cognitive science coincided with the development of computer science in the 1950s, leading early cognitive scientists to model theories of the mind on computational processes. Computers were understood as the best metaphor for the human mind; hence, the mind's working was assumed to be similar to computational processes. The key assumption was that cognition is a computational process operating on symbolic representations. Simply put, it argues that thinking or cognitive processes, in general, are the manipulation of symbols inside the brain. This computational process starts with the receipt of symbolic inputs, then some syntactic computation occurs in the brain, and finally ends with the production of again some kind of symbolic outputs.

In the cognitive realm, it begins with the input provided by sensory organs and ends with motor systems. This model shows that symbols are the most prominent aspects of cognition for computation to occur. Symbols are simply representations of the actual thing or concept. It can be a word, an expression, a colour, or just an image. The important feature of symbols is that they need not be like an actual thing to be qualified for the proper representation of that thing. Their functional role is to stand in for specific features (Clark, 1998). For example, the three letters 'D,' 'O,' and 'G,' when combined, form a word 'DOG,' representing an animal with particular features. Nevertheless, there is an equal possibility that the word 'DOG' might be associated with a very different animal because the word 'DOG' does not have any semantic value in itself. Thus, a separate system of rules is needed to attach meaning to the symbols.

Lawrence Shapiro argues that symbol can get their meaning in two ways (Shapiro, 2019, p. 11). The first one is through their functional value. For example, the symbol '8' represents the number 'eight' in English numerals, which is represented by 'VIII' too in Roman numerals, and it may represent a concept of 'infinity' (∞), and so on. The second way is by combining multiple independent symbols on the basis of some rules to form a new symbol. For example, a mathematical expression '2 + 3 = 5' can have a meaning and represent something by combining different independent symbols '2,' '+,' '3,' '=,' and '5.' This brings another important feature of symbolic representation that it works only within the given symbolic system. For instance, the English word 'DOG' will have no meaning for a non-English speaking person, and it will not invoke any kind of thought or image (unless 'DOG' has a very different representation of some other thing in a non-English symbol system). Therefore, for symbolic representation to work, a well-defined syntax or rule is necessary. Otherwise, one cannot understand what a circle 'o' will mean; is it a ZERO as in numerals, or is it a letter 'O' of the English language?

The key point to consider here is that symbols lack inherent semantic meaning. The significance of a symbol can vary depending on the specific system of rules in which it is utilized. This leads to the possibility of different interpretations in different contexts. Therefore, the relationship between a symbol and its representation is often arbitrary. In this sense, these symbols are amodal in nature (Shapiro & Spaulding, 2021). A symbol is amodal means that there is no definite correlation between symbols and the things they represent. For example, the symbol 'DOG' represents a specific animal in the English language, but it doesn't contain any physical resemblance to that animal. It is equally possible that the symbol could have represented something else if it was initially associated with different animals or objects in the English language. However, this arbitrary nature also has a benefit where symbols can be analysed and understood without direct sensory experience. This highlights the need for a system of rules that can connect symbols with their meanings and allow for shared communication. This implies that there must be a central computational system containing rules for computing symbols and generating their semantic values. In terms of human cognition, it suggests that there is a program operating in the brain that is regulated by certain rules. Jerry Fodor proposed a 'language of thought' for this purpose.

Jerry Fodor propounds the 'Language of Thought' hypothesis as part of the framework of computational representationalist approach to the study of the mind (Fodor, 1975). He asserts that all organisms utilize representation in their higher cognitive processes as computation cannot occur without representation.

He notes: "representation presupposes a medium of representation, and there is no symbolization without symbols. In particular, there is no internal representation without an internal language" (ibid., p. 55). This means that our internal mental language is similar to natural languages, such as Hindi or English, and has a universal grammar like those found in natural languages. Fodor, building upon Chomsky's views on syntax acquisition, argues that a language is learned through the formation of hypotheses and their confirmation with the assistance of an already-known language. Therefore, for a child in the pre-verbal phase to learn their first natural language, they must have access to an innate universal grammar. This argument, we can clearly see, is analogous to computational processing.

A basic computer uses two types of languages. The first is a compiler, which converts input and output signals into machine language. Once these signals are translated into the machine language (0s and 1s), they don't need further translation for computation to occur. This is because computers are designed to understand the computational language and have an innate system of syntax and semantics for the symbols in the machine language. In a similar manner, humans only need one natural language (such as Hindi or English) to translate environmental stimuli into symbols (representations) prior to mental computation because we have the innate ability to compute through the language of thought.

Now, without delving into the technicalities of symbolic representationalism, we can observe how traditional cognitive science tends to view cognitive processes through the lens of symbolic representationalism, positing that these processes mimic computational activities. In this framework, the mind is often likened to software running on the brain's hardware (Shapiro, 2007). However, it's crucial to understand that this conventional view emerged from broader philosophical currents, notably physicalism and functionalism, which advocated that mental states are physical states and that mental phenomena can be understood by their functional roles, respectively. It is also worth noting that the move from dualism to physicalism in the philosophy of mind did not necessarily imply a rejection of mentalism. Physicalism, especially the mind-brain identity theory, still emphasized the exclusive focus on the brain as the locus of the mind (Stoljar, 2023).

In this classical understanding, encapsulated in what Susan Hurley (1998) termed the 'classical sandwich model,' the focus is insularly on brain-centred cognitive activity. This approach fosters Methodological Solipsism, where only an organism's internal states are scrutinized for behaviour explanation (Fodor, 1980). Consequently, this limits the scope of cognition to input reception and output generation, obscuring any active participation in reality through bodily interaction. However, this perspective has been thoroughly scrutinized and found lacking, particularly by proponents of the embodied cognition approach. This approach disputes the brain-centric view and proposes a more holistic understanding of the mind, body, and environment. Even before the rise of the embodied cognition approach, symbolic representationalism was subject to substantial criticism from various quarters. I shall now outline the major problems of the classical approach, and in the following section, I shall explain how the embodied approach addresses these challenges and provides a more plausible explanation for human cognition.

1.2 *Problems with Cognitivism*

I shall present three major challenges to cognitivism that are relevant to our discussion of the embodied approach and its impact on education.

1.2.1 Problem with Semantics

The classical approach to cognition posits that it arises from the manipulation of symbolic representations according to rules. This approach is based on the belief that internal computation is necessary because the stimuli received from the world are limited and lack syntactic or semantic value. Therefore, this theory presupposes the existence of an innate Language of Thought to support computation and meaning making. This assumption is criticized by John Searle on the grounds that if a system can manipulate symbols correctly, it does not mean that it has the ability to understand the meaning of symbols. This means that a syntactic system cannot generate meaning, as it can only perform calculations with symbols and produce outputs based on prior set rules. To demonstrate this conceptual flaw, Searle used a thought experiment which is known as the Chinese room argument (Searle, 1980).

This thought experiment involves a scenario in which a person is locked in a room and given three sets of symbols in the Chinese language which the person cannot read or understand. The person is then provided with a set of rules in English to match the second set of symbols to the first set. The second set of symbols represents questions, and the third set represents answers to those questions, but the person does not know this. When the person returns symbols from the third set by following the rules, it may seem like they understand the Chinese language, but in reality, they are just following the rules in a language they understand. Thus, Searle posits that correct manipulations of symbols do not lead to an understanding of semantics too. Another simple example can be a computer program that can solve trigonometry problems using the Pythagorean theorem ($c = \sqrt{(a^2 + b^2)}$). While it may provide the correct result when given values for a, b, and c, it is unlikely that it truly understands the theorem.

To conclude, Searle's thought experiment highlights that mere manipulation of symbols does not amount to understanding meaning; thereby classical view of cognition cannot be considered a correct explanation for human cognition.

1.2.2   Problem with Cognitive Load

The classical approach considers that cognition can be explained by symbolic representations alone. This solipsistic approach is challenged by Terence Horgan and John Tienson by claiming that there are multiple soft constraints involved while performing a task that cannot be satisfied by the symbolic rule-based system alone (Horgan & Tienson, 1989). A cognitive system in the real-world need to process many planned and unplanned information (soft constraints) very quickly to perform efficiently. For instance, a thought experiment by Stan Franklin (1995) is noteworthy in this regard. A simple trip to the shopping mall involves a series of decisions based on prior information, such as the distance, transportation method, direction, route, entrance gate, parking lot, and more. Additionally, there are multiple pieces of hidden information in the process that can impact our actions, known as soft constraints. For example, one must consider if the vehicle has enough fuel, where to refuel, if necessary, how to handle traffic, which route is shorter and has less traffic, which parking spot to choose, and which parking spot will have the best exit position. And we can't deny the possibility of unexpected events, such as accidents or a full parking lot.

These constraints are considered 'soft' because they don't significantly impact the overall task, but they do affect the overall process. As a result, a separate set of rules is required to address these constraints. Moreover, these constraints can't be treated as isolated tasks. A cognitive system must consider all relevant constraints in regard to the situation and the ultimate goal of reaching the shopping mall. Additionally, as there may be multiple interrelated constraints, a system must be able to handle multiple activities simultaneously. These constraints increase the cognitive demand on the computer and make the tasks harder to perform as "the number of computations required expands exponentially with the number of factors" (Franklin, 1995, p. 115).

However, Franklin argues that having more soft constraints sometimes makes a task easier for humans because it provides extra logical points to make decisions. Contrary to it, extra constraints become an overload for computers because they have to test the consequences in every possible way for each constraint. Further, these extra factors put systems under a time constraint too as computers work in a sequential manner of input-process-result. Even though computers can calculate in milliseconds, they often need to process multiple pieces of information simultaneously, which can significantly impact the system's speed (Shapiro, 2019, p. 49). Therefore, computers cannot be said to work analogous to human beings because they are unable to handle this level of cognitive strain if they process information sequentially.

The significance of Horgan and Tienson's study is that the classical approach fails to effectively address the soft constraints and unexpected elements involved in the cognitive process, while humans are able to efficiently handle these types of constraints. That is why they claim "human intelligence is different in kind from computer intelligence" (Franklin, 1995, p. 115).

1.2.3 Problem with Adaptability

Classical cognitive scientists believe that all cognitive activities are based on rules, which are innate to the system. If the computational thesis is correct, it follows that a system should be able to perform any type of cognitive activity, provided it has the relevant information (symbols) from the world. These systems are considered self-sufficient and rule-based, making it easy for them to perform any task without much difficulty. This premise implies that every cognitive task must have its own set of rules. Hubert Dreyfus and colleagues mainly challenge this assumption by claiming that not every domain of cognition is rule describable (H. Dreyfus et al., 2000). They give an example of riding a bicycle. They argue that one responds to the unbalancing not based on some rules but due to the experiences acquired from practice. They call it 'know-how' and argue that it cannot be reduced to 'know that' which is based on rules (ibid., p. 16). There are some tasks that can be performed solely on the basis of 'knowing that' but not all tasks (especially learned skills) require the use of conscious abstract rules (ibid., p. 19). Though one starts learning with the rule-based system, once he or she becomes an expert in performing that behaviour, they do not require to be guided by rules to exert the behaviour. To validate his point, they illustrate five stages of skill acquisition.

Dreyfus et al. maintain that non-rule-based behaviour can be possible when an individual gains expertise by progressing through five stages of learning:

1. *The novice*: A novice learns new skills through instructions. The elements learned at this phase are context-free. That means this phase is simply information processing. For example, learning the mechanics of the car with the help of an instructor when learning to drive.

2. *The beginner*: In addition to the rules, they start to gain experience while dealing with real-life situations. These situations are in addition to the context-free elements. For example, knowing when to shift gears by just hearing the sound of the engine (situational element) but speed (context-free element).

3. *The competent*: Once one gets mastery over situational elements, they start to examine and filter out the most important ones from the pool of innumerate situational elements that are relevant to their goals. For

example, selecting a particular route with respect to distance, time, and traffic while going home from the office.

4. *The proficient*: A proficient would not need to examine and assess the situational elements, but they just know what to do at a particular point by just being in the situation. This ability works as intuition, and they react in a particular situation without any deliberate conscious decision-making because they have experienced similar kinds of situations multiple times in the past. This stage of intuition is termed as 'knowing-how.'

5. *The expert*: This is the stage where one just does it. An expert does not become aware of the various decision-making processes involved in the activities. That means the skills of the person are not much detached from him to be aware of. For example, anyone who is an expert in driving generally feels the boundary of the car as their own extension. This can be easily witnessed while rash driving or cutting corners. We typically tend to bend left or right as we are not trying to turn the vehicle, instead, we are trying to turn ourselves. Dreyfus et al. conclude that in a normal scenario, "experts don't solve problems and don't make decisions; they do what normally works" (ibid., p. 31).

Now, if Dreyfus et al. are correct about the expert stage that it does not require rule-based computation, then the classical approach cannot be considered a comprehensive model for human cognition. Most human behaviours are learned skills, and even if some of them (which are at the expertise level) do not rely on rule-based, then the classical approach will be inadequate for explaining these expert behaviours.

The above discussion shows the problem of adaptability. An expert generally adapts himself according to the situation and becomes a part of the situation. They perform and react in a given situation without deliberate conscious thinking or decision-making. Their behaviour becomes reflexive through continuous experiences in the past. This is the progression from a rule-based system to an autonomous system by continuous adaptation of the external elements. Humans typically behave like this, and we have to do the same activity multiple times to become experts by including various new elements during the whole process. That means if we want to describe a human cognitive system, then it should not and cannot be a rigid system. The system should be able to adapt to external factors and continue learning and improving itself to gain more and more expertise to face new challenges.

This line of explanation indicates that cognitive activity is not merely confined to a central processing unit, but it is the result of various internal and external factors. This is one of the central tenets of the embodied theory.

Embodied cognition approach makes a strong commitment to the experiences we gain through bodily interaction in the world. This framework is anticipated in phenomenology, especially in the thoughts of Merleau-Ponty, which fuelled further studies in the direction of embodied cognition. Therefore, let us briefly explore its phenomenological roots.

1.3   *Phenomenological Roots*

The phenomenological Movement can be considered a theoretical precursor to empirical studies exploring the bodily foundation of our existence. The embodied approach is influenced and driven by the seminal phenomenological ideas first introduced by Husserl and further advanced by Heidegger, Sartre, and Merleau-Ponty. The principal subject of phenomenology is an explanation of our conscious lived experiences, in short—"how do we experience" (D. W. Smith, 2018). It is a method in which every concept is investigated from within and aims to explain the intentional structure of consciousness. Intentionality is a feature that refers to and relates to objects or actions. For instance, if I think about a dog, it manifests in my consciousness. Similarly, thinking about running is directed towards an action related to bodily movement. This is why phenomenologists view intentionality as an integral aspect of conscious experiences. As a result, phenomenologists concentrate on investigating our subjective conscious experiences to understand the majority of our actions, thoughts, perceptions, motivations, etc. In this sense, an objective existence cannot be entirely divorced from our lived experiences. The obvious conclusion is that the body and the surrounding environment cannot be ignored as we experience the world through our bodily sensations. Therefore, our subjective cognitive experiences should be viewed and analysed in terms of our physical embodiment in the world.

Developing on the same line, phenomenologist Merleau-Ponty argues that our subjective consciousness cannot be considered separate from our physical embodiment in the world. He illustrates: "my existence as subjectivity is merely one with my existence as a body and with the existence of the world, and because the subject that I am, when taken concretely, is inseparable from this body and this world" (Merleau-Ponty, 1962, p. 475). This view is a substantial deviation from the solipsistic notion of mentality, which is conceived as completely detached from the body and world.

Merleau-Ponty argues that while actual experiences are dynamic, they are not taken into account in classical approaches. Classical approaches consider perceptual experiences as consisting of atomic sensations (Toadvine, 2019). Atomic sensations are the causal factors responsible for the projection of the world. Contrary to it, Merleau-Ponty utilizes gestalt psychology to explain the perceptual experiences and argues that a 'phenomenal field' is necessary for the whole perceptual experience because it contextualizes the experiences. Thus, an agent's direct engagement through the body with its phenomenal field is the true description of the experience constructed. That means an agent's body is an indispensable part of its phenomenal field. Moreover, for Merleau-Ponty, the notion of the body does not mean just a physical body; he calls it a 'lived body,' i.e. experiences of our own bodily actions.

Therefore, in Merleau-Ponty's view, experiences are not isolated, but they are infused with our bodily engagement in the world. This makes a shift from the view that subjectivity is purely mentalistic and the bodies are merely a tool to interact with the world. Instead, the phenomenological method focuses on the intertwining of the mind-body and the world. This intertwining opens up the possibility that not only the mind is embodied, but the body is also somehow part of the mind. This clearly shows how the phenomenological method creates the foundation for embodied approach. Moreover, the phenomenological stance doesn't make a hard separation between the experience of the world (as input) and engagement with the world (as output). Similarly, the Embodied approach does not make a substantial distinction between the mental and physical realms, and it claims that mental phenomena are constituted because of our engagement with the world. Phenomenology makes the foundation for further matured thoughts in this domain, and many empirical studies support the bodily basis of ourselves. That is why even recent embodied researchers such as Shaun Gallagher, Dan Zahavi, Evan Thompson, and Francisco Varela et al. frequently refer to thoughts of Merleau-Ponty or Phenomenology in general.

To sum up, it is clear that the classicist approach faces significant challenges from phenomenology with regard to complete distinction between the mental and physical realms. This brief historical review suggests that the classicist account fails to provide a plausible explanation for human cognition and mental processes. As a response, contemporary researchers in cognitive science argue for an embodied approach and claim that it provides a correct and convincing account of the human mind and cognition. Moreover, the embodied theory is well supported by empirical studies, which makes it more convincing. Therefore, let us discuss it in detail and build the case for our embodied nature.

2   Building the Case for Embodied Cognition

Andrew Wilson and Sabrina Golonka (2013) view embodied theory as the most exciting concept in cognitive science. This is because it challenges the long-standing belief that the human mind and body are ontologically separate entities. Historically, the body has been viewed as merely providing input through sensory organs and acting as an output tool through motor organs. In contrast, the mind has been seen as an autonomous processing unit with abilities such as cognition, memory, thought, and rationality. This differentiation creates a hierarchy, with the mind as the controller and the body as controlled. However, embodied theory challenges this idea and posits that the mind and body are deeply intertwined and that mental processes are shaped by and emerge from bodily experiences. The embodied approach challenges the belief in an autonomous and independent mind. Instead, it recognizes the integral role of the body and our environment in shaping mental processes.

As seen in the previous section, the concept of embodied cognition emerged as a challenge to traditional cognitive science in the latter part of the 20th century. Researchers from various fields, including philosophy, psychology, neuroscience, and artificial intelligence, contributed to its development. As a result, it is difficult to articulate a simple, comprehensive definition of embodied cognition. However, this lack of a specific theoretical foundation also allows researchers greater flexibility to explore various aspects of embodied cognition without strict adherence to any particular methodology. This has led to the emergence of various versions and interpretations of embodied theory, collectively contributing to our understanding of this approach. Furthermore, we also see a fluidity between different themes despite taking diverse routes. Therefore, it is necessary to briefly describe some of the fundamental assumptions that the majority of researchers share in order to comprehend what exactly this theory proposes.

To begin, let us first ponder upon the encyclopaedic definitions, which delineate the general characteristics of embodied thesis and give an idea of what precisely embodied thesis is.

For instance, an entry in the Stanford Encyclopaedia for Philosophy notes:

> Many features of cognition are embodied in that they are deeply dependent upon characteristics of the physical body of an agent, such that the agent's beyond-the-brain body plays a significant causal role, or a physically constitutive role, in that agent's cognitive processing. (R. A. Wilson & Foglia, 2011)

Similarly, the Internet Encyclopaedia of Philosophy entry defines embodied theory as:

> The general theory contends that cognitive processes develop when a tightly coupled system emerges from real-time, goal-directed interactions

between organisms and their environment; the nature of these interactions influences the formation and further specifies the nature of the developing cognitive capacities ... the central claim of embodied cognition is that an organism's sensorimotor capacities, body and environment not only play an important role in cognition, but the manner in which these elements interact enables particular cognitive capacities to develop and determines the precise nature of those capacities. (Cowart, n.d.)

Both definitions provide a quick glance at the central claims of embodied cognition, which are mainly conceptualized on the basis of some landmark literature on embodied theory (for example, Beer 2000; Clark 1998; Clark and Chalmers 1998; Gallagher 2005; Lakoff and Johnson 1980; Varela, Rosch, and Thompson 1991).

These core claims are:
- Cognition is dependent upon an agent's physical body, and the body is not restricted to the brain
- The physical body plays a causal as well as a constitutive role in cognition
- Cognitive processes are like tightly coupled system
- Cognitive capacities are the result of interaction between sensory-motor capacities of the body and the environment

The above claims, though not exhaustive, set the overall tone of the embodied approach in the broadest sense. Also, despite these being core claims, not every scholar ascribes to all of them. According to Andrew Wilson and Sabrina Golonka (2013), there are various co-existing notions of embodiment while focusing on one common strand of viewing the brain-body-environment as a single system.

Now, the first claim is simple to understand. According to the argument, cognition is dependent on the type of body that an organism has. Since every organism has a different set of bodily features and sensory-motor capacities, each organism will undergo a different kind of experience. Therefore, cognitive activity cannot work in isolation from the experiences that emerge from a particular bodily feature. Another vital point to note here is that an embodied approach doesn't restrict the body to the brain only; it includes other non-neural bodily parts too. As a result, the claim is that an organism's particular experiences gained through its bodily interaction with the outside world determine cognition.

Another important claim that must be understood carefully is that the body plays a causal and constitutive role in cognition. As previously mentioned, cognition is dependent on the body, and certain bodily experiences trigger cognitive processes. The challenge arises when considering the body's constitutive role in cognition. The embodied approach accepts the body as one of the constituents of cognitive activity. This minute but important aspect makes the embodied approach challenging to traditional views.

To grasp the commitments of this statement, let's look at the example of the photosynthesis process. We are aware that in the presence of sunlight, plants synthesize glucose from carbon dioxide and water. In this case, sunlight merely acts as a cause or catalyst for the reaction. But unlike carbon or hydrogen, it does not end up as a component of the finished product. Similar to this, the body is not regarded as a component of the cognitive system in traditional cognitive theories; rather, it is merely seen as a causal factor for providing the initial sensory inputs. Moreover, the brain alone was responsible for all cognitive functions, which were segregated from the body. An embodied approach, on the other hand, challenges this theory and recognizes non-neural bodily characteristics as a component of the cognitive system along with other constituents like the brain.

Advancing the above-mentioned arguments, embodied theories contend that cognitive system is a tightly coupled system of mind, body, and environment. Here, another important claim of the embodied approach that comes into the picture is the inclusion of the world (the surrounding environment) into the cognitive system. The embodied approach considers cognition as an emergent property that emerges when a body interacts and acts in the world. It implies that there is no central controller or processing unit separate from the body or the world. This is a fascinating viewpoint that claims that an embodied system is self-sufficient to perform cognitive activities and the mental realm is not separate from an embodied system. We saw earlier that it was thought that the body takes sensory input from the outside world, then the brain processes it, and finally we act in the world through our motor organs. Worldly objects, including our motor organs, were not part of the cognitive system. But the embodied approach argues that cognition emerges only because we are able to interact with worldly objects. Following similar lines, many researchers such as Andy Clark and David Chalmers argue that our mind is not restricted to the brain or body and even extends into the world (Clark & Chalmers, 1998).

The above claims summarize the overall intent and primarily lay the foundation of the embodied thesis, on which many researchers base their opinions. The main guiding principle is the recognition that our interactions with worldly objects and engagement with our surroundings play a constitutive role in our reasoning, which was overlooked in traditional approaches. Simply put, an embodied approach sees the body and world as an unavoidable part of our overall cognitive system. Yet, for the sake of defining the embodied theory in a single sentence, we can state it as follows:

Mental phenomena arise out of bodily interaction with the world.

Here the emphasis should be given to 'arise out of' and 'interaction,' because these are the main challenges for traditional views. 'Arise out of' connotes that cognition is not an isolated activity but the result of combined processes. And that process is 'interaction.' Although the fundamental assumptions are clear, further complexity lies with the issue of how mind, body, and world are tied together. Many researchers try to untangle this knot with diverse viewpoints. Some theories take the extreme route for the inclusion of beyond body objects into the cognitive system, which results in the extended mind hypothesis, whereas some are more radical towards the enaction aspect and claim that cognition cannot be separated from the actions in the world. However, despite being slightly different in focus, each version unravels the different aspects that contribute to an overall understanding of our cognition. Furthermore, almost every version converges on the central argument that human cognition cannot operate in isolation from body and world.

The claims discussed above form core guiding principles for almost every embodied cognition researcher, upon which multiple themes have been developed. Although embodied cognition is now well supported and validated by various empirical data, it is also suggested that it should be treated more like a research program than a well-defined theory (Shapiro & Spaulding, 2021). Moreover, this domain is relatively new, as most of the literature started to emerge only in the late 90s. This approach and its core assumptions were further developed by various researchers, resulting in some notable literature that helped establish the domain.

The landscape of contemporary cognitive science has increasingly embraced perspectives that reject the idea of the mind as a separate, non-material entity. Influential theories have emerged, variously highlighting the embodied, embedded, enacted, and extended dimensions of cognition—often referred to as the 4E cognition framework. For instance, Francisco Varela, Eleanor Rosch, and Evan Thompson (1991) put forth the enactive theme within the embodied cognition paradigm, emphasizing the importance of bodily interactions with the environment. Conversely, Andy Clark and David Chalmers (1998) introduced the concept of extended cognition, emphasizing the role of environmental elements in cognitive processes. Additionally, George Lakoff and Mark Johnson (1999) focused on the embodied basis of concepts and language through the lens of conceptual metaphor theory.

Despite the breadth and interconnectedness of the 4E framework, this discussion gives primacy to the embodied cognition aspect for a specific reason. The embodied approach serves as an ontological and epistemological foundation that allows for a nuanced understanding of the other E's—embedded, enacted, and extended. The embodied perspective serves as a grounding parameter, focusing on how bodily experiences shape and influence cognition, which can subsequently extend to understanding how these experiences are embedded in a larger context, enacted through actions, and potentially extended through environmental interactions. Each of these theories brings a unique perspective based on their origins in various domains. Still, they collectively contribute to a more integrated understanding of cognition within the framework of 4E cognition, with embodied cognition serving as a foundational cornerstone.

As a result, while keeping the scope and intent of the discussion in check, I shall now discuss three major themes that emerge from embodied theory in general. These themes are formulated by keeping our discussion related to problems with the classicist approach in mind. It will help us see how they provide more plausible explanations. Furthermore, these three themes are most important and relevant for our discussion related to education in the forthcoming chapters. It will help us to understand the commitment of embodiment more comprehensively and make us able to apply these findings in the field of education.

2.1   Mind-Body-World Coupling

The most common and central claim of the embodied approach is that cognition is the result of mind-body-world coupling. The three elements of this coupled system are the cognitive agent (the mind), the body that the agent inhabits, and the physical and social worlds in which they are situated. Here, the coupling means that each of these elements affects and is affected by the others. In that sense, unlike traditional views, cognition is seen as the result of a bidirectional process. This means that not only does the world influence the individual, but the individual also influences the world through their bodily interactions. Thus, an individual's interpretation of the world is based on the way they interact with it and the way they learn from it. Similarly, an individual's memories and understanding of the world affect the world too.

The concept of mind-body-world coupling emphasizes the way in which an organism is constantly drawing pieces of information from its environment to support its cognitive processes and how those cognitive processes, in turn, influence its perception and action in the world. The key point here is that cognition is not simply the product of the individual mind, body, and brain working in isolation but the result of their continuous interaction as one system. According to Anthony Chemero (2001), "it is only for convenience (and from habit) that we think of the organism and environment as separate; in fact, they are best thought of as constituting just one system."

Another important key point of the claim related to mind-body-world coupling is that cognition is an emergent property that arises out of the continuous mutual interaction between these three components. Andy Clark uses the phrase "continuous reciprocal causation" for this mechanism and argues that human cognition is a property that emerged from dense reciprocal causal influence among the brain, body, and world (Clark, 1998, pp. 163–165). This underlies the fact that cognition is not a static process but is constantly changing and evolving through interaction among its components (brain, body, and world). That means cognition is the result of the dynamic and ongoing interaction between an organism and its environment. That is why dynamical systems theory is claimed to be the best possible explanation for human cognition.

A dynamical system, in general, is a system of elements that changes over time. A dynamical system exists in a constant state of change, with its structure and behaviour being determined by the current environmental conditions. Randall Beer argues that a dynamic system is also able to adapt and learn from its previous experiences, meaning that it can change its behaviour in response to changes in its environment (Beer, 2000). In terms of cognition, this means that cognition is not a static process but one that constantly changes in response to the environment. This theoretical framework offers a way of understanding mental processes as emergent phenomena that arise from the dynamic interactions between various elements, such as the body and environment, in the system. In contrast to the computational perspectives, which see cognition as a process of information processing and pattern recognition, the dynamical systems perspective sees cognition as a process of self-organization.

Dynamical system theory (DST) is an area of study in mathematics used to describe the behaviour of complex dynamical systems such as planetary orbits, electronic circuits, etc. It was initially applied in cognitive science by Timothy Van Gelder in the 1990s. He uses the metaphor of Watt's centrifugal governor to explain the dynamical nature of human cognitive systems (Van Gelder, 1995). A Scottish engineer named James Watt designed a centrifugal governor in the eighteenth century to regulate the speed of a steam engine. The governor consists of a flywheel and two weights attached to it. Further, a throttle valve is attached to this system, which regulates the flow of steam going into the engine. The basic principle behind the governor is that as the speed of the engine increases, the centrifugal force acting on the weights attached to the radial arms of the governor also increases. This, in turn, causes the arms to rotate faster and the weights to move outward. The increased centrifugal force acting on the weights causes the governor to automatically adjust the position of the throttle valve, which regulates the flow of steam to the engine and, consequently, its speed. That means, when the engine generates more power, the flywheel rotates faster, which makes flyballs rise due to centrifugal force, consequently closing the throttle valve a little bit, which decreases the steam flow in the engine. In contrast, when the engine does not produce enough power, the rotation of the flywheel slows and the flyballs drop, causing the throttle valve to open wider to increase the flow of steam (Figure 1).

The key idea here is that the changes in the system are instantaneous and interdependent, as there is no sequential order to the operation of various elements as well as no clear starting point to the causal process. That is why cognitive scientists conceive of cognition as a circle of causality that does not have a separate, watertight partition between the beginning, middle, and end of the cognitive process (Shapiro, 2019, p. 156).

While applying DST in cognitive science, Thelen and Smith claim that this kind of system is capable of exhibiting coherent behaviour solely through the "relationships between the organic components and the constraints and

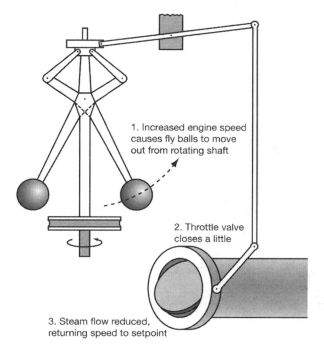

1. Increased engine speed causes fly balls to move out from rotating shaft

2. Throttle valve closes a little

3. Steam flow reduced, returning speed to setpoint

FIGURE 1
Watt's governor model
(Lawrence Shapiro, 2011, p. 121)

opportunities offered by the environment" (L. B. Smith, 2006). They also emphasize the concept of an open system in which the environment is treated as an equal component alongside others. Moreover, they argue for multicausality, in which no single element of the system has causal priority, whether it is internal or external. This is why these systems are considered self-organized because they can adapt automatically to environmental factors on the basis of continuous feedback loops. Similarly, cognition is conceived as a self-organizing, adapting phenomenon that emerges due to the circle of causality, which consists of the brain, the body, and the environment. That means the body and the environment are not only equally important as the brain, but they also have a concomitant relationship (Figure 2).

Randall Beer illustrates this conceptual framework by arguing that an agent's cognitive system is primarily evolved to coordinate its behaviour in the world. That means an agent's immediate physical and social environment cannot be divorced from its cognitive behaviour. Beer contends that because "nervous systems and bodies co-evolved with one another and with their environment," (Beer, 2003, p. 211); therefore, they should be regarded as a coupled system.

DST has inspired many researchers to conduct empirical studies in light of this new understanding. For example, Thelen and Smith (1996) studied the coordination of infants' legs for their stepping behaviour during the transition from crawling to walking; Beer (2003) studied the artificial agent's categorization behaviour in the detection of circles and diamonds; and Varela, Rosch, and Thompson (1991) analysed our experience of colour from phenomenological and physiological perspectives. These studies provide plausible support for the integrated perspective of mind-body-world and show that human

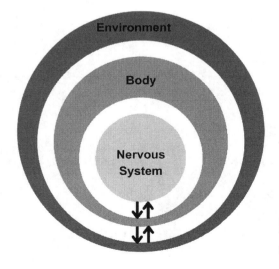

FIGURE 2
The environment, body, and nervous system are in continuous interaction

cognitive behaviour is the result of the active and dynamic engagement of an embodied agent in its physical-social environment. In recent years, the above claim has been frequently validated through numerous empirical studies in the areas of embodied robotics, vision, sport psychology, clinical psychology, and education (e.g., Farina 2021; Leitan and Chaffey 2014; Macedonia 2019). These studies demonstrate the maturity and plausibility of the embodied cognition approach and provide strong validation of the integrated mind-body-world approach for understanding and explaining human behaviour.

To sum up, these pieces of evidence pose a solid objection to the conception of a discrete mental process sandwiched between inputs and outputs. It shifts our attention to the continuous mental processes that evolve and adapt in response to a stream of inputs while simultaneously producing a stream of outputs. These empirical outcomes converge towards another crucial claim of the embodied approach: that mental phenomena such as perception and action are continuous. It implies that there is no clear boundary that delineates the cognition and action of an agent, as the whole process is one continuous event. Furthermore, the idea that human actions are the result of some thoughtful process happening in the brain would become obsolete as action and cognition are dynamically linked together, and inputs coming from the world will not play just a casual role but will be a constitutive part of the whole process.

I shall further discuss this claim in the following section on the basis of empirical studies done in the area of perception, which show that perception is a form of action. I shall also take cues from the perspective of enactive and extended approaches, which are typically considered more radical in the domain of embodied cognition.

2.2   *Mind Is Continuous*

We have seen how the fundamental assumption of an embodied approach broadens the definition of mind by incorporating body and environment into the entire cognitive process. Further, the cognitive behaviour of a cognitive agent acts as a dynamic system that continuously evolves and adapts according to new environmental challenges. Unlike traditional input-output information processing, it employs feedback loops. Therefore, an embodied approach shifts our focus from discrete mental states to continuous mental processes (Shapiro, 2019, p. 159). That means cognition and action are not to be considered separately in terms of mental and physical domains. Thus, the actions of an agent are inherently infused with cognition, and vice versa.

To illustrate this claim, I shall refer to the studies conducted in the domain of perception (vision). Traditionally, cognitive scientists generally considered that perception is an internal mental activity that takes place in the brain after receiving signals (data) from the sense organs, such as the eyes (ibid., p. 22). This explanation necessitates the requirement of symbolic representation and internal algorithmic computation to process the data arriving at the retina, just like the computational model. This approach was initially challenged by James Gibson's ecological theory of perception, which is usually seen as a precursor to the embodied approach (Gibson, 1966, 1979).

The fundamental tenet of Gibson's theory is that perception is an active process, meaning that we actively seek out information from the environment in order to construct our perceptual map. This contrasts with traditional theories of perception, which posit that we are passive recipients of sensory information. Gibson showed that the perceiver actively extracts information from the environment through our senses by actively navigating into it. There are two major constituents of his theory; one is the concept of resonating, and another is affordances. Gibson viewed the perceiver as a perceptual system that orients itself to gather necessary information from the environment. It is like a radio receiver. A radio has to be tuned to a specific frequency to get the correct information from the vast array of information by resonating it back and forth. Similarly, by reorienting and navigating in the environment, a perceptual system resonates or tunes itself in appropriate ways for the pickup of useful information from the environment. He argued that our visual system is tuned to certain aspects of the natural environment (including cultural aspects), which he termed "affordances" (Kaptelinin, 2014).

Affordances are the relationship between the characteristics of an object and the actions that can be taken with that object. For example, a chair affords the opportunity to sit, and a doorknob affords to turn. Likewise, a staircase affords the opportunity to walk up or down. Gibson argues that we perceive these affordances directly; that is, we can see what we can do with an object without having to think about it. It means that when we perceive an object, we are also aware of the object's affordances. For example, when we see a staircase, we immediately recognize that we can move up or down it without consciously thinking about it. We do not need to engage in any cognitive processes to understand the stairs' affordances; they are directly perceptible.

Another important aspect of Gibson's theory is that this entanglement of perceptual system and environment is not limited to the sensory organs but necessarily involves other bodily features. Gibson emphasizes the role of the body in perception by arguing that we use our bodies to explore the environment and gather information about it. He put it this way: "head movements, ear movements, hand movements, nose and mouth movements, and eye movements are part and parcel of the perceptual systems" (Gibson, 1966, p. 58).

The key takeaway from Gibson's ecological theory of perception is that the process of perception is not entirely dissociated from the actions of organisms. That means perception is essentially the process of making sense of the environment to guide the actions of the organism. That also means perception is not just about acquiring information about the world around us; it is about knowing what to do with that information. In other words, perception is goal-directed action. Gibson's theory served as a baby step towards an embodied approach, and it further inspired many cognitive scientists to conduct empirical studies that supported the assumption that thought results from an organism's ability to act in its environment.

For example, developmental psychologist Esther Thelen and colleagues conducted an experiment to determine "how infants learn to reach" (Thelen et al., 1993). They concluded from the study that action is the essential first step for cognition to develop. They examined four infants of different energy levels, of which two were quieter and the remaining two were relatively more spontaneous and energetic. Each infant had been exposed to the common problem of reaching for a toy. However, their solutions to the given problem differed because each infant faced the same problem uniquely and differently due to their individual energy level, body mass, and the various ways in which they first attempted to reach it. Given these different parameters, each infant had to find different solutions for controlling their arms, speed, and trajectory to reach the toy. This was, in a sense, required to convert head-eye coordinates into shoulder-hand coordinates. The study reported that the infants created movement patterns that were specific to the task and changed these patterns over time. Furthermore, they did not have predetermined movement patterns that they followed but instead actively explored different ways of moving that best fit the task. On the basis of this study, they suggested that infants' central nervous systems are not hardwired with specific programs for how to move their hands and arms but that these motions are the result of the natural dynamics of their bodies and the active exploration of the task at hand. Moreover, in a similar study, Thelen and Smith show that the infant's ability to control its body in order to perform various activities enables it to learn certain categories simultaneously. These studies conclude that "perceptual motor category formation is foundational for all cognitive development" (Thelen, 1995, p. 95).

The above experiment is just one example of why embodied accounts hold that action is the essential first step that makes cognition possible. There are many more influential psychological studies that further advance the idea of the interdependence of action and perception (e.g., Hurley 2001; Hutto & Myin 2012; Noë & Thompson 2004; O'regan & Noë 2001). At the same time, some scholars such as Varela, Thompson, and Rosch further advance this theme in their theory of enactivism, in which they build their arguments from the perspective of an organism's ability to enact in the world. Not only theoretically, but recent neuroscientific studies provide ample evidence showing the interdependence of action and perception on a neural level. For instance, canonical and mirror neurons are bimodal, possessing both motor and visual properties (Garbarini & Adenzato, 2004). Their defining characteristic is that they become activated when a person performs an action or when they observe someone else performing the same action. Moreover, experimentation with monkeys conducted by Evelyne Kohler and colleagues has demonstrated that mirror neurons respond in a similar manner even in different modalities (Kohler et al., 2002). This means that mirror neurons can detect and respond to the same action, regardless of whether it is performed physically or simply observed. Furthermore, these neurons will also activate in response to the sounds associated with the action. The conclusion is that the same neural region is capable of representing the meaning of an action, whether the animal has performed the action themselves or has simply seen or heard it. In other words, the nervous system's motor functions not only control and execute action but also serve to represent it (Garbarini & Adenzato, 2004).

These neuroscientific studies demonstrate and support the idea that mental and physical states are intimately connected and should not be viewed as separate entities. An organism constantly interacts with its environment to perceive, understand, theorize, act, and modify its surroundings to meet its needs. The organism is a perceptual system that is continually acting, perceiving, and adapting itself to the given situation. As such, the cognition of an organism should not be considered discrete and separate from its actions. This is why the embodied approach emphasizes the continuity of cognitive processes and argues that the mental realm, or the mind, should not be treated as separate from the world in which it interacts or its ability to interact through the body. That means, in this continuous loop of mental-bodily-environmental interaction, we can not specify where the 'mind' resides. Therefore, in the words of Michael Spivey, the mind should be treated "as a natural, continuous event" (Spivey, 2008, p. 29).

Now, if the mind or cognitive activity is viewed as a continuous natural event resulting from the interaction between mental, physical, and environmental factors, it follows that cognitive abilities can be influenced by the features of an organism's body and its environment. In other words, an organism can improve its cognitive abilities by increasing its opportunities for interaction with a well-organized social and physical environment. The surrounding environment not only helps us to improve our cognitive abilities but also helps us to ease our cognitive efforts. It is pretty evident that we use the surrounding environment (even the body) to ease our cognitive activity by distributing the cognitive load to the body and/or environment. For example, we typically use our fingers for simple mathematical calculations, and the use of a pencil and paper helps us solve more complex mathematical problems. In short, external factors such as bodily and environmental features provide us with a way to distribute our cognition. The real question is whether these external factors are a necessary part of cognitive activities or merely tools to aid cognition. We have discussed previously that one of the central claims of embodied cognition is that the world plays a constitutive role in cognitive activities. This claim has been adequately illustrated by the theory of the extended mind, which was initially developed by Andy Clark and David Chalmers and further advanced by many scholars such as Martin and Schwartz, Margaret Wilson, Lucy Suchman, and Edwin Hutchins.

The key tenet of the extended mind hypothesis is that the mind is not confined to the boundaries of the skull. That means cognition is not confined to the brain but extends to include processes and resources located outside the brain, such as in the body or the environment. For example, (Clark & Chalmers, 1998) argue that when we use a pencil and paper to help us remember something, the pencil and paper become part of our cognitive process and thus part of our mind. The important point here is that pencil and paper (the world) have not merely a causal role in the cognitive system; they are, in fact, constituents in the overall cognitive system. Moreover, the world can be a constituent of the cognitive process in two complementary ways. Firstly, features of the environment are constituents of our cognition; at the same time, our cognitive activity is extended in the environment too. This duplex relationship with the world can be further illustrated by the closely related concepts of cognitive scaffolding and cognitive offloading.

Cognitive scaffolding suggests that our cognitive abilities both depend on and are shaped by the resources in our environment (Sterelny, 2010). These resources are often built, preserved, or manipulated in a way that improves our cognitive skills. Cognitive offloading, on the other hand, implies that we frequently transfer information in the world in order to overcome cognitive limitations and/or reduce the load of cognitive activity (M. Wilson, 2002). This claim has been supported by various empirical studies, too. For instance, David Kirsh and Paul Maglio conducted a study related to the Tetris game. They reported that players use actual physical rotation movements to simplify the problem rather than attempting to solve it solely through mental computation (Kirsh & Maglio, 1994). In a similar kind of experiment, Taylor Martin and Daniel Schwartz showed that children are able to better understand and calculate 1/4 of 8 when they are able to actually manipulate and work with the pie pieces, as opposed to just looking at them (Martin & Schwartz, 2005).

These studies suggest that the use of the external environment can lead to a more efficient form of cognition by allowing us to offload some of the mental resources required for the task. Enactive approach and extended mind hypothesis together typically challenge the traditional view of the mind as a purely internal, mental realm, cut off from the rest of the world. On the basis of the above discussions, it is evident that cognition is the result of our inter-action with the environment in various ways. Further, we have seen that vari-ous psychological and neuroscientific studies converge on the fact that mental phenomena are rooted in the bodily interaction of an organism with its sur-rounding environment. This has important implications for our understanding of human concepts and rationality.

In the traditional view, rationality is a purely mental process carried out by the individual mind. But in embodied cognition (including enactive and extended approaches), rationality is a distributed process resulting from our enaction in the world. It is claimed by various proponents that most, if not all, mental concepts are embodied. This marks a paradigm shift from the tradi-tional approach, which considers symbolic representations as mental aspects dissociated from the action or external world. It is a crucial claim and one of the most controversial too. It is simply because most folk psychological theo-ries, beliefs, and even religions are based on this very assumption that humans have some innate feature of rationality. Moreover, our most social activities, including education, are based upon this very assumption, which we shall see in more detail in the forthcoming chapter. But before that, let us discuss another important central theme of the embodied approach, which claims that 'concepts are embodied.'

2.3   *Concepts Are Embodied*

'Concepts' are generally described as basic units of thoughts. They are the foundation of all of our thinking and reasoning, which enable us to make sense of the world and communicate with others. That is why concepts are considered the fundamental building blocks of cognition. Concepts can be concrete as well as abstract. For instance, the concept of a chair has more of a 'concrete' nature, which means the concept represents an object that has a physical existence in the world. In contrast, the concept of time or love is an abstract concept that might not have any physical existence. Typically, con-cepts are considered features of the mental realm of an organism, which is different from its physical realm. For instance, some ancient philosophers like

Plato believed that concepts, or forms, have an otherworldly existence and are ultimate, while worldly objects are just reflections of these concepts. In modern times, Descartes was the biggest proponent of a sharp division between mental concepts and physical existence. Although psychologists bring concepts back into the world, they limit them to the confines of the brain. In both philosophical and psychological perspectives, concepts are considered separate from bodily aspects. This raises a key issue: if concepts are completely disconnected from the physicality of an organism, how do they derive meaning?

Embodied theorists argue that most, if not all, concepts are embodied. That means concepts derive their meaning from the bodily experiences an organism has. This leads to an important conclusion: concepts cannot exist independently of an organism's body. This also means that different kinds of bodies may give rise to different kinds of concepts. As a result, there are no fixed and independent conceptual structures. This is the core claim by embodied theorists, well formulated by Shapiro as the "Conceptualization Hypothesis," in which he argues that "the kind of body an organism possesses constrains or determines the concept it can acquire" (Shapiro, 2019, p. 80). That means concept formation is dependent on an organism's specific sensorimotor experiences. For example, consider the simple task of grabbing a ball. A human baby will typically use their hands to pick up the ball, while a puppy will likely use its mouth. This difference in behaviour arises from the different physical characteristics of each organism, leading to distinct ways of interacting with the world. Thus, different kinds of "embodiment" shape different kinds of action patterns, which in turn shape the cognitive functionalities differently. To further understand embodied concepts, I shall focus on the work of George Lakoff and Mark Johnson, who provide one of the most influential recent formulations of the embodied approach.

Lakoff and Johnson (1999) argue that most of the Western tradition is based upon the assumption that humans have an autonomous, independent capacity to reason, and this view is part of what is called "faculty psychology." This faculty is believed to be autonomous and not dependent upon perception, action, or other bodily capacities. Lakoff and Johnson differ from this view on the basis of evidence in cognitive science. They argue that human reasoning is not all that different from that of other animals, but that it is the result of our evolution and the experiences we have had in the world through our bodies. Further, according to Lakoff and Johnson, the process of concept construction is based on the ability to categorize. They argue that, like other living entities, human beings instinctively categorize the world into subgroups, including "food," "predators," "potential mates," and "members of their own species," among others (Ibid., p. 17). This categorization process depends upon two factors: firstly, the way an organism interacts with its environment (i.e., walking, swimming, flying, etc.); and secondly, the kind of sensory apparatus they have (i.e., a heat sensor, infrared vision, rods and cones in the eyes, etc.). Moreover, they contend that most of the categorization process is not the result of conscious reasoning because we are evolved to do so naturally due to survival necessities.

They take help from findings in cognitive science to illustrate the necessity of categorization in humans. They note:

> Our brains each have 100 billion neurons and 100 trillion synaptic connections. It is common in the brain for information to be passed from one dense ensemble of neurons to another via a relatively sparse set of connections ... To take a concrete example, each human eye has 100 million light-sensing cells, but only about 1 million fibers leading to the brain. (Ibid., p. 18)

Therefore, the information transmitted to the brain through each fiber must be "reduced in complexity by a factor of 100." That means the information transmitted through each fibre comprises the information from about 100 cells. This process necessitates the grouping of information, which is described as "neural categorization" by Lakoff and Johnson. Moreover, they stress that this type of mechanism is not exclusive to the visual system but that this kind of neural categorization exists throughout the brain. Further, they argue that humans are able to mentally characterize and reason about categories, which are called concepts.

An important aspect of human neural structures is that they permit us to conceptualize categories in more than one way, which ultimately helps us make inferences or perform imaginative tasks related to the particular category. For example, the category "bird" can lead to inferring multiple meanings and understandings, thereby generating multiple concepts. They argue that our reality is determined by how we categorize the world, and "our concepts determine how we reason about those categories" (Ibid., p. 21). They also contend that this process of categorization and conceptualization is a mostly automatic and unconscious result of our functioning in the world. Moreover, the underlying structure of conscious categories is also shaped by unconscious categories.

This implies that even abstract categories, which we typically think we are consciously making, are built up by combining a group of more basic categories, which rely on our sensorimotor experiences. That means whatever category we form cannot be separated from our experiences, and thus, the process of categorization is not a purely intellectual activity isolated from bodily experiences. Therefore, human concepts cannot be considered as simple reflections of the world around us. Instead, they are crucially shaped by our bodies, including our brains, and especially by our sensorimotor systems. In other words, our conceptual system is embodied.

Lakoff and Johnson also claim that "most of our normal conceptual system is metaphorically structured" (Lakoff & Johnson, 1980, p. 57). That means one understands a concept on the basis of other concepts that are already understood. They show how important metaphor is by saying that it is all about understanding and seeing one kind of thing in terms of another. This implies that whenever we learn or try to understand any unknown concepts, we heavily rely on metaphorical reasoning. For example, we understand "relationship" through the metaphor of "journey," where a relationship can take a different path or might be bumpy, similar to a journey. Now, this raises the question: are all of our concepts comprehended through metaphor?

According to Lakoff and Johnson, there are some basic types of concepts that are based on our direct physical experiences in the environment. For instance, most of our spatial concepts are basic in nature and derive their meaning from our direct bodily experiences in the world. For example, we understand the concepts of "up" and "down," "in front of," "behind," and so on in terms of our bodily orientation and movement in the world. Another example is the concept of "in" and "out," which are basic metaphors derived from direct experiences in the world in which the body serves as a reference point and is conceived as a container. Since abstract concepts rely on basic concepts to derive their meaning, it is implied that abstract concepts are ultimately embodied too. The conclusion is that our concepts are not merely abstract mental objects that are separate from our bodies; instead, they are rooted in our bodily modalities, and we understand them metaphorically.

Lakoff and Johnson lay out a variety of such metaphors, which show the sensorimotor basis of most of our concepts. For instance, the conceptual metaphor "understanding is seeing" is based on our experience of visually perceiving and understanding the world around us. Another example is the conceptual metaphor "argument is war," which is based on our motor experience of physically engaging in combat. These conceptual metaphors are not just dead metaphors that we passively use; instead, they actively shape our cognition. In the case of "understanding is seeing," this conceptual metaphor shapes our cognition such that we tend to think of understanding as a process of gathering information in the same way that we gather information through our visual perception. Likewise, in the case of "argument is war," this conceptual metaphor shapes our cognition such that we tend to think of an argument as a competition in which we must vanquish our opponents.

There are numerous bodily-rooted metaphors that we use in our daily lives to construct and comprehend physical and emotional aspects. For example, the concept "affection is warmth" has a sensorimotor domain of temperature, the concept "Intimacy is closeness" has a sensorimotor domain of being physically close, and so on. More importantly, these metaphors are not simply linguistic conveniences but are instead deeply ingrained in the way we think and conceptualize the world. This results in a logical shift from the belief in the existence of independent symbolic representations to the belief that all symbolic representations have a bodily basis.

The above discussion related to the metaphorical construction of concepts suggests that concepts are modal in nature, unlike the traditional account, which holds that mental concepts are amodal and arbitrary. If concepts are amodal then their internal structures bear no correspondence to the states that produced them, and hence both are linked arbitrarily (Barsalou, 1999). But it is clear from the previous discussion that concepts contain information about their state of origin, i.e., a particular bodily experience, which is usually derived with the help of metaphors. The empirical pieces of evidence related to this claim come from various studies in cognitive science. These studies show that concepts are not completely dissociated from sensory-motor neural structures. The core hypothesis is that if concepts are modal, then a subject's conceptual thinking should have corresponding activity in the sensorimotor system in the brain.

Initial evidence comes from studies involving the observation of tasks performed in two groups (Barsalou et al., 1999; Kosslyn, 1980). Subjects are presented with two methods for completing tasks. Typically, one group is instructed to use mental imagery to resolve the task, while the other group is not given any specific directions. The outcome indicated that the creation of visual images stimulates the brain regions responsible for visual processing. Many such related studies have recently been conducted that demonstrate the sensorimotor basis of the concepts and confirm the modality of the concepts. For instance, Pierce Edmonton and Gary Lupyan conducted a study based on visual interferences (Edmiston & Lupyan, 2017). Subjects were asked two kinds of questions: one related to knowledge acquired visually (e.g., does a swan have a beak?), and another related to encyclopaedic knowledge that does not require visual knowledge (e.g., does a swan lay eggs?). In this study, a block of colours was projected just before the questions for interference. The data showed that subjects made more errors when using their visual knowledge than their encyclopaedic knowledge due to interference in their visual processing. But there was no significant difference in performance in the case of questions related to encyclopaedic knowledge. This study confirms that visual knowledge and perception are dependent on the same mechanism. Edmiston and Lupyan (2017) concluded that if concepts were amodal symbols, then they would not have sensorimotor origins.

Similarly, more direct evidence for embodied concepts comes from the studies related to the connection between the understanding of action-related words and the activation of respective motor areas in the brain. In a series of related experiments, researchers found that action-related words are semantically related to the stimulation of the motor system (e.g., Hauk, Johnsrude, and Pulvermüller 2004; Kana et al., 2012; Pulvermüller 2005). For example, reading the words "lick," "pick," and "kick" stimulates the brain area responsible for actions by the "tongue," "hand," and "leg," respectively. That means one understands the meaning of "kick" as related to the kicking behaviour of the person. This shows that thinking is not completely divorced from the bodily experiences of a person. Moreover, advancements in brain imaging technologies provide more empirical evidence to support the sensorimotor basis of most of our linguistic structures too. For instance, it is found that using an action verb activates the motor system of the brain, whereas the visual system of the brain gets activated when one thinks about a visual noun (Shapiro, 2019, p. 96).

Before ending this section, it is important to highlight that these novel findings indicate that our reasoning is not completely divorced from our bodily experiences. The traditional view of reasoning is based on faculty psychology, in which reason is considered a disembodied, logical process that has a separate mechanism from the sensorimotor system. On the other hand, empirical evidence from cognitive science shows that reasoning and many aspects of the human mind are not entirely isolated from the brain regions involved in sensorimotor activities. Moreover, in the faculty of psychology, social and emotional aspects of humans are generally neglected. In contrast, a growing body of research in this domain claims that emotion and feelings are required for individuals to make effective decisions. If we are talking about an organism's bodily interactions and experiences in the surrounding environment, then we cannot dismiss the social aspect of it. It is also important to clarify that the "environment" for embodied scientists includes both physical as well as social aspects. In this regard, the work of Antonio Damasio is notable.

Through his "somatic marker hypothesis," Damasio (1994) claims that emotions are necessary for adequate performance in at least one form of reasoning, i.e., decision-making. Somatic markers are physical sensations that are linked to certain emotions. For example, a racing heart might be associated with anxiety, or feeling nauseous might be linked to disgust. According to the theory, somatic markers (bodily signals or sensations) influence an individual's choices, decision-making, and voluntary actions. Damasio conducted a series of experiments on patients who had damaged pre-frontal lobes (the brain area responsible for emotional processing). He discovered that these patients had impaired decision-making capacities and were noticeably emotionally detached. The results show a strong connection between bodily sensations and the rational decision-making process. These findings also suggest that the brain regions involved in emotional processing are also important for decision-making. That means reasoning ability involves the interaction of multiple brain regions, including sensorimotor as well as emotional systems.

To sum up, the core claim of the embodied approach is that our physical bodies and the world we live in are not just the context for our reasoning but are actually essential for its shaping. This is because reasoning is not just a matter of manipulating symbols in our heads but is also a matter of interacting with the physical and social environment around us. This means that reasoning is not just a cognitive process but is also an embodied process. Moreover, the embodied approach has far-reaching implications for our understanding of the mind and its various functions. Now, based upon the above discussion, it can be argued that an embodied approach provides a plausible explanation for human cognition by taking into account the complex interplay between the body, environment, and experience. It appears more convincing because of the empirical support. As a result, it is more reasonable to accept human beings as embodied persons.

3   The Scientific and Philosophical Grounding of Embodiment

From the very beginning of this book, the fundamental assumption is that the nature of humans should be understood before designing any educational practices targeted for them. The core of the discussion till now was to understand humans, their abilities, their inherent features, and their overall working mechanism in the world. In the previous chapter, we have seen that traditional accounts of human nature do not provide plausible explanations, and most of the time, they are the result of just armchair reasoning. Moreover, most of the theories of human nature usually dissociate the mental realm from the physical realm, which leads to wrong assumptions about the nature and activities of human beings. But, as modern science gradually evolved to provide more just and convincing explanations in almost every domain, it provided us with the opportunity to explore and understand human beings more scientifically. Now, mere a priori judgments cannot be taken as sufficient to explain any phenomena, and human beings are no exception. Understanding cognition is one way to peek into human beings because this is the feature that primarily drives human beings and makes them understand as well as act in the world.

There are several reasons why the embodied cognition approach seems promising for explaining the nature of humans more accurately and comprehensively. One reason is that it provides a more holistic view of the human experience. Embodiment theory does away with the sharp division between the mental and physical realms. Instead, it suggests that the mind and body are intimately connected. Embodiment theory posits that our understanding of the world is rooted in our bodily experiences in the world. This means that our knowledge about the world is not just a product of some independent mental faculty but is shaped by our interaction with the world through our physical bodies. Another reason why embodied theory seems convincing is the abundance of empirical evidence. Apart from the numerous empirical pieces of evidence listed in previous sections, there are multiple cross-disciplinary studies being conducted that provide further support and validation for the plausibility of the embodied theory.

Vanessa Lux and colleagues provide a comprehensive list of such recent cross-disciplinary studies (Lux et al., 2021). These studies are from very diverse domains, but they all reveal the embodied nature of ourselves and provide further validation for embodied theory. For example, there are studies that show that age-related cognitive decline impacts motor control in humans (e.g., Cisek and Pastor-Bernier 2014; Gallivan et al. 2018; Krüger and Hermsdörfer 2019). Recent studies have also found a link between interoceptive perception and autism spectrum disorders (Nicholson et al., 2019), epigenetic mechanisms underlying long-term mental health effects of early life stress (Aristizabal et al., 2020), and epigenomic effects on gene expression related to stress during pregnancy (Provençal et al., 2020). Although these studies are in their early stages and many more studies are needed before a direct conclusion can be drawn, they do provide neurological evidence for human beings' embodied nature.

Another way to understand the plausibility of the embodied nature of human beings is by examining our evolutionary history. It is generally argued that embodied theories implicitly involve evolutionary reasoning. That means we can better understand the fundamental characteristics of humans and how they relate to the evolution of other animals by looking at our evolutionary past. A thorough analysis of our evolutionary history reveals that humans and other common ancestors share a lot of similarities with one another. Traditional abstract-symbol-processing views of cognition are unable to provide a reasonable explanation for continuity in cognitive skills with ancestors of the human species. Whereas the "embodied cognition" approach attempts to provide continuity between cognitively simpler creatures and modern humans (M. Wilson, 2008). In general, the evolutionary perspective on embodied cognition has its roots in Darwinian principles of natural selection.

According to evolutionary perspective, many aspects of human cognition are the evolved features that are most beneficial for survival and reproduction and are the ones that are most likely to be passed on to future generations. One of the most important claims of embodied cognition is that cognitive activities can be offloaded not only to the body but also to the environment. This feature of using bodily resources for cognitive activities can be traced to our evolutionary ancestors and other animals too. For example, Margret Wilson considers the "ability to exert flexible, voluntary control over particular articulators," "ability to see analogies," and "ability to imitate" crucial for the development of body-based cognitive abilities (ibid., pp. 381–387). Interestingly, there are several studies that show that these abilities are shared with our evolutionary ancestors in varying degrees and forms, which might be considered a precursor to the full-fledged development in humans.

The evolutionary aspect of embodied cognition is also supported by the fact that humans have evolved to be social creatures. We rely on others for our survival, and we have a strong desire to belong to a group. Yuval Noah Harari observes that various challenges like raising children, safety, etc. forced the human race to become social for their survival. He puts it this way: "Evolution favoured those capable of forming strong social ties" (Harari, 2014, p. 11). Thus, social cognition in humans is believed to have evolved along with other features that helped them with their survival prospects. Social cognition refers to our ability to understand other people and our social world. A key insight of embodiment theory is that our social cognition is rooted in our bodily interactions with other people. Shaun Gallagher claims that we have the innate capacity to understand the intentions and feelings of another person through perceiving their bodily movements, facial gestures, eye direction, etc. (Shapiro & Spaulding, 2021). Further, the discovery of mirror neurons substantiates this claim that the mere observation of a particular behaviour activates the same neurons as if we were producing the behaviour. Mirror neurons explain how a subject can understand what a target is doing or feeling without making any high-level inferences. One direct example that reflects the embodiment of social cognition is related to power posing. Dana Carney and colleagues found in one experiment that non-verbal expressions related to power not only influence one's behaviour but also affect neuroendocrine levels (Carney et al., 2010). Not only social, but there are studies related to moral cognition which further strengthen the case of embodied theory.

Recent research has also demonstrated that our moral judgments are shaped by our embodiment. That is, our moral judgments are influenced by the by-products of our physical experiences, such as the sensations we feel in our bodies and the motor processes that we use to interact with the world. For example, it has been shown that physical coldness promotes utilitarian moral judgments (Nakamura et al., 2014). Similarly, some evidence suggests that a bad smell in the environment causes a feeling of disgust, which influences moral judgments in a harsher way (Schnall et al., 2008). Additionally, recent research on the ventromedial prefrontal cortex (vmPFC) and somatic markers supports the idea that embodied cues deeply influence all forms of cognition, including social and moral cognition (Shapiro & Spaulding, 2021).

The key conclusion from the above evidence-based discussion is that humans are not fundamentally distinct from other animals, as Descartes theorized, with an innate reasoning ability. Instead, like all animals, we constantly move and interact with the world to gain understanding and adapt to the rapidly changing environment in order to increase our chances of survival. Our understanding of the world is shaped by our ongoing interaction with it through conscious and unconscious experiences rather than by a pre-existing reasoning faculty within the mind. That means human reasoning is not a universal and exclusive power of the soul or has some transcendental basis. Instead, it is an evolutionary emergent property that is shaped metaphorically by the peculiarities of our bodies, the neural structure of our brains, and our everyday functioning in the world. These findings fundamentally alter our understanding of what it means to be human. Lakoff and Johnson observe that major classical philosophical views of what a person is are at odds with what we now know. They observe that, in light of recent cognitive science findings, humans cannot be a Cartesian dualistic person: with an independent mind and body; nor a Kantian radically autonomous person: with absolute freedom and transcendent reason; nor a Fregean person: whose thought has been extruded from the body; nor a Chomskyan person: whose language is purely syntactical, independent of its meaning and context (Lakoff & Johnson, 1999, pp. 5–6). Instead, considering humans as embodied beings is more plausible, both evolutionary and empirically.

4   Conclusion

This chapter challenges traditional approaches to cognitive science by considering philosophical discussions and finding empirical backing for the arguments. Traditionally, Western philosophy has viewed the mind and body as separate entities, leading to debates over which one is more important. Cognitive scientists in the early twentieth century tried to establish a bodily basis for the mind, but this only restricted it to the brain. Computationalism and symbolic representationalism were based on the assumption that human minds are software running on brain hardware, but this leads to challenges related to semantics, adaptability, and cognitive load. An embodied approach tries to handle all three issues by integrating mind, body, and the world.

Embodied cognition theory is a promising theory to explain cognition and other inherent features of human beings. It suggests that cognition is deeply rooted in the physical body and its environment, and that our body plays a critical role in shaping our cognition. It also suggests that the mind is not restricted to the body and is sometimes extended to the world, making the mind a continuous natural event rather than a discrete faculty. This theory has been supported by empirical studies in cognitive science. The discovery of mirror neurons and studies related to brain damage further validate the claim that the mental and physical realms are closely related.

Now, once we move away from the classical disembodied notions of human beings, our educational practices too can be analysed in the light of novel understandings. If human beings are primarily embodied beings, then education must take into account the fact that the body is central to human cognition, emotion, and behaviour. Furthermore, education must recognize the importance of embodiment in human development and provide opportunities for students to develop their physical, emotional, and social skills.

The forthcoming chapters will explore the implications of an embodied view of human nature for education. As we will see, the majority of current mainstream educational practices are based on classical disembodied notions of human beings. But, once we appreciate our embodied nature, there is a lot to be assessed and restructured accordingly.

CHAPTER 5

Rethinking Education through Embodied Approach

Every society faces a range of challenges, issues, and difficulties associated with educational practices, which are acknowledged by both the general public and educators. There is no doubt that educators and governments make significant efforts to tackle the challenges through various reforms, where they generally focus on content, instructions, and school governance. While many of these reforms show positive results in different aspects of student learning, many problems have been persistent for decades. Any policy or reform typically has a finite life period, but learning and teaching methods remain remarkably constant despite multiple waves of change. A cursory overview of modern mainstream schools reveals similar problems as observed by notable thinkers and educators of the twentieth century, such as John Dewey, Paulo Freire, Jiddu Krishnamurti, et al.

Manuela Macedonia observes that modern mainstream education systems are heavily inspired by western principles, which are mostly rooted in mind-body dualism (Macedonia, 2019). She asserts that most educational programs adhere to mentalistic theories, which consider the mind and body distinct entities. It is also argued that a mentalistic education results in exam-oriented and achievement-based learning, which is not conducive to the development of critical thinking and an exploratory mindset among children. Although there have been a lot of pedagogical improvements in the past decades, the overemphasis on mentalistic education is still persistent in most schools. This implies that our efforts to tackle the issue have only produced surface-level changes and have yet to reach the core of the issue. Therefore, the main goal of this chapter is to analyse the prevalent dualistic assumptions in conventional education and propose potential modifications to integrate embodied practices.

I shall start by exploring the roots of dualistic (disembodied) biases that persist in the educational system. Multiple philosophical and psychological factors make it challenging for the education system to break free from a dualistic perspective. One of the significant reasons for our dualistic approach to education is that we typically give more emphasis to one way of looking at things due to our hemispheric differences. Additionally, various socio-political factors contribute to a dualistic approach being prevalent in our daily lives, leading to it becoming ingrained in our thinking and behaviour.

On the basis of these factors, I shall identify the main barriers that prevent most educational discourse from fully embracing an embodied perspective. The primary obstacle is the underlying dualistic assumption about ourselves, which is reflected in the design and delivery of educational practices. Furthermore, an education based on a dualistic approach reinforces this dualistic view of ourselves, obscuring our embodied nature. To break this cycle, intervention is required on two fronts. Firstly, through an "outside-in" approach where pedagogies are designed and delivered in accordance with embodied theory. Secondly, through an "inside-out" approach with the aim of realizing our embodied nature.

This chapter serves as a theoretical foundation for embodied education, paving the way for a more in-depth discussion of implementational aspects in the next chapter.

1   Uncovering Dualistic Biases in Traditional Education

A general examination of our current mainstream formal schooling shows that "society does not value embodied forms of knowing" (Nathan, 2022, p. 6). A disembodied and mentalistic bias leads to an incomplete and shaky foundation for school culture. A particular presupposition regarding what it is to be a human being has a significant influence on designing educational practices. As a result, it is not unreasonable to assert that the roots of body neglect (anti-body) in educational practices are based on philosophies and assumptions about human beings and their nature. In general, the foundation of modern formal schooling was laid in the seventeenth-eighteenth centuries in the West, and the model was spread to most areas of the world through colonial expansion. Nevertheless, even after three centuries, the fundamental way of imparting education has mostly stayed the same globally.

Although there are some educational centres that employ an integrated approach conceptually, they are few, and thus they are usually termed "alternative schools." These centres are mostly based on democratic values and employ collaborative and experiential learning, an integrated approach, hands-on practices, and a student-centric pedagogy for all-around human development. They are typically founded as an alternative to the traditional education system, drawing inspiration from the thoughts of many educational thinkers. Some notable examples include Summerhill School, founded by A. S. Neill in London; schools based on the educational philosophy of Rudolf Steiner, J. H. Pestalozzi, and Maria Montessori; Shanti Niketan by Rabindranath Tagore; Rishi Valley School by Jiddu Krishnamurti; Ashram Schools by Sri Aurobindo, and so on. While these schools do not explicitly mention embodied theory, at least in modern terminology, their practices demonstrate that they value human beings' embodied nature.

Despite this, the prevalent mainstream educational system nowadays, in general, frequently ignores our embodied nature in current teaching-learning practices and still adheres to the anti-body biases that have a long history. The culture of modern public schools has direct philosophical roots dating back to the seventeenth century. However, the factors that established and sustained public schooling at that time have evolved over thousands of years, and the underlying beliefs behind this creation have not significantly altered even today. Therefore, to understand the underlying dualistic assumptions in current mainstream schools today, it is crucial to examine the philosophical motivations behind them.

1.1   *Philosophical Perspective*

Conceptual dualism appears to be the main driving force behind anti-body biases and the preference for the mind over the body. This is because conceptual dualism creates a hard separation of the mind from the body, which then makes it appear like the body is less important than the mind. The idea of a distinct mind and body goes back to the thoughts of Plato, and the assumption that the mind is separate from the body has had a big impact on Western culture. In his allegory of the cave (Republic, book 7), Plato argues that ideas are real and physical things are just shadows of those ideas. Throughout his work, Plato makes it clear that the body is just a physical object that can change, decay, and die, while the mind is the only real thing. A pivotal implication of Plato's legacy is that it divorces us from our bodies and leads us to believe that there is an objective reality that is separate from our individual interpretation of events. As a result, since we have been taught to see our bodies as separate from ourselves, we also tend to mistrust our own experiences and instincts. Around two thousand years after Plato, in seventeenth century, Descartes emerged as a major proponent of mind-body dualism, from which most of the intellectual development in Western society has not been able to be completely free. If Plato is the thinker who laid the foundations for our epistemological objectification, René Descartes is the thinker who built on those foundations and brought them to fruition. This was also the period when public schooling began to emerge.

The emergence of modern public schooling coincided with the rise of physical science in the West, which endorsed objective methodologies (Reiss & Sprenger, 2020). Descartes' dualistic philosophy, which distinguished between matter (body) and mind, fortified the Western emphasis on objectivity

(Robinson, 2020). In Descartes' paradigm, matter becomes 'what is to be known' (the object), while the mind remains 'who knows' (the subject). This conceptualization ascribes distinct compartments to the mind and body, laying the philosophical groundwork for the mind-body dualism evident in educational practices of the time.

While it may not be directly causal, the Cartesian dualistic framework indirectly facilitated educational systems that undermine learner subjectivity. The prioritization of objective, verifiable knowledge in this framework devalues the learner's mental states and subjective experiences, pushing toward a "one-size-fits-all" educational model. Therefore, it can be argued that philosophical foundations in the West, particularly Cartesian dualism favoured objective, verifiable knowledge, which inadvertently sidelines the learner's subjective realm. This shift in focus is particularly observable in the development of standardized curricula that emphasize universally "true" knowledge, diminishing the role of individual subjectivity in learning. This system prioritizes a common curriculum and teacher-centered approach, an arrangement that Paulo Freire critiques as the 'banking model of education.' The characteristic of this model is that the teacher seems to be the active subject, while the students are merely passive objects. Through this analogy, Freire strongly criticized the existing dissociated model of education, where a teacher's task is to "fill the students with the contents of his narration—contents which are detached from reality, disconnected from the totality that engendered them and could give them significance" (Freire, 1970b, p. 44).

In the banking model of education, a teacher gives someone else's knowledge, and the knowledge is about objects which also belong to others or exist in the external environment. It is crucial to note that due to the over-reliance on objective truth, the education system overlooks the importance of multiple perspectives, including the subjectivity of learners, and the sharp division between subject and object results in a strong feeling of alienation from the world. This might be one reason for having a dichotomized view and increased alienation from the world as well as from people.

1.2   *Economic-Political Perspective*

It is also important to mention that Freire's conceptualization of the banking model of education was very much rooted in the after-effects of the colonial period, as his observations were largely based on the economic and political realities in Brazil. He believed that the banking type of education was an important instrument used by the colonial powers to oppress the people and dehumanize them. Not only Freire but many other theorists postulate that education is used as an important tool to fulfil colonial endeavours and consolidate foreign rule (G. P. Kelly & Altbach, 1984). Education has often been used to propagate cultural ideals, defend imperial policies, and empower natives to be powerful agents of colonial change. For instance, education served to advance the empire's wide-ranging economic and political objectives during the British colonial era in India.

In India, the British established a network of schools and colleges that were designed to train a new class of Indian administrators who would be loyal to the crown. These institutions often reproduced the values and beliefs of British colonial society, and they helped to spread the English language and culture throughout India. Colonial institutions helped to dominate native culture and thought while also disseminating British civilization. One relevant impetus behind culturally and intellectually dominating educational policies can be seen very clearly in the following statements of a British official working in the Bombay administration (as quoted in Viswanathan 1988):

> The Natives must either be kept down by a sense of our power, or they must willingly submit from a conviction that we are more wise, more just, more humane, and more anxious to improve their condition than any other rulers they could possibly have.

The above statement indubitably echoes the intention of British officials to create a caricature of a superior "Ideal Englishman" (Viswanathan, 1988). Thomas Babington Macaulay, who is thought to be the father of the modern education system in India, made a statement with similar goals:

> We must at present do our best to form a class who may be interpreters between us and the millions whom we govern, a class of persons Indian in blood and colour but English in tastes, in opinions, in morals, and in intellect.

The outcome of these intentions was the development of an education system to literate the Indian population in the English language to make them interpreters and possibly to satisfy the clerical needs of the colonial government. It is obvious that an education system that only aims to make people literate in a foreign language would not focus upon other aspects of education such as cognitive or intellectual developments or, in the words of Freire, "critical consciousness" (Freire, 1970b, p. 9). Furthermore, in order to fulfil these colonial endeavours of oppressing Indians and making them only "interpreters," an education system will necessitate a common objective curriculum and teacher-centric pedagogy to impart it. Undoubtedly, education became one of the most important tools to help fulfil colonial endeavours, but that does not mean the colonizer's own education system was immune to these issues.

An imperial outlook was the basic motif in these colonizer countries (especially Britain), and the native population was trained accordingly. Ruth Watts observes that an imperial outlook sprang from many diverse sources, such as the economic desire to find and exploit; impulses to convert, civilize, and dominate; and so on (Watts, 2009). These motivations often encourage an urge to pass on the knowledge that has an implicit imperial mindset. Furthermore, starting from the seventeenth century, Western society was very much inclined toward scientific knowledge because it started giving exclusive attention to scientific ways of knowing (Gaukroger, 2006). This perspective eventually got infused with underlying assumptions in education.

Scientific knowledge is produced and refined through research, experimentation, and analysis. Science relies on the external forces of nature and is believed to produce knowledge that is universal, objective, and systematic. At the same time, it tends to minimize the role of individual experience and subjective knowledge in the construction of knowledge. As a result, Western education systems place greater emphasis on scientific knowledge than subjective experience, which may lead to students learning in a limited way and having difficulty engaging with the world outside of the confines of their educational environment. This is one of the major reasons for an overemphasis on the acquisition of objective knowledge without giving much importance to understanding it. This type of educational environment undervalues the importance of subjective experience, which alienates children from active participation in knowledge creation and makes them mere accumulators or passive agents.

Now, any educational program built on these divisive presumptions will conceptually distance children from the real world. And to be clear, their body would also be a part of the physical reality. This type of education would naturally prioritize intellectual activities over real-world experiences. Simply put, the focus would be on acquiring knowledge of the world instead of direct experience. This approach can be observed in any educational institution where pupils spend hours memorizing facts from textbooks. Currently, most of the educational activities are concerned with providing "second order experiences," which are descriptions of experiences instead of direct experiences (Laurillard, 1993, p. 55). These second-order experiences put the body and bodily activities on the periphery of the main activity, which leads to an overemphasis on the mind and mental activities. In the words of Manuela Macedonia (2019), it is a kind of mentalistic education. In this environment, bodily activities are no longer considered important for meaning-making and knowledge creation.

In short, mentalistic education does not consider our embodied nature and, hence, does not put much effort into embodied practices.

Now, the underlying theoretical assumptions behind mentalistic education have been challenged by recent advancements in cognitive science that demonstrate our embodied nature. Despite the numerous pieces of evidence in support, we still do not fully acknowledge or appreciate our embodied nature. It is evident from the studies presented in the previous chapters that we do not have two ontologically distinct aspects, such as mind and body. Instead, mental phenomena arise out of bodily experiences in the world. At the same time, despite much criticism of conceptual dualism in general, it is prevalent in our everyday lives and speech in one form or another. Therefore, it is also crucial to explore and understand the reasons behind this un-realization of our own embodied nature, despite the abundance of evidence available. Once we understand the root cause of this inherent dualistic mindset, we can redesign our educational activities to overcome it.

2   The Roots of Dualism in Human Thought

In this section, I shall outline the prominent reasons for the non-realization of our embodied nature. I shall focus more on the psychological and neurological perspectives of this inherent dualistic outlook. Moreover, there are various social reasons why a dualistic approach becomes prominent in our everyday lives, and therefore, it becomes tacit in our thinking and actions.

2.1   *Psychological Perspective*
One of the prominent claims for the explanation of our inherent dualistic approach is that we might be naturally born dualists. This theory comes from the nativist child psychologists, such as Paul Bloom (2005). Bloom's thesis is based on the simple premise that we are born dualists who perceive the world in terms of bodies and souls. The premise is rooted in Darwin's evolutionary theory, and Bloom postulates that perceiving the world on dualistic lines is a by-product trait of evolutionary adaptations. That means dualist thinking is natural to humans, which can be observed from the very beginning of childhood. This is an interesting viewpoint, which argues that a dualistic viewpoint comes naturally to us rather than being the result of philosophy or religion. Bloom substantiates his claims through various studies on human babies related to their "looking time," and it is found that babies, even very young ones, do not consider people in the same way as they consider physical objects.

Studies exhibit that children look at people for longer periods of time than any other object.

According to Bloom, this occurs because children are born with an innate ability to distinguish between a person and an object. They are born with an innate ability to recognize human faces and infer that humans possess some form of psychological state, unlike other objects. Bloom argues that this kind of behaviour involves an ability of mindreading, which is innate and exclusive to human beings. Mindreading, also known as the "theory of mind," is the ability to infer the mental states of others based on their behaviour (Forstmann & Burgmer, 2015). Owing to this special trait, we have a natural tendency to derive inferences about the mental processes of others that are not directly perceivable with the senses. This fosters the development of two modes of belief: observable bodies and unobservable mental processes.

Hence, Bloom argues that children's initial experiences make them perceive worldly things on dualistic lines. Children, from the very beginning, start to differentiate between their internal and external realms. This happens due to their initial experiences in the world, where they interact with objects, play with toys, and control them. This creates a sense of duality in which only a few things (objects) can be controlled by them (the controller). Further, as they get older, this dualistic perspective becomes stronger due to the maturation of the brain as well as through societal conditioning. This might be the reason why we become intuitive dualists over the course of time, as we become disposed to look at tangible things in terms of objects (even the body, as it is controlled) and intangible subjects (the mind, which is the real controller). This distinction between tangible objects and intangible subjects can be termed "body" and "soul," although Bloom uses the term "soul" in a broader sense, which refers to all mental states of humans. It can also be termed "self" or "mind" interchangeably.

Bloom's hypothesis seems plausible if we analyse it in terms of evolutionary adaptations. There are compelling reasons to believe that this mind-reading trait evolved during the course of evolution because it may have aided in survival. Like some other primates, humans have evolved to live in large social groups and cooperate with each other for mutual benefit. As a result, understanding the minds and mental states of others has become crucial. Likewise, comprehending material objects is also essential to interact with and utilize them for our benefit. Thus, this intuitive dualistic approach of viewing the body and mind as distinct appears to be necessary and critical for our survival, adaptation, and evolution. However, even if it is accurate, this assertion does not establish whether infants regard the soul as something distinct from the body or merely perceive it as different in some way (Andre, 2022). While it is plausible that children perceive the body and the soul differently (as argued by Bloom), it is unclear if they view both as distinct entities. Furthermore, there is no evidence to support the notion that children innately perceive the body and soul as separate entities. It is entirely possible for two things to have different characteristics without being completely distinct (Andre, 2022).

Therefore, it can be argued that we somehow fall into believing that body and soul are separate because we naturally tend to perceive both differently. It is some kind of false, or at least illusory, experience. Let's consider a simple example related to colour perception. A particular surface reflects the light after partially absorbing it. Then it reaches our retina and travels to the brain. After processing the information, the brain presents us with a specific colour. In this case, we cannot assert with complete certainty that our experience of colour (a mental phenomenon) exists separately from the ray of light (a physical phenomenon). Similarly, if we perceive the body and the soul differently, it does not necessarily mean that they are ontologically separate from each other.

The above example also illustrates that interaction is the key here for a mental phenomenon to arise. Even though there is a similar kind of relationship between the body and the soul, it is often overlooked when the subject or soul is perceived as an independent entity. That is to say, in summary, that our intrinsic capacity to perceive others' mental states and form judgments about those states is a by-product of our tacit knowledge of mind and body as two entirely separate substances (mindreading). It is like any other cognitive ability that assists us in comprehending and engaging with the world to meet our survival needs. However, it may also be deceptive, as it has the potential to prejudice our thinking in various domains.

Peter Carruthers (2020) considers mindreading as a faculty that gives rise to a theory of mind. He argues that our capacity for mindreading is deeply ingrained and widely utilized in our daily lives, which is why Cartesian dualism appears intuitive to us. It creates a bias that influences our thinking and inquiry in other domains, and we tend to perceive everything through a dualistic lens. For example, all humans in all cultures believe in mind and body as two separate ontological entities (Boyer, 2001; Cohen et al., 2011; Roazzi et al., 2013). Moreover, mental and physical aspects are perceived as separate because they are experienced in very different ways. This gives rise to the notion of a distinct self, which links all mental traits with this identity. This has also given rise to new concepts, such as the idea of an afterlife, among others. Furthermore, Carruthers argues that there is always a mental agency that is causally linked to the physical, which further widens the gap between the mental and physical domains. In addition to this, the ineffability and first-person experience of mental states make them unique and appear very different and distinct from bodily or physical states. According to Carruthers, our dualistic perception of the universe is due to our capacity for mindreading, and this dualistic notion is implicit in our cognitive processes.

The key takeaway from Carruthers's arguments is that ontological dualism may not be an accurate portrayal of reality, and it is possible that the concept of the independent existence of the mind or self that is entirely separate from bodily existence is merely an illusion. A similar argument can be observed in Miri Albahari's theory of the two-tiered illusion of self, which is rooted in Buddhist philosophy and incorporates psychological research (Albahari, 2006). Albahari's argument is based on Buddhist thought, which denies the existence of an ontologically separate self. Instead, the five aggregates, including form, feeling, perception, mental formation, and consciousness, are the components that make up an individual. Albahari posits that the sense of a distinct self is an illusion created and sustained by each individual to fit their particular life circumstances, which are largely influenced by cultural norms. This mistaken idea is made stronger by cultural beliefs that support the idea of a permanent, unified, and continuous self.

Consequently, we reflexively assume the existence of a separate and distinct self, which is, in fact, a construct created by our thoughts, emotions, and sensations resulting from our day-to-day experiences (Albahari, 2006, p. 2). While the idea of a separate, distinct self is considered an illusion according to Albahari's theory, it is so deeply ingrained in our day-to-day lives that it feels natural for us to conceive of a separate self. This makes it challenging for us to acknowledge our own embodied nature, which becomes illogical when we maintain a belief in a separate self-conception. Because of this, this dualistic way of thinking becomes a part of most of what we think and do.

However, the notion that a separative self is an illusion also raises the possibility that it can be changed. Albahari and many other researchers propose that eliminating this additional psychological layer and realizing our true nature can transform our perspective and help us appreciate our embodied nature. One option is to use meditation techniques, such as mindfulness, which will be discussed in the next chapter. Before that, let's briefly discuss the neurological basis of this dualistic approach to our thinking and behaviour in the world.

2.2   *Neurological Perspective*
The brain is often considered the seat of the mind. While recent research in cognitive science has challenged this view to some extent, the importance of the brain cannot be overlooked. It undoubtedly plays a crucial role in shaping how we perceive and interact with the world. Therefore, studying the structure of the brain can be a critical starting point in understanding our nature

and behaviour. Like many other creatures, the human brain is divided into two hemispheres: the left and right. It is claimed that certain aspects of the human experience dominate while others are suppressed due to ongoing disparities between the hemispheres of the brain. These disparities ultimately manifest in our perception of the external world and of ourselves.

The left hemisphere is commonly associated with analytical and rational thought, while the right hemisphere is responsible for creative, holistic, and intuitive thought. Additionally, the left hemisphere is specialized in language and speech functionalities, while the right hemisphere is more concerned with perception and emotional aspects (Corballis, 2014). Although each hemisphere functions asymmetrically, this division is not rigid (Beaumont, 2008, p. 113). Any mental activity involves complex processing, including components on both sides that frequently interact with one another. Nevertheless, Iain McGilchrist argues that the left hemisphere has gained dominance in modern society by diminishing the importance of the right hemisphere.

Iain McGilchrist (2009) argues in his book "The Master and His Emissary" that how an imbalance between the two hemispheres of the brain was vital in the development of the Western world. The central premise of McGilchrist's analysis is that

> there are two fundamentally opposed realities, two different modes of experience; that each is of utmost importance in bringing about the recognizably human world; and that their difference is rooted in the bi-hemispheric structure of the brain ... they are in fact involved in a sort of power struggle. (p. 3)

McGilchrist contends that just because both hemispheres are involved in different functions does not mean they work in isolation. In fact, both parts of the brain are interdependent and provide different perspectives on reality. However, one hemisphere may take precedence over the other in certain functions. McGilchrist suggests that the brain's bi-hemispheric structure is linked to an organism's attentional capacity, which is essential for survival.

The left brain usually yields localized, narrow, and focused attention to cater to our immediate needs, such as food. Simultaneously, the right hemisphere yields broad, flexible, open, and vigilant attention to construct a broad perspective, which might be directed towards forming bonds with potential partners, emotional understanding, etc. Both kinds of attention are essential to human beings as they construct the reality of the world in different but complementary ways. These two different kinds of attention are rooted in the way our brain is formed. McGilchrist uses neurological findings such as EEG (electroencephalogram) tests to support the claim. EEG tests exhibit that the left hemisphere has closer interconnection within regions of itself than the right. It explains why the left hemisphere has more self-referring characteristics. Furthermore, because of this internal connectivity, it produces a unique worldview that it has developed for itself. By contrast, the right hemisphere exhibits stronger intracranial connectivity, extending beyond the cortex to other regions of the brain. As a result, the right hemisphere provides a broader perspective on the world. McGilchrist has provided a thorough explanation of how our brain's bi-hemispheric organization gives rise to two types of attention, which shape the majority of our conceptualizations and behaviours. However, without digressing, I shall now specifically discuss the trait of self-conception.

Several pieces of evidence suggest that conscious self-awareness is a relatively recent development in evolutionary history. For example, several studies have shown that some of our closest evolutionary relatives, such as chimpanzees and orangutans, can pass the mirror test, indicating some level of self-awareness. Recently, it has also been revealed that the right prefrontal region is crucially involved in self-recognition (Keenan et al., 1999; Sugiura et al., 2000). This is a compelling claim because other animals that lack self-awareness lack or have very little development of the prefrontal area. This correlation is supported by cases of autism, in which patients have difficulty with self-awareness pronouns such as 'I' and 'me,' and damage to their right prefrontal region has been observed. Although McGilchrist maintains that both hemispheres are equally involved in objective self-recognition, they exhibit two distinct forms of self-conception.

The right hemisphere conceives the self as inseparable from its world, where it has relations with others, whereas the left hemisphere conceives the self as separate in an objectified manner. That means the right hemisphere pays attention to other things that exist beyond ourselves—and accepts life in terms of relationships with other things. In comparison, the left hemisphere is more concerned with the virtual world it creates, which is self-contained and disconnected from others. In summary, the left hemisphere creates a worldview that is explicit, abstracted, compartmentalized, fractured, and static, whereas the right hemisphere creates a vision that is more continuous, interconnected, and not limited to subjective isolation.

The above discussion implies that the right hemisphere is more connected with our bodily existence, and therefore it is predisposed to thinking of the self as an embodied being. The left hemisphere, in contrast, imagines a body that is analogous to other material things from which the self is relatively detached. Additionally, research on brain damage demonstrates that the right parietal lobe carries an image of the entire body, in contrast to the left hemisphere, which only retains an image of the right half of the body. That is why the right hemisphere exhibits greater proprioceptive awareness than the left. It is clear from the above discussion that the bi-hemispheric structure of the brain constructs two different aspects of reality. Even though both ways of looking at the world are important for getting things done in the world, one side sometimes tries to win out over the other.

According to McGilchrist, the left hemisphere has exerted a dominant influence on modern Western culture. He posits that in the last few hundred years, the left brain has progressively taken control, resulting in a society that is rational and efficient but also superficial and materialistic. This imbalance has given rise to several issues, such as the prevalence of scientism, materialism, and a failure to comprehend the human experience in all dimensions. McGilchrist examines how the left hemisphere of the brain has risen to prominence in our culture, which values certainty, linearity, and control. Consequently, the left hemisphere has a restricted and narrow perspective on the world. Moreover, this has led to the amplification of specialized and technical knowledge (McGilchrist, 2009, pp. 428–429). Most notably, an overreliance on the left hemisphere weakens our embodied perspective, which encompasses both our body and the environment surrounding us. However, according to McGilchrist, if we want to get the most out of life and our relationships with one another, we must learn to balance the two hemispheres of the brain.

Apart from neurological roots, we cannot deny the societal influence on our increased dichotomized behaviour. It is true that our innate inclination is towards a disembodied outlook, but our way of life and social surroundings have a critical influence on our over-mentalistic or disembodied approach to life. Social conditioning is a key factor through which our inherent tendency to categorize things in dualistic terms becomes prevalent in our daily lives, leading to significant changes in our thoughts and actions.

2.3 *Social Perspective*

Human beings are subject to cultural conditioning, similar to biological conditioning. However, societal conditioning, unlike biological conditioning, influences humans through ideologies, religions, and even education, which are, in fact, a result of social development. Ashwini Kumar notes that social conditioning has a crucial influence over human lives through which "people build images about themselves and others" (Kumar, 2013, p. 48). People tend to construct and adopt images that derive from the dominant culture and its norms, values, and beliefs, which reflect the expectations and assumptions of their social environment. Most importantly, people frequently form relationships with these psychological images, which are essentially a result of the abstraction of real personalities. That is why there is a perpetual tension between images and reality because individuals form relationships with these abstractions rather than with actual human beings. Moreover, the images that we construct for ourselves and others are fictitious, leading us to live our lives away from reality. That means whatever we tend to consider reality is instead a projection of reality (ibid., p. 53).

In this regard, Erving Goffman observes that people present themselves to others in their daily lives, and this impacts their relationships and interactions with others (Goffman, 1956). Goffman suggests that people engage in a type of performance in everyday life by presenting a "front" or a version of themselves to others. He refers to this as the "presentation of self" and posits that individuals do this to create a particular impression in the minds of others and to manage the impression that others have of them. People present themselves in various ways to enhance their performances and create a particular impression on others. Physical cues and symbols, such as appearance, grooming, and body language, contribute to the image one projects. However, these projections or images can be restrictive, prompting individuals to act in ways that conform to social expectations or the image they have created. That means that if society's standards favour conceptual dualism, then individuals will attempt to construct an image based on these norms, representing a particular idea about themselves and others in their day-to-day lives. Moreover, our actions are also based on these projected images, which may not accurately represent reality. Education provides a good example of this phenomenon, as it is often used to perpetuate societal projections while also being a product of societal projections. Therefore, education is frequently viewed as a tool for societal conditioning. Oren Ergas uses the term "pruning" to illustrate the societal conditioning of the mind through the means of education itself (Ergas, 2017).

Ergas asserts that education is a societal tool used to inculcate specific beliefs in the human mind. This can be understood through the metaphor of a kaleidoscope, where all of our knowledge and understanding are coloured by society's beliefs. In other words, society shapes our minds to understand and function in the world in a particular way through education. Moreover, our minds can be shaped differently to see the world based on any narrative. Despite the fact that the human mind can be grown and moulded in any way due to its neuronal plasticity, starting in early childhood, it is pruned and shaped by the values and expectations of a given culture. Ergas argues that during this process, the mind is diminished from universality to particularity.

The notion of particularity creates a fertile ground for the sprouting of dichotomized perspectives, such as the experience of subject-object differentiation, where "this" is located either "in here" (like mental objects) or "out there" (like physical objects), and is either part of "me" (mental objects) or "not-me" (physical objects). According to Ergas, these kinds of spatial distinctions give rise to a psychological sense of "self" that implicitly distinguishes between two levels and two forms of selfhood in terms of "I" and "me," as well as between "me" and "not-me," where "I" is the essential self and "me" is the narrative self that centres on "I." This kind of distinction is similar to Miri Albahari's two-tiered self. Moreover, similar to Albahari's position, Ergas also advocates for un-pruning the mind through mindful attention and contemplative inquiry. He argues that these practices can help free the mind from societal conditioning and enable individuals to realize their true nature.

Besides psychological, neurological, and societal factors, we may fail to recognize our embodied nature due to our inclination to focus on the past or future. As humans, we tend to shift our temporal focus by default (Shipp & Aeon, 2019). We often dwell on past events or worry about future events. This preoccupation with the past or the future prevents us from being fully present in the here and now. As a result, we develop the notion of a continuous self that constructs a narrative from the threads of the past and future. Our everyday experiences link together past events (in the form of memories) and future events (in the form of plans and expectations), giving rise to what Antonio Damasio (2010) terms the autobiographical self or what Shaun Gallagher (2000) refers to as the narrative self. Gallagher describes this day-to-day self as "a more or less coherent self (or self-image) that is constituted with a past and a future in the various stories that we and others tell about ourselves" (ibid., p. 15). However, this is not to suggest that it is inappropriate to reflect on the past or anticipate the future. Rather, the point is that by failing to live in the present moment, we risk losing awareness of our embodied nature.

Additionally, we may not be aware of our embodied nature because we are often disconnected from our surroundings. We live in a fast-paced, technologically advanced society where we are constantly bombarded with stimuli. We are often so caught up in our own thoughts and experiences that we are not really aware of our surroundings. This disconnection from our surroundings often leads to a disconnection from our bodily awareness. When we are disconnected from our environment, we are not fully conscious of our bodies and their sensations. However, there are ways to overcome these obstacles and become more aware of our embodied nature and the role that the body plays in our experience of the world.

To sum up, it is now clear that our perspective is divided because of both the structural differences in our brain hemispheres and the way society has conditioned us. Our brain naturally creates a particular worldview to help us function and survive in the world. While trying to construct a worldview, we sometimes prioritize one perspective over another, leading to a bias in our thoughts and actions. This (mis) perception does not only seem to apply to the field of education. The world is becoming more dispersed and atomized as a result of our (through the left brain) concern with control, and it is in danger of losing contact with the ground of being, which is the right hemisphere's domain. To that, McGilchrist goes on to argue that the only way to heal the effects created by the split between the two hemispheres is to rediscover the importance of the right hemisphere and to learn to live in a more balanced way. Training our attention can be one way to balance out the conceptual rift that is deeply ingrained in our way of living. Furthermore, because these studies show that our overemphasis on the mentalistic world is caused by both nature (bi-hemispheric differences) and nurture (social and emotional conditioning), there is the possibility of shifting our perspective from being separated to embodied and becoming a more balanced creature.

Now that we have examined the roots and reasons behind a disembodied or mentalistic education system, we can now outline the basic principles of embodied education. However, in order to fully appreciate the challenges facing the implementation of embodied educational practices, we must also address the major obstacles. Therefore, in the next section, I shall outline the major contentions of an education system inspired by an embodied approach while also identifying the primary challenges related to implementing embodied education. I shall highlight a four-step challenge that creates a cycle of dualistic education and propose a two-way model for breaking this cycle for the implementation of embodied education.

3   Towards an Embodied Approach in Education

The embodied approach has significant implications for education, as its major claim is that humans make sense of the world and learn about it through embodied experience. According to John Dewey, education is understood to be a process that proceeds from concrete experiences to abstract concepts (Dewey, 1910). Concrete means anything which is tangible. Abstract things are mostly intangible, such as mathematical calculations, the idea of justice, and language. It is argued that when teaching anything new, it is important to begin with tangible objects and gradually progress to abstract concepts. This approach helps students to build their abstract knowledge based on their experiences with concrete objects. For instance, if a child is not familiar with a certain animal, it is better to show them some real animals rather than simply describe their features. The sensory experience gained from observing actual

animals can help the child conceptualize the shared characteristics of different animals and apply this information in the future to construct additional
knowledge.

The embodied approach encourages these kinds of learning environments,
where students can use the knowledge acquired through embodied experience to understand new concepts by applying them to new situations. According to the embodied approach, learning occurs primarily at the level of bodily
experiences we have in our daily lives, and all subsequent abstractions we
generate can be traced back to those experiences. This means that learning is
not dissociated from bodily experiences but is deeply ingrained in them. The
embodied approach recognizes the importance of sensory-motor interaction
in learning and overall cognitive development. It is now commonly argued
that embodied theory provides a more accurate understanding of human
nature by bridging the gap between mind and body, and between humans and
the world. This means that an embodied approach to education can ultimately
reduce the sharp division between subject and object. Therefore, overlooking
embodiment is no longer tenable in educational endeavours, as it is now well-
supported by ample empirical evidence. In this context, the term "embodied
approach" is used in a general sense to refer to approaches that consider the
mind and body as inseparable.

Now, when the mind itself is embodied and extended even to the environment, there is no longer any justification for continuing the "banking model of
education." The mind is not some vessel to be filled in. Instead, it is something
that arises out of rich interactions with the world. Hence, what is of primary
importance is that children are encouraged to remain open more and more
towards the environment, paying more attention to whatever takes place in and
around them. In this scenario, knowledge and sense-making become primarily
the result of interaction with the environment, and even abstract concepts are
grounded in our embodied engagement with the world (Lakoff & Johnson, 1999).
As a result, a child with a whole body, including the mental realm, becomes central to the learning process, and education should not be conceived solely as a
matter of mind. This has the potential to dispel the narrow conception of education that says knowledge is only found in books and is imparted by teachers.
Instead, learning is viewed as a continuous activity that involves multiple ways
of acquiring knowledge, such as through the use of our sense organs, within
the much broader context of ongoing engagement with the world. In this way,
embodied education aligns with the constructivist theory of education.

According to the constructivist theory of education, knowledge and understanding are created by individuals through a combination of their own experiences, interactions with others, and the assimilation of new information

into what they already know (Bada, 2015). It challenges the notion of knowledge being passed down in a direct way and instead emphasizes the building of understanding through active engagement. Therefore, in this type of educational setup, subjects are seen as active participants in the formation of knowledge, and consequently, the whole process of education becomes more student-centric. Hence, for the learning process to flourish fully, education must attend to both the body and the environment. This is indeed a far cry from the typical classroom setting, where learning is treated as the imparting of information by the teacher based on some textbooks.

In the embodied learning environment, as David Nguyen and Jay Larson (2015) argue, learners are simultaneously sensory-motor bodies, reflective minds, and social beings. This approach also helps in enhancing interpersonal communication among students, which ultimately makes children more socially active. Therefore, an embodied learning approach makes it possible to combine conventional classroom instruction with a variety of student-centred activities and cutting-edge technologies. Moreover, the collaboration between the teacher and students in these classrooms is crucial for embodied learning. Tutors are not viewed solely as instructors in this context; rather, they serve as both facilitators and providers of learning environments.

Now, it is also true that, despite considerable evidence and arguments in favour of embodied education, it has not been widely embraced in most conventional schools. It doesn't mean that no school appreciates or follows an embodied approach. There are various small educational centres, often termed "alternative schools," which do incorporate the embodied approach in pedagogy in various capacities. Although they may not be aware of or concerned with the most recent empirical evidence supporting this perspective, they conceptually adopt it in practice. However, the majority of public schools continue to use a mentalistic approach to education. Therefore, it is important to understand the barriers that prevent the embodied approach from being implemented in the mainstream education.

3.1   *Obstacles in Implementation of Embodied Education*

There are several reasons why the embodied view has yet to enter the educational discourse. Firstly, our current educational practices are primarily disembodied, leading to increased detachment from our bodies and the world. As a result, children, teachers, and policymakers often fail to recognize the significance of incorporating our embodied human nature in education. Another significant reason is the failure to integrate recent empirical studies on human cognition and nature into the educational discourse. Given these major reasons, there can be four notable obstacles in traditional education that prevent it from acknowledging the embodied nature of learning in practice.

These are:

1. Underlying assumptions of mind-body duality, giving rise to
2. Overemphasis on the mentalistic approach in traditional educational practices, which in turn
3. Failure to recognize the wholeness of learners and the integration of mind-body-world, which results in
4. Ignoring the body in educational research, which in turn, again, strengthens the assumption of mind-body dualism

These four obstacles have distinct importance, but at the same time, they are interrelated and can directly or indirectly influence each other (see Figure 3). This creates a vicious cycle in which each obstacle supports and aggravates the others. Several authors (for example, Merriam and Kim 2008; McClelland, Dahlberg, and Plihal 2002; Nguyen and Larson 2015) have emphasized the underlying Cartesian dualistic approach in philosophical thought, particularly in the West, which is embedded in educational discourse. Sharan Merriam and Young Kim note that since the seventeenth century, the West has emphasized learning as a purely cognitive activity taking place in the brain. Consequently, "the mind has been privileged as the site of learning and knowing" (Merriam & Kim, 2008, p. 76). This creates a sharp distinction between the knower (specifically the mind) and the known (all worldly knowledge, including the body). As a result, knowledge became an independent, objective truth in this paradigm.

Furthermore, Brian Bukhart examines how knowledge became propositional in Western epistemology, which means knowledge is true, separate from

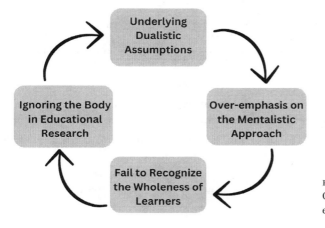

FIGURE 3
Obstacles in implementing embodied education

the self, and can be written down and directly conveyed through statements (Burkhart, 2004). This kind of assumption leads to the conception that most of our knowledge learning is centred on the mind, and that cognitive processes are limited to acquiring, storing, and making meaning of new information. This type of conception also fails to recognize the wholeness of learners, and learning is reduced to merely reflecting on the experiences, which is a mental activity. On the other hand, Sharan Merriam and colleagues claim that learning is "learning in an experience as it occurs" rather than "reflecting on the experience after it occurs" (Merriam et al., 2007, p. 187). Reflection on experiences is a rational activity that excludes the body and aspects beyond the body. The majority of Western educational models are based on reflecting on experiences, resulting in a rationalistic approach that is characterized by reason and objectivity. As a result, pedagogy and curriculum still consider learning in an abstract format, dissociated from the body and the world.

Despite several educational theories as well as modern empirical evidence, the rationalist perspective has dominated educational research until recently (Merriam & Bierema, 2014, p. 120). However, in recent years, the importance of embodiment in learning has come to the foreground in educational research. Yet, despite these developments, embodied learning still tends to be under-theorized and under-appreciated in many educational contexts. One classical reason is that the body is often seen as a hindrance to learning. Usually, the mind is viewed as the seat of intelligence, and the body is seen as a tool that the mind uses. This perspective often leads people to believe that the body is a hindrance to learning and that the mind should be the sole focus. Another important reason is that people may not be aware of the significance of the body in learning. The body plays an essential role in processing information and navigating the world. If people are not aware of this importance, they may not recognize the necessity of embodied practices for effective learning. This leads to the final reason, which is one of the most significant in today's context: that people involved in the educational domain may not be fully aware of the research on the embodiment.

Embodiment is a relatively new field of academic research, and many people are not familiar with the findings of this research. Educators and educational researchers may fail to consider the embodied nature of learners in educational discourse due to a lack of awareness of the educational implications of embodiment. Additionally, researchers in the field of embodiment may not effectively communicate their findings to educational stakeholders (Nathan, 2022, p. 7). If people are not aware of the educational implications of embodiment, they may not realize the need for policies that align with the embodied nature of children in order to learn effectively. This perpetuates the underlying dichotomized assumptions and continues to be reflected in educational discussions, practices, and research.

The lack of awareness of the embodied nature of learners is a serious problem, as it leads to a number of negative consequences. For example, people may believe that the body is a hindrance to learning, that it is not capable of complex thought, or that it is separate from the mind. Such beliefs can lead to the development of learning strategies that are based solely on the mind, ignoring the importance of the body in learning. The negative consequences of learners' lack of awareness of the embodied nature can be mitigated by raising their awareness of the embodied concept. This can be achieved through exposure to the theory of embodiment itself, education, and research. A greater awareness of the embodied nature of learners is more likely to result in the development of learning strategies that incorporate the body and involve it in the learning process. Now, let us discuss how to tackle the aforementioned challenges.

3.2   Two-way Model for Implementing Embodied Education

As discussed in the second chapter, education is a two-way process. When viewed as a product, it refers to a deliberate practice designed by humans to impart various types of knowledge about the world and society, as well as equip a child with all the necessary skills and information to better adapt to a changing world. Furthermore, viewing it as a process implies transforming the human, revising the fundamental assumptions about themselves, and as a result, calibrating their activities. Interestingly, both of these approaches are interdependent, as a particular assumption about oneself will eventually get reflected in the design of teaching-learning practices. Thus, the design of teaching-learning practices is often influenced by the assumptions that individuals hold about their own embodied nature. Now, if individuals do not appreciate the importance of their own embodied nature, it can be difficult to develop a pedagogy that aligns with this nature.

Therefore, to create educational environments that acknowledge the embodied nature of human beings, we need to intervene on two fronts. Firstly, it is necessary to develop teaching methodologies that align with the principles of the embodied theory. Secondly, it is equally important to educate educational stakeholders about their own embodied nature. These two approaches can work together and complement each other, helping to break the vicious cycle of underlying assumptions of mind-body duality. Furthermore, it is important to note that these interventions should be evidence-based and not solely based on philosophical debates. As Steven Stolz notes, "former philosophical debates have either privileged the mind over the body (rationalism) or viewed the body as a type of sensorial instrument where knowledge is verified (empiricism)" (Stolz, 2015, p. 484). However, both viewpoints fail to recognize the role of embodiment in learning. Using evidence-based practices is crucial to overcome these obstacles and correct the misguided educational system, which is often fuelled by outdated philosophies that create an unnecessary rift between mind and body (Nathan, 2022, p. 36).

As stated earlier, this two-way approach to embodied education involves a focus on two aspects. The first part of this two-way approach to embodied education involves designing pedagogies based on an embodied approach, which is an "outside-in" approach. The second part is focused on changing individuals' perspectives about themselves and helping them recognize their own embodied nature. This approach can, in turn, facilitate the design of embodied pedagogies, which is an "inside-out" approach. The approaches can be referred to as the "outer embodied curriculum" and the "inner embodied curriculum," respectively. Here, it is important to note that implementing the outer embodied curriculum is a relatively manageable task, and many educators already incorporate it in various capacities in the classroom through project-based learning, experiential methods, and learning by doing. Moreover, in the science subjects, laboratory activities are often used to confirm theories learned in the classroom. Additionally, newer technologies such as virtual reality and haptic feedback devices are increasingly being utilized in teaching, making learning more immersive and engaging (Richard et al., 2006). In contrast, the inner embodied curriculum is a more challenging and urgent need of the hour. Changing one's perspective on oneself and recognizing one's own embodied nature is a herculean task that very few schools address. Undoubtedly, the inner curriculum requires significant attention since it has a fundamental impact on a person's overall perspective, and its effects get reflected in the outer curriculum.

4   Conclusion

The aim of this chapter was to analyse the dualistic conceptions prevalent in conventional education and propose potential modifications to integrate embodied practices. Education systems, in general, face many challenges, issues, and difficulties that are acknowledged by both the general public and educators. However, despite multiple reforms, many problems have persisted for decades. One of the core issues is that most educational programs adhere to mentalistic theories, which are not conducive to the development of critical thinking and an exploratory mindset. Moreover, in recent years, society has become increasingly focused on intellectual achievement and a mentalistic outlook, which gets reflected in the form of disembodied education. It is also visible that modern mainstream education mainly implies a dualistic approach that considers the mind as separate from the body. This kind of dualistic outlook emerges partly due to our own brain hemispheric structure and societal conditioning based on dualistic lines. Further, as we become more dependent on a fast-paced society, we lose touch with our bodies and the physical world around us. All of these factors are responsible for a disembodied approach in education.

Now, there are ample evidence available which show that human mental phenomena are not completely divorced form the body. Therefore, it is time to redesign and calibrate our educational system as per embodied theories. There are several reasons why embodied education is relevant. Firstly, our bodies are the means by which we interact with the world and gather information, as well as how we express ourselves. By including the body in education, we encourage students to interact with their surroundings in a more holistic manner and to use their bodies to express themselves and gather information. Secondly, research has shown that bodily-based learning can be more effective than abstract learning. To implement embodied-based learning environments, we need to adopt a two-way approach to educational intervention. The first is an "outside-in" approach, where pedagogies should be designed with the embodiment of children in mind. The second part of the intervention involves changing one's outlook, which constitutes an "inside-out" approach. Without realizing one's own embodied nature, individuals may not be fully committed to design and implement the embodied education. Therefore, it is important to work directly with stakeholders. I shall now discuss the practical aspects of embodied education related to classroom implementation of both approaches in the upcoming chapter.

CHAPTER 6

Embodied Education in Practice

Designing Holistic Learning Environments

As we have seen, embodied education is based on the concept of an "embodied view of the mind," which recognizes the significance of both neural and non-neural bodily components, as well as the environment, in the formation of mental processes. As a result, educational approaches that do not actively involve the body fall short of their potential to transform the mind. On the other hand, embodied learning emphasizes the importance of students having direct experiences with their bodies. Furthermore, traditional educational practices place a greater emphasis on reflecting on direct experience. But, in an embodied learning environment, students engage fully with the world through thoughtful bodily movement, allowing for a genuine and direct experience. Therefore, the primary goal of this chapter is to investigate the development of a pedagogy that recognizes human beings' embodied nature.

The chapter is divided into two sections: the outer curriculum and the inner curriculum. The first section is devoted to developing a pedagogy that recognizes humans' embodied nature. The first section demonstrates, using several empirical studies, that human thinking is not solely a mental and isolated process but is inextricably linked to our bodily characteristics and surroundings. This connection is exemplified by gestures, which are used unconsciously in the learning process. This section also uses examples from two subjects, English and mathematics, to demonstrate how linguistic and mathematical learning is fundamentally embodied.

The second section of the chapter delves into the more complex issue of recognizing our own embodied nature, which is reflected in our educational conversations and obstructs the development of an education that respects the embodied nature of human beings. This section relates to the inner curriculum and aims to help us become more aware of our own embodied nature. According to recent contemplative research, we can develop this ability by increasing our self-awareness, and mindfulness practices can help with this process. The chapter concludes by arguing that incorporating mindfulness exercises into standard classroom curricula can assist students in recognizing their embodied nature.

© AKHIL K. SINGH, 2025 | DOI:10.1163/9789004724372_006

1 The Outer Curriculum: Aligning Education with Embodied Human Nature

A discussion about embodied cognition theory in the fourth chapter suggests that cognitive grounding and offloading are key principles of embodied cognition. These principles emphasize the interconnectedness of the mind, body, and environment in shaping cognitive processes. Through these two forms of relationship between an agent and the world, environmental features (including the body) are used to ground thoughts and offload cognitive load onto the environment for efficient cognitive processing. In short, offloading and grounding are the two methods by which the body and environment influence cognition. Therefore, using these two methods in the classroom becomes crucial to facilitate an embodied learning approach.

Grounding is the most important and primary way to facilitate learning in the early stages. Grounding is the process of connecting an abstract concept to a more concrete referential object (Barsalou, 2008). Coldness, for example, is represented by the concrete object ice. Several researchers (for example, Glenberg and Robertson 1999; Lakoff and Johnson 1980; Lakoff and Núñez 2000; Vega, Glenberg, and Graesser 2008) contend that we derive the meaning of an abstract idea through sensorimotor grounding in immediate perception and action. For instance, George Lakoff and Mark Johnson (1999, pp. 45–73) argue that simple, as well as complex concepts metaphorically derive meaning from bodily experiences. Simple metaphors are primary in nature, which means they are directly grounded in our daily lives. We acquire them unconsciously and without our knowledge. For example, the abstract concept of "knowing is seeing" is based on our visual sensory organ's primary experience of receiving information through vision. Complex metaphors, on the other hand, are constructed from primary metaphors that may or may not have direct sensory-motor grounding. Complex metaphors may also include popular cultural beliefs and folk theories (ibid., p. 61). For example, "a purposeful life is a journey" is a complex metaphor that combines the cultural belief that "purposes are destinations" with the primary metaphor "actions are motions." These examples demonstrate that grounding is an important component of embodied learning, which is typically facilitated by concrete objects, metaphors, signs, and pointing to something tangible.

Cognitive offloading, on the other hand, is a mechanism that uses external resources to overcome a person's cognitive and attentional limitations. It is also a method of preserving and/or expanding one's limited memory capacity for storing information, as well as enhancing information manipulation due to limited cognitive capacity. For example, we use a pen and a notebook to capture information as well as to solve complex mathematical problems. Cognitive offloading is typically accomplished by offloading cognitive demands both "onto-the-body" and "into-the-world" (Risko & Gilbert, 2016). For example, we use our fingers to point or nod our heads to mark positions in sequential tasks (R. A. Carlson et al., 2007). Similarly, we use objects from the outside world to supplement our limited memory capacity. Furthermore, cognitive offloading can improve problem-solving abilities in cognitive constraint situations (Tran et al., 2017).

David Kirsch and Paul Maglio's study on Tetris game-playing behaviour is a classic example of cognitive offloading (Kirsh & Maglio, 1994). In this experiment, subjects were asked to play Tetris, a game in which they had to rotate the falling blocks to find an appropriate orientation to fit at the lower level. This game necessitates quick action because the block must be rotated to the proper position before touching the lower blocks. To overcome time constraints, players rotated a Tetris shape physically on the game console rather than mentally. This observation demonstrates that cognitive offloading into the world is a common feature of our daily lives.

The above two embodiment methods, either alone or in combination, can help to facilitate embodied forms of education. Although there may be a variety of instructional methods based on both modes of embodiment, I shall concentrate on the discussion of "gestures" due to their importance in the learning environment. Gestures are a type of action that occurs in both everyday communication and instructions, and they are regarded as an unavoidable tool for teaching and learning. Furthermore, in terms of subject-specific discussion, I shall limit myself to the domains of language and mathematics simply because these are considered the most abstract domains in educational discourse.

Additionally, I shall employ the "translational learning sciences research" (TLSR) model, conceptualized by Sheila Macrine and Jennifer Fugate (2021). The core intention of this model is to highlight empirical studies on embodiment and translate them into educational contexts to inform educators and teachers about potential classroom applications. Some of the main goals of TLSR are to make sense of empirical research findings in the context of education, close the gap between knowledge and practice in the classroom, and improve teaching and learning by promoting curriculum, designs, and technologies that are based on embodied learning.

1.1   *Gestures*

Gestures are a type of nonverbal communication that involves movement of the body, typically the hands and arms, to convey meaning. They can be used to supplement or replace verbal communication and convey a range of meanings (Ekman & Friesen, 1969). Embodied education emphasizes the integration of first-hand and second-hand knowledge, and gestures appear to be an important tool for imparting this type of education. Gestures can convey thoughts and ideas while also providing context and meaning for spoken language. There is no doubt that gestures are ubiquitous in our everyday lives as they occur automatically and spontaneously in response to changes in our external and internal environments (Goldin-Meadow & Singer, 2003).

Our bodily movements, facial expressions, eye direction, and so on are all part of our daily lives and have an impact on our thinking and behaviour. In other words, our body language, hand gestures, and facial expressions reveal information about our inner thoughts. For example, when we see someone furrowing their brow and thinking hard, we know they are trying to solve a problem. Similarly, a person's posture can reveal information about their confidence level; someone who slouches is perceived as less confident than someone who stands up straight. Gestures encompass more than just movements of our arms and hands. They also include our facial expressions and body language, which communicate meaning in various ways. A person nodding their head, for example, usually indicates agreement with what is being said, whereas someone shaking their head indicates disagreement.

In recent years, there has been an increasing interest in the role of gestures in teaching and learning, particularly in the area of embodied education. A number of studies conducted by Goldin-Meadow and her colleagues have demonstrated the significance of gestures in learning (for example, Goldin-Meadow and Sandhofer 1999; Iverson and Goldin-Meadow 1998; Goldin-Meadow et al. 2001; Goldin-Meadow and Wagner 2005; Cook and Goldin-Meadow 2006; Goldin-Meadow and Beilock 2010). Interestingly, some of these studies suggest that gesture not only duplicates or supplements the information conveyed verbally but also contributes to the transmission of information that is typically not present in speech (Shapiro & Stolz, 2019). Moreover, it is also reported that gestures are overtly used by congenitally blind people for communication despite their lack of a visual model (Iverson & Goldin-Meadow, 1998).

These findings argue that gestures are more than just hand-waving while talking. They are deeply embedded in our cognitive processes and influence how we think and communicate. Furthermore, recent studies indicate that gestures made during verbal communication influence thinking and can serve as a link between action and abstract thoughts (Goldin-Meadow & Beilock, 2010). That means when we use gestures in communication, we not only express our thoughts but also shape our thoughts and speech simultaneously. In this sense, gestures engage in a dialectic relationship with speech and thought, exhibiting as well as shaping thoughts in real time (McNeill, 2005). In other words, gestures are not a byproduct of thought but an essential component of it. That is to say, gestures are an inseparable part of our embodied nature, and any teaching-learning efforts should take this into account.

This perspective on gestures have significant educational implications. It implies that gestures can be used to aid learning. We frequently use gestures to help us understand and internalize information when we want to learn something. In a study conducted on third and fourth-grade children, it was discovered that including gestures during instructions encourages children to produce their own gestures, which leads to improved learning (Cook & Goldin-Meadow, 2006). In a related study with adults, it was further reported that people who use gestures have better recall memory than those who do not use gestures (Cook et al., 2010). Additionally, using gestures to explain a concept assists teachers in lightening their cognitive load and redirecting cognitive resources to the memory part (Goldin-Meadow et al., 2001). These studies show that learning is more than just acquiring knowledge; it is also about learning how to use our bodies to interact with the world. This means that learning is an embodied activity, with gestures playing an important role.

Gesture-based learning offers a multi-faceted approach to instruction across a variety of classroom settings. Teachers can utilize gestures to clarify content, provide feedback, and assess student comprehension. Effectiveness hinges on the consistent, repetitive use of meaningful and memorable gestures. These gestures can range from iconic, which visually represent a concept or object, to deictic, which point to something in the environment, to metaphoric, which convey abstract ideas. Teachers can utilize these gestures across a range of instructional formats, including whole-class, small-group, and one-on-one settings. They can also be applied across various subjects and educational levels, from primary school to college, including in online teaching modes (Kang et al., 2013; Kang & Tversky, 2016; Kessell & Tversky, 2005; Khan & Réhman, 2015; McCafferty & Rosborough, 2014; Novack et al., 2014; Roth, 2001; Singer & Goldin-Meadow, 2005). For example, a mathematics teacher might use iconic gestures to represent parallel lines, while a language arts teacher could employ metaphoric gestures to discuss conflict. Studies such as those by M. W. Alibali et al. (2014) and Hostetter (2011) underscore the importance of using appropriate gestures to enhance comprehension and retention of complex topics.

It is essential, however, that gestures are employed not sporadically, but meaningfully and consistently for maximum effectiveness. Additionally, the age and developmental stage of learners must be taken into account, as the impact of gestures can vary depending on the educational context. Studies like those by Cook, Mitchell, and Goldin-Meadow (2008) and Goldin-Meadow, Cook, and Mitchell (2009) indicate that age and cognitive development influence how gestures are internalized and processed. A gesture that is effective in a primary school setting may not have the same impact at the college level. That means the receptivity to gestures varies from elementary to high school to college settings. Having said that, it is not enough to use gestures only by the teachers while explaining concepts. Students also need opportunities to practice using their own gestures for improved learning. Students should also be encouraged to integrate gestures into their learning, facilitated through interactive activities that prompt them to use specific gestures to explain concepts, thereby reinforcing their own understanding.

To summarize, the theory of embodied learning proposes that our bodily experiences and environment influence our thoughts, emotions, and behaviour. This means that incorporating gesture-based learning into instruction can be a powerful tool for improving learning. Gestures are an important component of embodied education because they allow educators to connect physically with their students and create a more interactive learning environment. Gestures, when used correctly, can help students understand complex concepts, remember information, and stay engaged in the classroom.

These studies on gestures mentioned above show how the theory of embodied cognition can be used to improve learning in the classroom. There are some empirical studies available in the domains of mathematics and language that provide ample evidence for the embodied nature of learning. To emphasize the importance of the outer curriculum, I shall briefly discuss these two domains. Furthermore, because mathematics and language are often considered abstract domains, it is necessary to investigate these domains in order to appreciate the plausibility of embodied learning in humans.

1.2   *Embodied Language*

In previous chapters, we discussed how the mentalistic approach dominated many fields, including studies related to language acquisition, during the eighteenth and nineteenth centuries. However, towards the end of the last century, there was a significant challenge to the notion of language as an innate phenomenon. We have already seen in the fourth chapter that the argument for an innate "Language of thought" (LoT) was challenged, and evidence reveal the embodied aspect of language. Therefore, in this section, I shall focus on studies that are centred around classroom settings and demonstrate the embodied nature of both basic and complex aspects of language.

Language acquisition is a continuous, step-by-step process that begins with letter learning and progresses to more advanced skills, such as sentence formation and comprehension in later stages. The initial step in the process of learning letters includes visual recognition and linking those visual codes with corresponding sounds (Whitehurst & Lonigan, 1998). Therefore, early childhood educators in preschools should focus more on the practices that enhance children's letter recognition skills. According to Karin James (2022), handwriting can be one such method because it involves fine-motor skills that are similar to the self-generated actions. In particular, handwriting necessitates a visually guided and goal-directed movement of the hand. That means, handwriting, which refers to writing by hand, is essentially an embodied activity. This is because handwriting not only allows children to interact with objects, such as a pen and paper, but it also empowers them to create objects. By creating letters stroke by stroke, children engage their sensory-motor brain network.

In a series of studies involving functional magnetic resonance imaging (fMRI), researchers have elucidated the neurobiological foundations of letter recognition and learning. One seminal study by James and Gauthier (2006) revealed that the process of perceiving or writing letters activates multiple brain regions responsible for visual perception, kinaesthesia, proprioception, fine motor control, in-hand manipulation, and eye movements. This suggests that the conception of a letter is not merely an abstract process, but inherently involves motor activities as well. Subsequent research (James, 2010; James & Engelhardt, 2012; Li & James, 2016; Vinci-Booher & James, 2016) has shown that activation patterns differ when typing is used for letter learning instead of handwriting.

It is pertinent to clarify that typing may not be considered an equivalent form of embodied learning compared to handwriting. While both activities involve motor functions, the differences lie in the richness of the sensory-motor experiences they offer. Handwriting involves a complex orchestration of muscle movements, touch, proprioception, and visual feedback that create a rich neural imprint (Longcamp et al., 2003). Typing, on the other hand, while engaging some of these elements, may lack the fine motor skills and kinaesthetic feedback associated with writing by hand. Consequently, the neural activations in typing and handwriting are different (James & Engelhardt, 2012; James & Gauthier, 2006). Shiela Macrine and Jennifer Fugate (2022) further argue that the sensory-motor activation linked to handwriting correlates with improved reading performance as well.

Vocabulary is another important feature of the language, and there is no doubt that rich vocabulary knowledge influences language comprehension (Proctor et al., 2012). During the initial phase of vocabulary acquisition, various sensory-motor actions are involved. These include hearing and repeating the sequence of sounds (combination of letter sounds), associating the written sequence of letters with the corresponding sequence of sounds, and understanding the meaning of the whole word by linking it with an object or symbol that can be experienced with the senses. For example, the word "APPLE" has a visual sequence of certain letters, and it needs to be linked with the corresponding sound. Children accomplish this by repeating the word multiple times. Studies have shown that like learning letters, acquiring vocabulary is also an embodied experience and not just an abstract mentalistic activity (Gómez & Glenberg, 2022). Furthermore, neuroimaging techniques have demonstrated that comprehension while simply reading sentences stimulates the sensory-motor areas that are typically responsible for actions. These studies imply that we cannot ignore the possibility of a sensory-motor basis for language comprehension.

We have seen in the previous chapter that words are not merely abstract symbols, and their meanings are not arbitrary. But they are, in fact, grounded in our sensory-motor modalities and our embodied experiences in the world. Let us consider some studies to illustrate this. In an experiment, it was found that reading the words "Kick" and "Pick" are linked with different motor regions responsible for the movements of legs and hands, respectively (Hauk et al., 2004). Similarly, an experiment conducted by Shirley-Ann Rueschemeyer and colleagues (2010) demonstrated the use of the perceptual system in comprehending meaning while reading. They presented motion-related sentences to participants, such as "the car drives toward you," "the car drives away from you," and "the car looks big." The interesting outcome of this study was that the researchers found more activity in the V5/MT area (the fifth visual area located in the middle temporal lobe responsible for the perception of visual motion) while comprehending motion-related sentences than in no-motion situations. In a separate experiment, it was found that only reading the word "cinnamon" activates olfactory brain regions (González et al., 2006). Furthermore, in another experiment, it was also found that not only sensory-motor areas support sentence understanding, but the emotional system is also involved in processing sentences with emotional content. For example, David Havas and colleagues (2007) demonstrated that participants processed sentences with pleasant situations faster when they were smiling.

These findings suggest that our sensory-motor system is involved in semantic processing. Benjamin Bergen refers to this process as "embodied simulation," where we create mental experiences of perception and action without external manifestation (Bergen, 2012). He argues that we understand language by simulating the expected experience we would have through our sensory-motor activities. This claim is well validated through various studies that show that during simulation or imagination, we make use of the same brain regions that are responsible for interacting with the world. That means language comprehension is not an isolated activity, as it is very much grounded in the sensory-motor modalities of humans, including soft features such as emotions. In addition to this, Peter Gärdenfors (2017) analyzed archaeological evidence and found that pantomime, which involves expressing thoughts using only gestures, played an important role in the evolution of language. He argues that imitation using gestures is an important component of human communication and, therefore, "showing how to do" cannot be separated from intentional teaching and learning activities.

Although the above brief review of some studies shows the embodied basis of language acquisition and comprehension in the context of native language (L1), the behavioural outcome of the embodied language position can be more directly seen in relation to second language (L2) learning. Gestures are inevitable components while learning L2, and they have been used for centuries in L2 lessons, long before any empirical underpinnings were found related to them (Macedonia, 2019). This could be because gestures may have demonstrated improvements in the progress of second language learners.

Manuela Macedonia and Thomas Knösche (2011) conducted a study on second language (L2) learning and found that attaching gestures to L2 words was able to transfer their meaning without invoking L1 words. They also found that gestures could transfer not only the meaning of concrete objects but also abstract concepts such as "theory." These experiments demonstrate that speech and gesture are part of an integrated system in which both work together to enhance language comprehension. That means, in this integrated system, speech and gesture are two sides of the same coin (S. D. Kelly et al., 2010).

Based on above-mentioned empirical studies, it is clear that linguistic cognition is very much grounded in action and perception. These are some examples from the pool of many empirical findings resonating with the idea of embodied cognition and the embodied nature of our thoughts, especially those concerning language. When it comes to classroom applications, educators can implement teaching methods following the above principles. To name a few, they can encourage word learning and language comprehension through "acting-out," learning vocabulary or sentences through play and gestures, and in the writing domain, teachers can encourage students to handwrite their notes because writing aids in memorization. Teachers can also encourage learners to use physical gestures while reading, speaking, or using language in communication activities. Furthermore, storytelling and physical activities, such as role plays, can be used to help students understand more abstract concepts, as it is clear that we learn language through mental simulations.

Incorporating physical activities into the language learning process can also help promote the development of target language skills such as reading comprehension, writing, speaking, and listening, as linguistic cognition is not separate from sensory-motor activities. But, it is important for teachers to ensure that these activities are tailored to the needs and abilities of each learner to ensure that this approach enhances linguistic learning in a meaningful and effective way.

1.3   *Embodied Mathematics*

Mathematics, like language, is considered to be one of the most abstract domains of human cognition (Soylu et al., 2018). Hence, the way mathematics is traditionally taught in schools often isolates it as an individual activity. Students work alone at their desks on problems that are often abstract and disconnected from real-world applications. For most children, mathematics involves memorizing arbitrary rules and practicing them repeatedly with different numbers. This can be challenging for children, as the subject is abstract and disconnected from their day-to-day experiences, which requires discipline and concentration. As a result, children, as well as teachers, tend to focus more on mental aspects and overlook the role of the body in the learning process. But, as the theory of embodied cognition has matured, it has been applied in various domains, including mathematics. There is now a growing body of evidence that suggests that not only human's mathematical capacities are linked with their bodies, but also that the embodied approach can be highly effective in mathematics education in schools.

Using brain imaging techniques is one way to demonstrate the close relationship between mathematical thinking and bodily activities in humans. Transcranial magnetic stimulation (TMS) is one such method of brain imaging that has been used frequently to show this link. TMS is a non-invasive process to stimulate the brain with magnetic fields. It can be used to measure how a particular cognitive task influences motor activity. Additionally, studies show that repetitive application of TMS can even alter the functioning of the stimulated brain area. Several studies based on TMS have shown that there is a direct connection between human mathematical ability and motor capacities, and TMS can even modulate mathematical ability (Glenberg, 2008). The basic premise for these studies using TMS is that a cognitive task such as mathematical activity should activate the neurons in the primary motor cortex and/or influence motor activity, and vice versa.

Michael Andres, Seron, and colleagues (2007) conducted a study on counting tasks using TMS. In this study, participants had to count the number of dots in a given series while receiving transcranial magnetic stimulation (TMS) to brain areas related to hand, arm, and leg movements. At the same time, neural activity was recorded from the hand, arm, and leg muscles, respectively, to observe any correlation between the neural activity and counting performance. It was discovered that an increased activity was measured in hand during counting but not in the arm or leg. This result indicates that there is a possible link between hand motor circuits and counting activity. There are various other related studies that establish the link between basic mathematical abilities and motor activities, especially hand activities. For example, Marc Sato and colleagues (2007) conducted a study related to odd/even judgments using TMS, and the findings indicate a close relationship between hands and numerical representations. These studies suggest that there is a close relationship between mathematical and motor processes, which eventually challenges the conception of mathematics as an abstract subject dissociated from perception and action.

Another way to counter the abstractionist account of mathematics and show the embodied basis of it is by exploring the causal link between actions, especially gestures, and the mathematical performances of children in the classroom. Martha Alibali and Mitchell Nathan (2007) argue that classroom instruction is a communicative act in which gestures are not only ubiquitous but influential too. Further, it is also contended that gestures help in symbolic offloading while conveying complex and abstract ideas, as well as providing grounding for abstract ideas and representations (Nathan, 2008). In relation to mathematics, the work of George Lakoff and Rafael Núñez is notable. They argue that for a mathematical symbol to be understood, it must be associated "with a concept—something meaningful in human cognition that is ultimately grounded in experience and created via neural mechanisms" (Lakoff & Núñez, 2000, p. 49). They stress that mathematical understanding is no different from the everyday understanding of the world, and as everyday understanding is embodied, mathematics too is embodied in nature.

There are various other studies (e.g., J. I. D. Campbell 1994; J. I. D. Campbell and Fugelsang 2001; Goldstone, Landy, and Son 2008; Crollen and Noël 2015) that support the arguments presented above. These studies demonstrate that perception-action, including gestures, is not entirely separate from mathematical performance. For example, Wagner Cook and colleagues conducted a study on children related to learning basic mathematical calculations (Cook et al., 2008). In this experiment, children were divided into two groups and taught to solve new mathematical problems such as "4 + 9 + 3 = 4 + ?" or "4 + 3 + 6 = ? + 6," etc. One group was taught using only verbal instructions, while for another group, verbal instructions were integrated with relevant hand gestures. Four weeks later, the children were tested again, and it was found that the children who had been taught using gestures were able to retain the knowledge for a longer period of time than the children who had been taught using verbal instructions only. On the basis of these results, Cook, Mitchell, and Goldin-Meadow (2008) make a strong claim that gestures play a causal role in learning. Therefore, they suggest that children's mathematical learning ability may be improved just by encouraging them to move their hands.

Recently, many such experiments have been conducted that show the direct causal relationship between hand movement and mathematical performances. For instance, Ilaria Berteletti and James Booth (2015) presented the neural underpinnings for finger representations in learning and understanding arithmetic. Interestingly, they also found that complex subtraction problems lead to greater somatosensory activation than smaller problems, suggesting a greater reliance on finger representation for larger numerical values.

These behavioural as well as neurological studies demonstrate the link between embodied cognition and mathematics. It is clear that mathematics is not a mere manipulation of symbols in the mind but has a bodily basis in our actions and perception. Therefore, there is no point in treating mathematics as an abstract subject, and a mentalistic way of teaching it will not do justice to mathematical learning. The embodied approach to mathematics has the potential to revolutionize the way we think about mathematical education. By taking the role of the body in mathematical cognition into account, educators can design teaching methods and materials that are better aligned with students' natural learning processes. This could help students to learn math in a more effective and interesting way.

Now, to sum up, there can be many reasons why embodied education is relevant. First and foremost, bringing the body back into education encourages students to interact with their surroundings in a more holistic way and to use their bodies to express themselves and gather information. Furthermore, research has shown that body-based learning can be more effective for many subjects, such as language and mathematics. This leads to the ultimate conclusion that pedagogies should be based on embodied principles. However, changing pedagogies for various subjects alone will not be sufficient to tackle the persistent problem of a dualistic perspective. It is also necessary to work on changing one's outlook simultaneously. Until people realize their own embodied nature, they will not be fully committed to their actions, including designing and practicing education. With these intentions, in the next section, an "inner curriculum" will be discussed with the aim of changing one's perspective about oneself and, in turn, changing educational activities.

2   The Inner Curriculum: Fostering Self-Awareness and Embodied Learning

The key to realizing our embodied nature is rooted in our awareness of ourselves and our surroundings. Historically, it has been widely claimed that regular awareness practices help us realize our true nature and connection with the world. Realizing our true nature is also said to help us break free from illusions and see ourselves as embodied beings. Therefore, there is a need for an inner curriculum with the goal of transforming one's understanding of themselves. Meditative practices are claimed to be significant in this regard. Therefore, I shall now focus on the possibility of including meditative practices in an educational setting, which I consider to be a core element of an inner curriculum.

I shall begin by drawing from Oren Ergas's thoughts for the simple reason that one can find an amalgamation of Buddhism, psychological studies, neuroscience, and contemplative studies in his work. The title of this section, the "inner curriculum," is also credited to him.

2.1   *Turning the Attention Inward*
It is important that any educational effort should align with our embodied nature, as it is now widely acknowledged that humans are inherently embodied. However, due to certain social and psychological reasons, people may not be fully aware of their embodied nature. As Oren Ergas (2017) points out, our experience of life is shaped by attending to objects, whether they are mental objects arising from within or physical objects from the external world. This suggests that our experiences are a product of both the external and internal worlds, which contribute to our outer and inner lives, respectively. Therefore, educational efforts should take into account both aspects and align with the embodied approach. The objective should be to raise awareness of our embodied nature and, as a result, foster practices that reduce the divide between us and the world. However, sometimes, though not always, education itself can serve as a tool for disconnection from the world.

As noted by Ergas, the current educational system tends to view knowledge as something that can be found only in textbooks, which often results in a lack of attention given to lived experiences that unfold in the present moment. He notes that knowledge is mostly seen as "out there, not in here" (ibid., p. 97). It occurs primarily because we, as stakeholders (teachers, students, and policymakers), are unaware of our own embodied nature. We have discussed the outer embodied curriculum in the previous section, focusing on the pedagogies related to outer world knowledge. But what about educating our inner world? As I argued earlier, in order to do full justice to our embodied nature in education, we need to reorient our perspective to include the inner world. Therefore, it is crucial to design a curriculum that enables us to recognize and embrace our true nature—our embodied nature. This could be referred to as an "inner curriculum" since its objective is to change one's perspective from the inside out.

Inner curriculum amounts to paying attention to the whole field of inner experience, which comprises thoughts, emotions, hopes, worries, prejudices, or any other mental state. A typical educational setup does not give importance to these dimensions because knowledge is seen as "out there" and the student simply has to get it. The inner curriculum, on the other hand, does not lead to any fixed knowledge but instead provides an avenue to look at things as they are. It helps in appreciating the role that inner processes play in the overall experience, including the production of knowledge. Therefore, it advances a more balanced and accommodating approach, making one realize that "in here" and "out there" are not sharply separate but rather continuous. Such a realization might also amount to a reduction in the thickness of the psychological boundary between the self and the world.

To achieve this, Ergas urges us to turn our attention inward instead of outward (ibid., p. 9). Attention is the capacity through which our experiences are shaped, depending on whether it is directed outwards or inwards. Our entire experience, knowledge, and memory are nothing more than the accumulation of numerous moments of attention over something. As our attention is limited in terms of temporal and spatial parameters, it is necessarily selective. Ergas uses the metaphor of a "flashlight of attention" to describe it (ibid., p. 29). There are numerous things available at a given moment to pay attention to, but only those things become part of our conscious experience upon which this light of attention shines. This also means that many things that are often dismissed as irrelevant may become significant and part of our reality. Now we need to focus on how to direct this flashlight of attention inward.

Ergas suggests that meditative practice is one way to turn our attention inward and explore our first-person experience (ibid., p. 14). Similarly, Miri Albahari (2016, 207) advocates for meditative practices in order to dismantle one's false sense of self and reflexively recognize one's true nature. Self-reflexivity is the process of turning one's attention inward, being both the observing subject and the observed object, through self-knowledge and self-monitoring (Pagis, 2009). This process can be referred to as "self-awareness." Although practicing self-awareness is an important way to foster self-reflexivity, it is also claimed that outward practices such as journaling (Barbezat & Bush, 2014; Brady, 2007) and listening to external sounds can inculcate self-reflexivity (Kleinberger, 2014). Many thinkers have expressed similar views, emphasizing the importance of self-awareness in cultivating an independent, clear, and meaningful perception of reality.

2.2 Developing Self Awareness

Ashwini Kumar describes self-awareness as the state of pure observation "that involves neither translating the state of being into words nor judging it with predetermined ideals, but rather observing it with full attention" (Kumar,

2013, p. 79). Generally speaking, self-awareness is defined as the ability to be aware of oneself, both physically and mentally. This includes the awareness of one's physical sensations, emotions, thoughts, and beliefs. Self-awareness also includes the ability to reflect on these elements and to understand how one's thoughts and decisions affect one's life, as well as the lives of those around them. Further, self-awareness is a way to truly examine one's innermost thoughts, feelings, and beliefs, which is essential for deep self-understanding. Therefore, it is important to become more aware of our thoughts and feelings through a conscious effort of self-awareness. Consequently, one can begin to recognize that many of our thoughts, feelings, and beliefs are largely conditioned and habitual. By recognizing this fact, one can free the mind from these patterns and allow for greater insight and understanding. Hence, by becoming aware of the movement of one's own thought, one could see the effects of conditioning and realize that various divisions between observer and observed, thinker and thought, and experiencer and experience are merely an illusion.

In general, there are several methods for achieving self-awareness such as meditation, observation, concentration, and contemplation. At their core, these practices are intended to develop "effortless or choiceless awareness of one's self in relationship to ideas, people, and nature from moment to moment" (ibid., p. 90). Choiceless awareness is believed to be helpful in cultivating a state of non-judgmental awareness, allowing one to break free from the conditioning of society and connect with their true nature. Non-judgmental or choiceless awareness can be cultivated by practicing choiceless attention to things. This involves perceiving things as they are without any distortion caused by past experiences, memories, or preconceived notions. Such pure perception can be fostered through activities such as pure visual observation and attentive listening.

According to Jiddu Krishnamurti (1954; 1969), we usually listen to our own noise rather than to what is actually being said because we attach our own thoughts, past experiences, prejudices, and pre-formulations to it. That is why he considers listening to any sound, as they are, crucial to becoming self-aware. Similarly, pure visual observation is the art of looking at anything objectively without any association of prior knowledge, opinions, judgments, and so on. According to Krishnamurti, this activity of pure observation will eventually lead to the realization that there is no separate observer and that only attention exists.

According to Kumar (2013), there are several ways to free ourselves from conditioning and become aware of our true nature. These include engaging in choiceless observations, playfulness, meditative thinking, imagination, and paying close attention to our body, thoughts, and emotions in the present moment. Moreover, he explicitly emphasizes developing awareness of the body and its functions. He notes that "having an awareness of one's body is basically a way to be at home—body is our home—to allow centering to happen at a deeper level" (ibid., p. 109). He argues that there is unity in life since the body is our home and ecology is the home of the body. This implies that human thoughts are not entirely separate from the body or the environment. This is why becoming aware of our own bodily states is considered one of the important, if not central, steps to realizing our true nature. Based on this perspective, it can be argued that the body somehow mediates between our inner nature and the external world. Therefore, focusing on the body can have profound results in terms of recognizing and embracing our true nature, i.e., our embodied nature.

In terms of modern cognitive science terminology, I believe that practicing awareness techniques and attention training would aid in the development of body-consciousness. It is evident from the empirical studies presented in previous chapters that the body not only provides a medium for stimuli-induced reactions but is also active in interpreting and comprehending reality. Now, if self-awareness is defined as awareness of what is happening in a given place at a given moment, then the question arises: what exactly are we aware of? Building upon Kumar's position, I contend that we are primarily aware of the body and its various states including our inextricable connection with the world. If the body is considered as our home, then the body itself becomes the primary object for our observation. This brings us to the final question: how can we incorporate these exercises into educational settings to help children develop body awareness, cultivate body-consciousness, and ultimately realize their unity with nature? In this regard, various meditation practices, such as mindfulness, can be of immense importance.

2.3   *Meditation and Mindfulness*

Nowadays, the term "meditation" is broadly used and has various connotations. Modern definitions generally emphasize over self-regulation practices, attention training, voluntary control of mental processes, the development of mental capacities for calmness and concentration, etc. Collectively, modern societies ascribe various meanings to the term "meditation," such as a state of concentration or a state of relaxation. These meanings typically refers to moving away from one's usual mundane, unfocused, and unrelaxed state (Varela et al., 1991, p. 23). On the other hand, traditionally, meditation was explained using metaphors such as "purifying the mind," "freeing from illusion or conditioning," "awakening," "healing," "calming," "unfolding," "uncovering," "enlightening," etc. (Walsh, 1999).

It goes without saying that meditation has taken many forms, been developed in various countries, evolved within various cultural contexts, and been modified to meet societal needs. This diverse range of meditative practices mostly varies on the basis of the type of attention, the relationship to cognitive processes, and the goal. However, I am going to consider one such version from the large set of meditative practices: what is called awareness or mindfulness practices.

Jon Kabat-Zinn defines mindfulness as "the awareness that emerges through paying attention in a particular way: on purpose, in the present moment, and nonjudgmentally ... to nurture greater awareness, clarity, and acceptance of present-moment reality" (Kabat-Zinn, 2009, p. 14). Mindfulness is the process of experiencing one's own thoughts and sensations as they arise in moment-to-moment awareness through conscious attention. The importance of mindfulness can be understood by analyzing its typical behaviour, as the natural tendency of the mind is to wander. Research indicates that mind-wandering accounts for almost half of our regular stream of thoughts (Killingsworth & Gilbert, 2010).

A person's thought can be considered "mind-wandering" if it is not related to the present task and/or decoupled from the surroundings. For instance, we usually notice mind-wandering when we try to accomplish any task, and wandering hinders it. Additionally, one might also be surprised to know that they have completed a pleasurable activity without noticing it. In both cases, our mind or attention got shifted to something else or went somewhere else, and was not available in the present moment. Now, going back to what mindfulness means, the most important parts of mindfulness practices are being in the present and not judging.

Present-centeredness is related to keeping our attention in the present moment, i.e., now. Shinzen Young (2016) describes three attentional skills that are involved in developing present-centeredness. First is focusing attention on physical elements such as sight, sound, and bodily physical sensations, which is termed as "concentration power." Next is focusing on subtler bodily sensations, such as the sensation of a breath at the nostrils, termed "sensory clarity." In both cases, the practitioner's attention becomes entangled in a chain of thoughts and must be intentionally brought back. Thoughts can be about the past, future, or fantasy, but like other mental states, they occur in the present. Therefore, it is crucial to be attentive to thoughts as well.

This brings us to the third skill or step of being attentive to thoughts without being carried away by them, termed "equanimity." It requires two major things to be done: 1) be clearly aware of when each thought begins and when it ends; 2) not be caught in the content of the thought as it is happening. Young argues that reaching to the third level is a real present-centeredness state, which is a kind of "balance point that avoids both pushing down and grasping on" (ibid., p. 32). Although these skills are important to realizing present-centeredness, they do not necessarily need to be practiced in sequence because the effect is just a consequence of applying them in certain ways.

Likewise, non-judgment is the state of non-reactivity to any sensations, thoughts, or emotions. Young (2016, 33) notes that judgments and reactions arise constantly and naturally whenever we turn our attention inward. Now, there are two possibilities to avoid this. One strategy is to keep our attention away from the judgments until our natural reactive tendency ceases on its own. It is like going to a much deeper level, seeing your judgments as well as the fact that you are judging. Another possibility is to attend to judgments and deconstruct them into their finer elements, such as mental talk, emotional sensations, etc. One can then observe each component in detail until it eventually dissolves. Clearly, experiencing a non-judgmental state necessitates considerable preparation in terms of present-centeredness. In more refined words, mindfulness is "self-regulation of attention and a particular orientation towards one's experiences in the present moment, characterized by openness and acceptance" (Bishop et al., 2004). That means in order to cultivate mindful awareness, attention must be combined with a non-judgmental attitude toward openness to the flow of one's experiences. This indicates the obvious implication that training attentional functions is an essential aspect of mindfulness practices.

Further, it is also frequently argued, based on several neurological studies, that mindfulness meditation practices can help to balance out the effects of the left and right hemispheres of the brain. Studies have shown that meditation increases the amount of white matter and the size of the corpus callosum, facilitating enhanced communication between different areas of the brain (Tang et al., 2010). Simply put, the corpus callosum is the primary connecting region of the brain, made up of white matter tracts that connect the left and right cerebral hemispheres. It has been observed that people tend to have either a left or right-dominant brain structure because our day-to-day activities often require different types of focus, such as narrow attention of the left hemisphere and broad attention of the right hemisphere. Consequently, one brain hemisphere typically receives more activity than the other, leading to an over strengthening of one side of the brain while neglecting the other. However, studies suggest that long-term meditation practice can strengthen the connection between the hemispheres by thickening the callosal regions (Luders et al., 2012), and increasing connectivity among various regions of the brain (Hasenkamp & Barsalou, 2012).

Moreover, although research in this area is in its preliminary stages, some initial results indicate morphological changes in the brain due to the effects of various meditation practices, particularly in brain areas related to exteroceptive and interoceptive body awareness (Fox et al., 2014). This suggests that meditation practices have the potential to alter our brain structure and enable us to realize our embodied nature. Such changes may also help in overcoming the various factors, discussed in the previous chapter, that often lead us to overlook embodiment, especially in the realm of education. Mindfulness practices encourage nonjudgmental awareness of our experiences and reduce our tendency to view the world in dualistic terms. By focusing on the present moment, we become more attuned to our thoughts, emotions, and bodily sensations, and learn to observe them without reacting or identifying with them. As we continue to practice mindfulness, we begin to recognize the interdependent nature of our experiences and see how everything is interconnected. This can foster open-mindedness and compassion towards others, as we acknowledge that everyone's experiences are unique and intertwined. Studies have demonstrated that mindfulness training can result in more pro-social and empathetic behaviour (Berry et al., 2018; Rosenberg et al., 2015). Therefore, mindfulness may help reduce the overemphasis on the left hemisphere, which is primarily concerned with overpowering, domination, and control.

Interestingly, a study found that individuals who practice mindfulness are less concerned with their self-image in relationships, likely due to the development of non-judgmental present-moment awareness (Stewart et al., 2018). These empirical results suggest that regular mindfulness meditation may help minimize the effects of social conditioning and divisive behaviour in our everyday lives, which can lead to false relationships with self-representations. Furthermore, even brief mindfulness training can reduce implicit racial bias, leading to increased kindness towards others (Luberto et al., 2018; Lueke & Gibson, 2015). These studies suggest that regular mindfulness practice may aid in overcoming controlling tendencies and racial oppressions that have led the world to suffer through colonialism. While our natural tendency is to comprehend the world on dualistic lines, recent studies in the contemplative domain suggest that we can reduce the effects of societal conditioning that amplify our dualistic outlook, and lead more balanced lives by realizing our interconnected relationship with the world.

Now, let us explore specific practices that can be utilized to become more mindful and move us one step closer to realizing our embodied nature.

There are various practices being used to train attention and cultivate mindfulness, depending on different traditions and settings. Antoine Lutz and colleagues (2008) club this diverse range of attention training into two broad categories: one is focused attention (FA), and the other is open monitoring (OM). These two styles of attention training are found in one way or another, with some variations, in most of the classical meditative traditions. Moreover, these styles are crucial (obviously with variations) to target both elements of being mindful, i.e., present-centeredness and non-judgmental approach.

The first style, FA practices, entail the voluntary focusing attention on a chosen object in a sustained fashion; in contrast, OM practices involve nonreactive monitoring of the content of experience from moment to moment to recognize the nature of emotional and cognitive patterns. In brief, FA meditation practices involve the following steps: directing and sustaining attention on a selected object, such as breath sensations; detecting mind wandering and distractors, such as thoughts; disengaging attention from distractors and shifting it back to the selected object; and finally, a cognitive reappraisal of the distractor, such as recognizing it as "just a thought" or "it is okay to be distracted." On the other hand, open monitoring (OM) practices involve no explicit focus on any object and require nonreactive meta-cognitive monitoring in terms of labelling experiences. Additionally, OM require nonreactive awareness of automatic cognitive and emotional interpretations of sensory, perceptual, and endogenous stimuli. As a result, executing FA seems more effortful than OM due to more deliberate one-pointed attention, whereas OM is relatively more effortless due to its unfocused monitoring, something like choiceless awareness (Austin, 2009, p. 4).

In the past few decades, there has been a surge of empirical studies showing the positive effects of mindfulness practices in various domains of human life (Keng et al., 2011). Specifically, in the educational domain, studies have shown that mindfulness practices can improve attention and focus (Baijal et al., 2011; Napoli et al., 2005; Semple et al., 2010); cognitive development (Sanger & Dorjee, 2016); empathetic and social behaviour (Schonert-Reichl et al., 2015); in addition to academic performance (Magalhães et al., 2022). Studies also indicate that mindfulness practices can help students regulate their emotions by reducing anxiety, stress, depression, and post-traumatic symptoms (Etherington & Costello, 2019; Mendelson et al., 2010; Metz et al., 2013; Raes et al., 2014; Sibinga et al., 2016). Furthermore, mindfulness practices have demonstrated significant improvements not only in students but also in educators' personal and professional lives. For example, teachers who learned mindfulness experienced less stress and burnout, performed better at work, and organized their classrooms more effectively, resulting in a more emotionally supportive environment for their students (Flook et al., 2013; Jennings et al., 2019; Roeser et al., 2013; Zarate et al., 2019).

While it is beyond the scope of this work to discuss the numerous positive benefits of mindfulness practices, it is worth noting that these practices have been shown to have a significant effect on improving social, emotional, and psychological well-being; enhancing concentration; and reducing mind-wandering (Brown & Ryan, 2003; Chiesa & Serretti, 2009; Davidson et al., 2003; Hayes et al., 1999; Xu et al., 2017). Further, various studies have shown that attention training, including mindfulness, helps individuals to be present at the moment. These practices can help students, teachers, and educators reduce the conceptual gap between the body, mind, and environment and better realize their embodied nature. However, the main challenge right now is figuring out how to incorporate these attentional practices into the regular modern educational curriculum. While some alternative educational settings emphasize mindfulness practices, more cross-cultural research across ages is required to develop a secular, common, and feasible inner curriculum for children.

In the end, it is also important to highlight that being mindful can help us realize our interconnectedness and interdependence with nature, which is a crucial aspect of being embodied. William Van Gordon and colleagues observe that we are intimately connected with nature and that being human means appreciating our lives through this connection (Van Gordon et al., 2018). They put it this way:

> When we breathe in, we breathe in the out-breath of plants, shrubs, and trees. When we breathe out, we breathe out the in-breath of flowers, animals, and birds. When we drink water, we drink the clouds, rivers, and oceans. When we eat a meal, we eat plants, vegetables, and fruits that have grown out of the earth. (Van Gordon et al., 2018, p. 1655)

To appreciate this symbiotic relationship, it is suggested to practice mindfulness in natural environments and enhance meditative awareness by observing and contemplating specific properties of the natural environment. For example, simply observing a river while walking or a tree while sitting in a park. While it is important to appreciate the beauty of the present moment, these observations should not be used to raise questions or analysis, but rather should be solely focused on enjoying the experience. This kind of pure observation practice helps us to become one with nature and eliminates the conceptual boundary between us and the natural world. In the words of Jiddu Krishnamurti, "If it is pure observation ... there is no division ... there is no observer" (Krishnamurti, 1985). This implies that we become aware of our unity with nature. In short, we can realize, we are embodied and embedded in the world. It is about living with the fact, as Andy Clark and David Chalmers famously put, "we are creatures of the world" (Clark & Chalmers, 1998).

3 Conclusion

Embodied education is founded on the idea that the mind is embodied, recognizing the importance of both neural and non-neural bodily components in the formation of mental phenomena. That is why it highlights the need to provide learners with direct experiences that engage their bodies. The main objective of this chapter is to explore the development of a pedagogy that acknowledges the embodied nature of human beings. By drawing on empirical studies, the chapter demonstrates that human thinking is closely intertwined with our bodily characteristics and the environments we inhabit. To address implementation, the chapter proposes a two-way approach that includes both an outer and an inner curriculum.

The outer curriculum relies on the core principles of embodied cognition theory, which are the cognitive grounding and offloading of mental processes through the body and environment. These concepts highlight the interdependence of the mind, body, and environment in shaping cognition, which is often facilitated by gestures. As gestures are an integral part of our embodied nature, they should be respected and incorporated into teaching and learning practices. Additionally, studies have shown that subjects traditionally considered to be abstract, such as language and mathematics, are, in fact, embodied and should be taught as per embodied methods.

However, the success of educational activities based on embodied principles depends on our ability to recognize our own embodied nature. Thus, the inner curriculum is concerned with helping students, teachers, and other stakeholders to become aware of their own embodiment, allowing them to design effective outer curricula. The main purpose of the inner curriculum is to help children to connect with their bodies and the world, and to appreciate the benefits of their embodied nature for learning. Several studies have shown that mindfulness meditation is an effective tool in assisting individuals to become aware of their experiences and to gain insight into their interconnected embodiment, in addition to its therapeutic and psychological benefits.

Mindfulness meditation encourages individuals to observe their present-moment experience of their body and mind, leading to awareness of the unity and interconnectedness of the two. By focusing on the present moment rather than thoughts about the past or future, mindfulness meditation can help individuals become aware of their bodily sensations and their mind's connection to these sensations. In addition, mindfulness meditation can help individuals become aware of the relationship between their thoughts, emotions, and bodily experiences in the present moment. By being aware of their bodily sensations, feelings, and thoughts, individuals can observe their embodiment and interconnectedness.

Realizing the embodied nature of one's experience can lead to several physical and psychological benefits for students. Studies show that those who recognize their embodied nature also learn to appreciate their internal and external environments. Through mindfulness meditation, students can become more aware of their own thoughts, feelings, sensations, behaviours, and the outside world. This awareness can help students form healthier relationships with their environment by means of engaging with a deeper understanding of themselves and their inner experience. In the long run, awareness of one's embodied nature will help students realize that they are not dissociated from nature but are a part of a larger whole.

Having said that, it is crucial to recognize that the inner and outer curricula are not isolated but are interdependent aspects of a holistic educational experience. Developing an inner curriculum that encourages embodied self-awareness can significantly influence how students and teachers interact with the outer curriculum. For instance, mindfulness practices in the inner curriculum can enhance one's perception and awareness, thereby making the use of gestures in the outer curriculum more intentional and effective. Moreover, policy-level interventions can bridge this gap by advocating for the inclusion of both inner and outer embodied curricula in mainstream educational systems. This would entail revising teacher training modules, updating learning materials, and promoting awareness programs that emphasize the interconnection between these two dimensions of embodied learning.

CHAPTER 7

Conclusion

A Path Forward

This work is centred around the close link between educational practice and a theory of human nature. Humans are social species, and most of their activities occur in their relationships with other human beings and their environment. Further, a person's beliefs and dispositions are the primary drivers of their activities and behaviour towards others. Hence, it is reasonable to assert that every human being has certain assumptions about their own fundamental nature that influence their actions and behaviours, which, in turn, has a significant impact on various aspects of their social life, including education. This interconnectivity between specific assumptions about human nature and educational practices is clearly found in the works of most educational theorists worldwide. With this issue in mind, in the second chapter, I engaged with the first research question "how does a particular assumption about human nature impact the way education is conceived?"

Particularly, I reviewed ideas related to human nature and education in three prominent educational thinkers of the twentieth century—Paulo Freire, John Dewey, and Jiddu Krishnamurti. Upon examining the views of these three thinkers, it was found that there is a close connection between their views on human nature and education. Further, a close analysis of their philosophy clearly shows that their views on education directly stem from their views on human nature. Thus, this study's initial hypothesis, "to comprehend and transform education, it is necessary first to comprehend human nature," appears to be correct. Moreover, education emerged as a significant social institution in human societies that aims at changing human behaviour. Therefore, understanding human nature must be a top priority before designing any educational activities intended to transform individuals. This leads to the next question "How can we formulate a comprehensive theory of human nature based on available evidence?," in the third chapter.

The term "human nature" refers to the essential qualities or characteristics that define human beings. While it is commonly defined as the characteristics that all humans share, there is no single definition of human nature, leading to the development of various theories based on discipline-specific explanations. A brief historical excursus about major theories of human nature reveals that two major themes underlie their claims: the mind-body relationship and

© AKHIL K. SINGH, 2025 | DOI:10.1163/9789004724372_007

the nature vs. nurture debate. The debate concerning the mind-body problem mainly assumes a dualistic viewpoint that regards mental and physical properties as real and having independent existences. Similarly, the nature versus nurture debate focuses on whether a particular aspect of human behaviour is innately fixed or can be influenced by sociocultural and environmental factors. These debates often result in two extreme positions that create a division between the mind and body, as well as between nature and nurture. As a result, they lead to a divided picture of human beings.

Another crucial point to consider is that most past theories regarding human nature were the result of speculative reasoning and may not offer a complete understanding of the topic. These theories tend to view humans through a dualistic lens, assuming that humans are composed of two distinct substances: a physical body and an immaterial mind. This perspective is still prevalent in many educational institutions, which assume a complete separation between the learner's mind and body. Such a divisive approach to education undermines the wholeness of the learner and impedes the development of critical thinking and an exploratory mindset among children.

On the other hand, recent empirical studies in cognitive science offer a more comprehensive perspective on humans and propose reconciliation as a solution to divisive debates. A body of contemporary research focused on embodied and embedded aspects of cognition (often referred to as 4E cognitive science), questions the idea that there is a separate, transcendental mental entity that is entirely detached from the body and the world. Based on various pieces of evidence, it is now argued that mental properties emerge from bodily activities and sensory-motor interaction with the world, establishing a connection between humans and their environment. This means that humans are inherently embodied and deeply embedded in the world.

Hence, it is more appropriate to define human nature in terms of embodiment without making a hard separation between their physical and mental characteristics and their environment. This perspective asserts that all mental properties arise from a person's bodily interaction with the world. Therefore, it is preferable to view humans as embodied, thinking, and acting agents in the world, rather than sharply distinguishing between their thinking and acting activities. This perspective represents a significant paradigm shift in our understanding of human beings and their nature, as well as their behaviour. Therefore, it is essential to explore this perspective in depth and breadth to understand its fundamental claims. This brings us to the third question, "How does embodied cognition theory provide a compelling explanation of human nature?" which is examined in the fourth chapter.

The embodied cognition approach emerged as a critique of traditional cognitive science, which viewed mental processes as purely computational, operating on symbolic representations. It has roots in the phenomenological tradition too, particularly in the ideas of Merleau-Ponty. Currently, this approach is supported by several empirical studies, making it one of the most prominent theories to explain human cognition. The central claim of embodied cognition is that "mental phenomena arise from bodily interaction with the world."

The embodied theory challenges the notion of an autonomous and independent mind and posits that the mind and body are deeply intertwined. It also recognizes the integral role of the environment in shaping mental processes, contending that mental processes are shaped by and emerge from bodily experiences in the world. Importantly, the definition of the body in embodied cognition is not restricted to the brain but includes other non-neural bodily parts, such as motor organs as well. Additionally, one of the distinctive features of the embodied approach is that it considers the world as constitutive in cognitive processes, in contrast to traditional views of cognition that only consider the world as causally responsible. Thus, cognitive activity is said to result from the dynamic coupling of the mind, body, and world.

The key point is that cognition is not simply the product of the individual mind or brain working in isolation but rather the result of their continuous interaction with the external world as one system. This implies that no single element of the cognitive system has causal priority, in contrast to the traditional approach that prioritizes the mind over the body or world. On the contrary, as per embodied approach systems are capable of self-organization since they can automatically adapt to environmental factors based on continuous feedback loops. Therefore, it is more appropriate to view cognition, and the mind as a natural, continuous event rather than a separate entity completely cut off from the body and the world, operating in isolation.

If the mind or cognitive activity is viewed as a continuous, natural event resulting from the interaction between mental, physical, and environmental factors, it follows that an organism can enhance its cognitive abilities by increasing its opportunities for interaction with a well-organized social and physical environment. The surrounding environment not only helps us improve our cognitive abilities but also facilitates our cognitive efforts. That is why cognitive scaffolding or grounding, and cognitive offloading are considered essential components of cognitive activity. Cognitive scaffolding suggests that our cognitive abilities depend on and are shaped by the resources in our environment, whereas offloading implies that we often transfer information to the world to overcome cognitive limitations and/or reduce cognitive load.

An embodied approach toward cognition also provides a novel understanding of human concepts and rationality. It is argued that we often understand a concept based on our particular bodily features, and this process happens automatically and unconsciously. We understand the meaning of concepts metaphorically, as they arise from our direct bodily experiences in our day-to-day activities.

This shift in our understanding of human beings has significant implications for how we approach educational activities. As with the traditional view of a distinct mind and conceptual structures being challenged by recent empirical evidence in cognitive science, it is necessary to reexamine our educational discourse. If humans are fundamentally embodied beings, then the crucial role of the body and the world in teaching-learning activities must be acknowledged in education. This brings us to our final research question: "in what ways can we restructure our educational practices based on the evidence-based (embodied) theory of human nature?," which is the subject of discussion in the fifth and sixth chapters.

While exploring the diverse range of issues present in education, many researchers have observed that most modern educational setups do not value the embodied nature of human beings. Now, it is obvious to ask, if embodied theory provides a plausible account of human cognition and their basic nature, why it has not been widely adopted in the educational domain? Despite a significant body of evidence supporting an embodied approach, mainstream educational systems are often heavily influenced by Western ideas that are often based on mind-body dualism.

The modern education system, in general, began to take shape during the seventeenth century in the Western world when society was influenced by conceptual dualism and scientific objectivism. Conceptual dualism gained prevalence in modern society due to its alignment with the development of scientific methodologies in the Western world, leading to a rigid separation between the mind and body, and the devaluation of the body. This dualistic perspective resulted in an education system that prioritized bookish knowledge and teacher-led instructions over the subjective experiences of learners, which has been criticized as oppressive.

Additionally, various socio-economic and political factors contributed to the education system overlooking the bodily existence of children, leading to a prioritization of intellectual activities over real-world experiences. However, despite recent findings in the field of embodied cognition that challenge these theoretical assumptions and historical reasons behind mentalistic education, our dualistic approach in everyday life remains prevalent. One explanation for this dualistic outlook is that it is an innate trait in human beings. This innate trait of understanding the world on dualistic lines is claimed to be an evolutionary trait that helps humans better survive and adapt. Empirical studies using neuroimaging techniques demonstrate that we may develop a divisive outlook due to structural differences between the left and right hemispheres of the brain.

The left brain typically yields localized, narrow, and focused attention to meet our immediate needs, such as hunger. Meanwhile, the right hemisphere provides broad, flexible, open, and vigilant attention to construct a broad perspective. Both forms of attention are essential to humans and construct our reality in different, yet complementary ways. Studies have also found that the left hemisphere has closer interconnections within its own regions than the right hemisphere, resulting in more self-referring characteristics. Owing to this close internal connectivity, the left hemisphere produces a unique worldview that it has developed for itself. In contrast, the right hemisphere exhibits stronger intracranial connectivity, extending beyond the cortex to other brain regions, providing a broader perspective on the world.

There is nothing inherently problematic with having two worldviews, but issues arise when we emphasize one aspect at the cost of the other. It has been observed that the modern world emphasizes a more logical, rational, and narrow outlook, which is a function of the left brain. Iain McGilchrist (2009) asserts that over the past few hundred years, the left brain has progressively taken control, resulting in a society that is rational and efficient but also superficial and materialistic. This imbalance has given rise to several issues, including the prevalence of scientism, materialism, and a failure to fully comprehend the human experience in all its dimensions.

Further, overemphasizing the left-brain results in narrow attention, and a virtual worldview, and undermine the effects of the right hemisphere, which help us appreciate our intimate relationship with the world. Additionally, overemphasizing the activities of the left brain further strengthens the left brain and may cause us to lose our connection with our body. This is because the right hemisphere has a full body schema, in contrast to the left hemisphere, which has a body schema only for the right side of the body. Most notably, an overreliance on the left hemisphere weakens our embodied perspective, which encompasses both our body and the environment surrounding us because its relationship with the world is not direct but through representations such as language.

In addition to our neurological roots, our society significantly influences our dichotomous behaviour. Even if there is a natural tendency to approach the world in two ways, our way of life and social environment plays a crucial role in making us more divisive and amplifying the effect of the left brain. Social conditioning is a significant factor that aggravates the divisive tendency in ourselves, leading to significant changes in our thoughts and actions. Furthermore, as human beings, we have a tendency to focus on the past and future, leading us to disconnect from the present moment and our bodily sensations, as well as our surroundings, thereby overlooking our embodied nature.

These aforementioned factors create various obstacles in appreciating our embodied nature and its role in educational activities. The first and most pressing issue is that we live in our daily lives with the underlying implicit assumption of mind-body dualism, which leads to an overemphasis on the mentalistic approach to education as seen in mainstream approaches. This, in turn, results in a failure to recognize the wholeness of learners and the integrated outlook of the mind-body-world. Consequently, the body is often ignored in educational research, which further strengthens the assumption of mind-body dualism and perpetuates the mentalistic approach to education. While these obstacles are distinct and important, they are also interrelated and may directly or indirectly influence each other, creating a vicious cycle in which each obstacle supports and exacerbates the others.

I have formulated a two-way approach to break the cycle of ignoring our embodied nature and create educational environments that acknowledge the embodied nature of human beings. The first aspect is the "outer embodied curriculum" where we need to develop teaching methodologies that align with the principles of the embodied theory. It involves designing pedagogies as per embodied principles, which is an "outside-in" approach. The second aspect is the "inner embodied curriculum," where we also need to educate educational stakeholders about their own embodied nature. It emphasizes on changing individuals' perspectives about themselves and helping them recognize their own embodied nature, which is an "inside-out" approach. These two approaches can work together and complement each other, helping to break the vicious cycle of underlying assumptions of mind-body duality.

The outer curriculum is primarily focused on applying embodied theory to create a more integrated learning environment that acknowledges children's embodied nature of learning. It relies on two key principles of embodied cognition: cognitive grounding and offloading. These principles emphasize the interconnectedness of the mind, body, and environment in shaping cognitive processes. We have seen in the fourth chapter that environmental features, including the body, are used to ground thoughts and offload cognitive load onto the environment for efficient cognitive processing. That means, offloading and grounding are two methods by which the body and environment participate in the process of cognition. There are many ways to utilize the principles of cognitive offloading and grounding in the classroom. However, I have specifically shown how gestures can be used to implement these concepts and discussed evidence that they are not just verbal conveniences, but an integral part of our everyday communication. I have also specifically discussed the embodied aspect of learning in two subjects: language and mathematics. These subjects have long been considered purely mental, but recent research in cognitive science has demonstrated that they are actually embodied in nature. Utilizing body and environmental features has shown significant improvement in learning in both subjects.

Now, it is certain that bringing the body back into education encourages students to interact with their surroundings holistically and use their bodies to express themselves and gather information. Therefore, it is recommended that pedagogies be designed in accordance with embodied principles. However, changing pedagogies for various subjects alone will not be sufficient to tackle the persistent problem of a dualistic outlook in the educational domain. It is also necessary to work on changing one's outlook simultaneously. Until people realize their own embodied nature, they will not be fully committed to their actions, including designing and practicing education. Therefore, changing one's perspective about oneself is also crucial in order to change educational activities. This requires an "inner curriculum" that helps us realize our own embodied nature and reduces our disembodied outlook in the domain of education.

The key to realizing our embodied nature is rooted in our awareness of ourselves and our surroundings. In a typical educational setup, knowledge is mostly seen as "out there, not in here," and therefore, students are expected to acquire it simply. This approach overlooks the inner world of the learner and makes a complete distinction between the knower and the knowledge. On the other hand, an inner curriculum emphasizes the role of subjective involvement in the process of knowledge construction. To achieve this, we need to turn our attention inward.

Attention is the capacity through which our experiences are shaped, depending on whether it is directed outwards or inwards. It is widely suggested that turning our attention inward results in diminishing the difference between subject and object and thereby realizing our interconnectedness with the world. This practice is also helpful in fostering self-awareness, which is the awareness of one's own physical and mental states.

Self-awareness allows for a deeper understanding of one's physical sensations as well as their innermost thoughts, feelings, and beliefs. As a result, one begins to recognize that many of our thoughts, feelings, and beliefs are largely conditioned and habitual. Recognizing this fact can free one from these patterns and allow for greater insight and understanding. Therefore, by becoming aware of the movement of one's own thoughts, one can see the effects of conditioning and realize that various divisions between observer and observed, thinker and thought, and experiencer and experience are merely illusions.

Mindfulness practices are considered an important activity to achieve self-awareness that can help us realize our embodied nature reflexively. Mindfulness is the moment-to-moment awareness of our thoughts by paying attention to the present moment without judgment. Its most crucial components are present-centeredness and a non-judgmental attitude, which involve keeping our attention in the present moment and being non-reactive to any sensations, thoughts, or emotions. These two aspects help us to stay present and become more open to our own thoughts and others. In essence, mindfulness is a self-regulation of attention and a specific orientation towards our present experiences, characterized by openness and acceptance. This openness and acceptance of our physical and mental states have tremendous benefits in terms of improving our social, emotional, and psychological well-being.

Besides the several obvious benefits, mindfulness meditation may also help address the various causes of a dualistic education system. As discussed in the fifth chapter, an overemphasis on one side of the brain, particularly the left hemisphere, can lead to an elevated dualistic approach in our outlook, which is also reflected in our education systems. However, studies have shown that practicing mindfulness can help balance the effects of the left and right hemispheres of the brain by altering the brain's structure. Such changes at the neurological level may help us to overcome the isolating approach that typically emerges due to overemphasizing one hemisphere at the cost of another and help in realizing our embodied nature.

Contemplative studies have also demonstrated that by focusing on the present moment, we can learn to observe our thoughts without reacting or identifying with them. With continued mindfulness practice, we can begin to recognize the interdependent nature of our experiences and see how everything is interconnected. Mindfulness training is also found to cultivate more prosocial and empathetic behaviour in human beings, which can help reduce the overpowering effect of the left hemisphere, which is primarily concerned with dominance and control.

It has been also observed that the modern education system was primarily shaped during the colonial expansion and that oppressive behaviour is still present in most schools. This was fuelled by racial biases and a notion of superiority, which can still be observed in modern education. However, several studies have shown that even a brief period of mindfulness practice can reduce implicit racial bias, leading to increased kindness toward others. This suggests that regular mindfulness practice may also help in overcoming controlling tendencies and racial oppressions that have led the world to suffer through colonialism.

These various studies suggest that mindfulness practices have the potential to significantly reduce dualistic assumptions arising from both our brain structure (nature) and societal influences (nurture). By focusing on the inner curriculum and incorporating mindfulness practices in education, we may be able to see a change within individuals and in their actions. Furthermore, mindfulness also helps us realize our symbiotic relationship with the world, enabling us to appreciate our interconnectedness and interdependence with nature. This, in turn, helps us recognize that the mind, body, and world are one system and that we, as human beings, are not disconnected from the world. By reducing the sharp division between subject and object, we become aware of our unity with nature and minimize our tendency to control and exploit it. This is because we realize that we are not dissociated but an essential part of the larger whole.

This work addresses a significant issue in modern education and suggests a solution. This issue arises out of an incomplete conception of learners and learning, where learners are often viewed as disengaged minds that simply record and compute information. However, I argued that learners are more than this; they are fundamentally embodied beings who are embedded within their surroundings and learn in conjunction with the world, rather than simply from it. Additionally, I also argued that instructional methods for subject-specific knowledge must be grounded in ways in which learners already perceive, interact with, and imagine to construct meaning with their embodied minds.

It is evident that an embodied approach to education helps to realize the vision presented by prominent thinkers, specifically the three whose ideas serve as the foundation for this work. Jiddu Krishnamurti was more concerned about problems arising due to societal conditioning, and he wanted education to help individuals to become free from this conditioning. We have seen how the inner curriculum directly helps us to overcome our habitual ways of looking at the world. According to Krishnamurti, education should be a process of self-discovery, where students learn to observe themselves and the world around them without preconceived notions. The inner embodied curriculum facilitates this process by encouraging students to explore their experiences and sensations, which can help them become more aware of their thoughts and emotions. This, in turn, can free them from conditioning and make them more open in their relationship with the world. As a result, the rift between the learner and their environment gets reduced. Owing to this, learning becomes a continuous event, as knowledge is no longer seen as a separate object in the world, making learning an active process that happens at each moment. In this regard, when knowledge is no longer primarily seen as a separate entity to be accumulated, there is no real difference between the knower and the known. This amounts to what Krishnamurti calls "freedom from the known." Thus, the difference between the observer and the observed, as well as the division between humans and the world, can be significantly reduced with the help of inner embodied education.

When learning becomes a continuous process, it gives rise to the collaborative learning environment envisaged by Paulo Freire. Freire believed that education should be a democratic process that promotes participation and collaboration. In this collaborative learning environment, there is an obvious reduction in vertical hierarchy and promotion of dialogue between various stakeholders such as teachers and students. In this way, education becomes a liberating experience that empowers individuals to critically analyse the world around them and take action to change it. Embodied education can facilitate this process by providing opportunities for students to engage in experiential learning through the process of praxis and dialogue grounded in real-world experiences. This can help students connect their learning to the real world and develop a sense of agency and purpose instead of being mere passive recipients of knowledge. Thus, an embodied approach to education can provide opportunities for students to engage in a democratic learning environment, which may help in realizing the vision of John Dewey.

Dewey believed that learning should be an active process that engages the learner in exploring their environment and making meaning from their experiences. Embodied education can facilitate this process by providing opportunities for students to engage in hands-on activities, explore their environment, and make connections between their physical experiences and their academic learning. This, in turn, can help us build more democratic educational institutions where students are encouraged to ask questions, explore multiple perspectives, and seek out answers. In addition to this, a collaborative learning environment built upon an inner embodied curriculum fosters interconnection among people and the world at large, which in turn strengthens democratic values in society.

The present work primarily aims to make a case for restructuring educational practices by examining our fundamental assumptions about human beings in light of empirical studies in cognitive science. Consequently, the focus has been mainly on studies that explore aspects of human understanding and relationships with others and the world from a scientific perspective. However, this approach has led to the overlooking of several other aspects that contribute to the problems in education. While psychological and neurological factors are often cited as explanations for the roots of our divisive outlook, there are other dimensions that can also contribute to the problem. Although the socio-political moorings of our divisive outlook have been briefly touched upon, these areas require further exploration. Sociological aspects such as gender issues, inequality, the post-colonial world order, colonial legacies, and the relationship between power and knowledge in the new world order are some areas that need separate examination but are beyond the scope of this work.

I view this work as an intermediary between theoretical and empirical research, in which I have attempted to translate empirical findings from diverse domains into the educational discourse. However, there are many domains that have been overlooked in this process. For instance, I have presented examples from two subjects, language, and mathematics, to demonstrate the embodied nature of learning. But there is already a substantial amount of evidence emerging from other disciplines that convincingly demonstrates the benefits of an embodied approach to learning. Additionally, the implementation of such pedagogies requires specialized infrastructure, resources, and teacher training, which have not been thoroughly discussed in this work, and therefore invite further study. Although emerging technologies, particularly immersive learning technologies, offer potential, their proper utilization in the regular school curriculum needs to be explored.

Last but not least, I have presented mindfulness practice as a way to break free from the vicious cycle of underlying dualistic assumptions about ourselves. However, the incorporation of these practices into the regular curriculum and their appropriateness for different age groups have not been discussed. There is a need to explore the appropriate design of meditative practices based on the mental level and age of the students. In addition to meditative practices, other methods can also help instil self-awareness and enable individuals to realize their embodied nature, such as journaling or simple observation in natural environments.

While some "alternative schools" use meditative practices to help children become more aware of their physical and mental states, we need to conduct more research, particularly ethnographic studies, to understand how these practices are integrated into their regular curriculum. As researchers, our goal should be to incrementally advance the discussion and open up new avenues for further work in the future. With this intention, I hope to explore these limitations in future works and contribute, even in a small way, to the transformation and improvement of humans, education, and society.

References

Albahari, M. (2006). *Analytical Buddhism: The two-tiered illusion of self.* Palgrave Macmillan.

Alibali, M., & Nathan, M. J. (2007). Teachers' gestures as a means of scaffolding students' understanding: Evidence from an early algebra lesson. In R. Goldman, R. Pea, B. Barron, & S. J. Derry (Eds.), *Video research in the learning sciences.* Routledge.

Alibali, M. W., Nathan, M. J., Wolfgram, M. S., Church, R. B., Jacobs, S. A., Johnson Martinez, C., & Knuth, E. J. (2014). How teachers link ideas in mathematics instruction using speech and gesture: A corpus analysis. *Cognition and Instruction, 32*(1), 65–100. https://doi.org/10.1080/07370008.2013.858161

Ambrose, S. A., Bridges, M. W., DiPietro, M., Lovett, M. C., & Norman, M. K. (2010). *How learning works: Seven research-based principles for smart teaching.* John Wiley & Sons.

Andre, S. (2022). Descartes' baby and natural dualism. *Open Journal of Philosophy, 12*(2), Article 2. https://doi.org/10.4236/ojpp.2022.122014

Andres, M., Seron, X., & Olivier, E. (2007). Contribution of hand motor circuits to counting. *Journal of Cognitive Neuroscience, 19*(4), 563–576. https://doi.org/10.1162/jocn.2007.19.4.563

Aristizabal, M. J., Anreiter, I., Halldorsdottir, T., Odgers, C. L., McDade, T. W., Goldenberg, A., Mostafavi, S., Kobor, M. S., Binder, E. B., & Sokolowski, M. B. (2020). Biological embedding of experience: A primer on epigenetics. *Proceedings of the National Academy of Sciences, 117*(38), 23261–23269

Austin, J. H. (2009). *Selfless insight: Zen and the meditative transformations of consciousness.* MIT Press.

Bada, S. O. (2015). Constructivism learning theory: A paradigm for teaching and learning. *Journal of Research & Method in Education, 5*(6), 66–70.

Baijal, S., Jha, A. P., Kiyonaga, A., Singh, R., & Srinivasan, N. (2011). The influence of concentrative meditation training on the development of attention networks during early adolescence. *Frontiers in Psychology, 2*, 153. https://doi.org/10.3389/fpsyg.2011.00153

Bandura, A., & Walters, R. H. (1977). *Social learning theory* (Vol. 1). Englewood cliffs.

Barbezat, D. P., & Bush, M. (2014). *Contemplative practices in higher education: Powerful methods to transform teaching and learning* (pp. XXIII, 231). Jossey-Bass.

Barsalou, L. W. (1999). Perceptual symbol systems. *Behavioral and Brain Sciences, 22*(4), 577–660.

Barsalou, L. W. (2008). Grounded cognition. *Annual Review of Psychology, 59*(1), 617–645. https://doi.org/10.1146/annurev.psych.59.103006.093639

Barsalou, L. W., Solomon, K. O., & Wu, L.-L. (1999). Perceptual simulation in conceptual tasks. *Amsterdam Studies in the Theory and History of Linguistic Science, Series 4,* 209–228.

Beaumont, J. G. (2008). *Introduction to neuropsychology.* Guilford Press.

Beck, F. A. (1964). *Greek education, 450–350 BC.* Methuen.

Beer, R. D. (2000). Dynamical approaches to cognitive science. *Trends in Cognitive Sciences, 4*(3), 91–99.

Beer, R. D. (2003). The dynamics of active categorical perception in an evolved model agent. *Adaptive Behavior, 11*(4), 209–243.

Bergen, B. K. (2012). *Louder than words: The new science of how the mind makes meaning.* Basic Books.

Berry, D. R., Cairo, A. H., Goodman, R. J., Quaglia, J. T., Green, J. D., & Brown, K. W. (2018). Mindfulness increases prosocial responses toward ostracized strangers through empathic concern. *Journal of Experimental Psychology General, 147*(1), 93–112. https://doi.org/10.1037/xge0000392

Berteletti, I., & Booth, J. R. (2015). Perceiving fingers in single-digit arithmetic problems. *Frontiers in Psychology, 6.* https://www.frontiersin.org/articles/10.3389/fpsyg.2015.00226

Bishop, S. R., Lau, M., Shapiro, S., Carlson, L., Anderson, N. D., Carmody, J., Segal, Z. V., Abbey, S., Speca, M., Velting, D., & Devins, G. (2004). Mindfulness: A proposed operational definition. *Clinical Psychology: Science and Practice, 11*(3), 230–241. https://doi.org/10.1093/clipsy.bph077

Bloom, P. (2004). *Descartes' baby: How the science of child development explains what makes us human.* Arrow Books.

Boyer, P. (2001). *Religion explained: The evolutionary foundations of religious belief.* Basic Books.

Boyette, A. H., & Hewlett, B. S. (2018). Teaching in hunter-gatherers. *Review of Philosophy and Psychology, 9,* 771–797.

Brady, R. (2007). Learning to stop, stopping to learn: discovering the contemplative dimension in education. *Journal of Transformative Education, 5*(4), 372–394. https://doi.org/10.1177/1541344607313250

Bransford, J. D., Brown, A. L., & Cocking, R. R. (2000). *How people learn* (Vol. 11). National academy press.

Brown, K. W., & Ryan, R. M. (2003). The benefits of being present: Mindfulness and its role in psychological well-being. *Journal of Personality and Social Psychology, 84*(4), 822.

Burkhart, B. Y. (2004). What Coyote and Thales can teach us: An outline of American Indian epistemology. *American Indian Thought: Philosophical Essays,* 15–26.

Campbell, J. (1995). *Understanding John Dewey: Nature and cooperative intelligence.* Open Court Publishing.

Campbell, J. I. D. (1994). Architectures for numerical cognition. *Cognition, 53*(1), 1–44. https://doi.org/10.1016/0010-0277(94)90075-2

Campbell, J. I. D., & Fugelsang, J. (2001). Strategy choice for arithmetic verification: Effects of numerical surface form. *Cognition, 80*(3), B21–B30. https://doi.org/10.1016/S0010-0277(01)00115-9

Campos, A. I., Mitchell, B. L., & Rentería, M. E. (2019). Twins can help us understand how genes and the environment shape us. *Frontiers for Young Minds.* https://kids.frontiersin.org/articles/10.3389/frym.2019.00059

Carlson, N. R., Buskist, W., Enzle, M. E., & Heth, C. D. (2005). *Psychology: The science of behaviour.* Pearson Allyn & Bacon.

Carlson, R. A., Avraamides, M. N., Cary, M., & Strasberg, S. (2007). What do the hands externalize in simple arithmetic? *Journal of Experimental Psychology: Learning, Memory, and Cognition, 33*, 747–756. https://doi.org/10.1037/0278-7393.33.4.747

Carney, D. R., Cuddy, A. J., & Yap, A. J. (2010). Power posing: Brief nonverbal displays affect neuroendocrine levels and risk tolerance. *Psychological Science, 21*(10), 1363–1368.

Carruthers, P. (2020). How mindreading might mislead cognitive science. *Journal of Consciousness Studies, 27*(7–8), 195–219.

Chemero, A. (2001). Dynamical explanation and mental representations. *Trends in Cognitive Sciences, 5*(4), 141–142.

Chiesa, A., & Serretti, A. (2009). Mindfulness-based stress reduction for stress management in healthy people: A review and meta-analysis. *The Journal of Alternative and Complementary Medicine, 15*(5), 593–600. https://doi.org/10.1089/acm.2008.0495

Churchland, P. M. (1999). *Matter and consciousness.* MIT press.

Cisek, P., & Pastor-Bernier, A. (2014). On the challenges and mechanisms of embodied decisions. *Philosophical Transactions of the Royal Society B: Biological Sciences, 369*(1655), 20130479.

Clark, A. (1998). *Being there: Putting brain, body, and world together again.* MIT press.

Clark, A., & Chalmers, D. (1998). The extended mind. *Analysis, 58*(1), 7–19.

Cohen, E., Burdett, E., Knight, N., & Barrett, J. (2011). Cross-cultural similarities and differences in person-body reasoning: Experimental evidence from the United Kingdom and Brazilian Amazon. *Cognitive Science, 35*(7), 1282–1304.

Coleman, W., & Coleman, W. R. (1977). *Biology in the nineteenth century: Problems of form, function and transformation* (Vol. 1). Cambridge University Press.

Combs, A. W. (Ed.). (1962). *Perceiving, behaving, becoming: A new focus for education* (pp. VIII, 256). National Education Association. https://doi.org/10.1037/14325-000

Cook, S. W., & Goldin-Meadow, S. (2006). The role of gesture in learning: Do children use their hands to change their minds? *Journal of Cognition and Development, 7*(2), 211–232. https://doi.org/10.1207/s15327647jcd0702_4

Cook, S. W., Mitchell, Z., & Goldin-Meadow, S. (2008). Gesturing makes learning last. *Cognition, 106*(2), 1047–1058.

Cook, S. W., Yip, T. K., & Goldin-Meadow, S. (2010). Gesturing makes memories that last. *Journal of Memory and Language, 63*(4), 465–475. https://doi.org/10.1016/j.jml.2010.07.002

Corballis, M. C. (2014). Left brain, right brain: Facts and fantasies. *PLoS Biology, 12*(1), e1001767. https://doi.org/10.1371/journal.pbio.1001767

Cowart, M. (n.d.). Embodied cognition. In *Internet Encyclopedia of Philosophy*. Retrieved 5 August 2022, from https://iep.utm.edu/embodied-cognition/

Crollen, V., & Noël, M.-P. (2015). The role of fingers in the development of counting and arithmetic skills. *Acta Psychologica, 156*, 37–44. https://doi.org/10.1016/j.actpsy.2015.01.007

Dale, J., & Hyslop-Margison, E. J. (2010). *Paulo Freire: Teaching for freedom and transformation: The philosophical influences on the work of Paulo Freire* (Vol. 12). Springer Science & Business Media.

Damasio, A. (1994). Descartes' error: Emotion, rationality and the human brain. *New York: Putnam, 352.*

Damasio, A. (2010). *Self comes to mind: Constructing the conscious brain.* Pantheon Books.

Darwin, C. (1909). *The origin of species.* Fingerprint Publishing.

Darwin, C. (2004). *The descent of man.* Penguin Classics.

Dasgupta, S. (1922). *A history of Indian philosophy* (Vol. 1). Cambridge.

Davidson, R. J., Kabat-Zinn, J., Schumacher, J., Rosenkranz, M., Muller, D., Santorelli, S. F., Urbanowski, F., Harrington, A., Bonus, K., & Sheridan, J. F. (2003). Alterations in brain and immune function produced by mindfulness meditation. *Psychosomatic Medicine, 65*(4), 564–570. https://doi.org/10.1097/01.PSY.0000077505.67574.E3

Dawkins, R. (1976). *The selfish gene.* Oxford University Press.

Descartes, R. (2006). *A discourse on the method.* Oxford University Press.

Dewey, J. (1910). *How we think* (pp. VI, 228). D C Heath. https://doi.org/10.1037/10903-000

Dewey, J. (1916). *Democracy and education: An introduction to the philosophy of education.* Aakar Books Classics.

Dewey, J. (1929). *Experience and nature.* George Allen & Unwin.

Dewey, J. (1980). *Art as experience.* Minton, Balch and Co.

Dewey, J. (2021). Does human nature change? In E. T. Weber (Ed.), *America's public philosopher: Essays on social justice, economics, education, and the future of democracy* (pp. 185–192). Columbia University Press.

Downey, G. (1957). Ancient education. *The Classical Journal, 52*(8), 337–345.

Dreyfus, G., & Thompson, E. (2007). Asian perspectives: Indian theories of mind. In P. D. Zelazo, M. Moscovitch, & E. Thompson (Eds.), *The Cambridge handbook of consciousness* (pp. 89–114).

Dreyfus, H., Dreyfus, S. E., & Athanasiou, T. (2000). *Mind over machine*. Simon and Schuster.

Duignan, B. (2016). Human nature. *Encyclopaedia Britannica*. https://www.britannica.com/topic/human-nature

Edmiston, P., & Lupyan, G. (2017). Visual interference disrupts visual knowledge. *Journal of Memory and Language, 92*, 281–292.

Ekman, P., & Friesen, W. V. (1969). The repertoire of nonverbal behavior: Categories, origins, usage, and coding. *Semiotica, 1*(1), 49–98. https://doi.org/10.1515/semi.1969.1.1.49

Ergas, O. (2017). *Reconstructing 'education' through mindful attention: Positioning the mind at the center of curriculum and pedagogy*. Palgrave Macmillan.

Etherington, V., & Costello, S. (2019). Comparing universal and targeted delivery of a mindfulness-based program for anxiety in children. *Journal of Psychologists and Counsellors in Schools, 29*(1), 22–38. https://doi.org/10.1017/jgc.2018.22

Farina, M. (2021). Embodied cognition: Dimensions, domains and applications. *Adaptive Behavior, 29*(1), 73–88.

Flook, L., Goldberg, S. B., Pinger, L., Bonus, K., & Davidson, R. J. (2013). Mindfulness for teachers: A pilot study to assess effects on stress, burnout and teaching efficacy. *Mind, Brain and Education : The Official Journal of the International Mind, Brain, and Education Society, 7*(3), 10.1111/mbe.12026. https://doi.org/10.1111/mbe.12026

Fodor, J. A. (1975). *The language of thought* (Vol. 5). Harvard university press.

Forstmann, M., & Burgmer, P. (2015). Adults are intuitive mind-body dualists. *Journal of Experimental Psychology: General, 144*(1), 222–235. https://doi.org/10.1037/xge0000045

Fox, K. C. R., Nijeboer, S., Dixon, M. L., Floman, J. L., Ellamil, M., Rumak, S. P., Sedlmeier, P., & Christoff, K. (2014). Is meditation associated with altered brain structure? A systematic review and meta-analysis of morphometric neuroimaging in meditation practitioners. *Neuroscience & Biobehavioral Reviews, 43*, 48–73. https://doi.org/10.1016/j.neubiorev.2014.03.016

Franklin, S. (1995). *Artificial minds* (1st ed.). MIT Press.

Freire, P. (1970a). *Cultural action for freedom*. Penguin Education.

Freire, P. (1970b). *Pedagogy of the oppressed*. Penguin Random House.

Freire, P. (2015). *Pedagogy of indignation*. Routledge.

Gallagher, S. (2000). Philosophical conceptions of the self: Implications for cognitive science. *Trends in Cognitive Sciences, 4*(1), 14–21. https://doi.org/10.1016/S1364-6613(99)01417-5

Gallagher, S. (2005). *How the body shapes the mind*. Clarendon Press.

Gallivan, J. P., Chapman, C. S., Wolpert, D. M., & Flanagan, J. R. (2018). Decision-making in sensorimotor control. *Nature Reviews Neuroscience, 19*(9), 519–534.

Garbarini, F., & Adenzato, M. (2004). At the root of embodied cognition: Cognitive science meets neurophysiology. *Brain and Cognition, 56*(1), 100–106.

Gärdenfors, P. (2017). Demonstration and pantomime in the evolution of teaching. *Frontiers in Psychology, 8.* https://www.frontiersin.org/articles/10.3389/fpsyg.2017.00415

Gaukroger, S. (2006). *The emergence of a scientific culture: Science and the shaping of modernity 1210–1685.* Clarendon Press.

Gibson, J. J. (1966). *The senses considered as perceptual systems* (Vol. 2). Houghton Mifflin Boston.

Gibson, J. J. (1979). The theory of affordances. The ecological approach to visual perception. In *The People, Place and, Space Reader* (pp. 56–60). *Routledge.*

Gilson, E. (1950). *The unity of philosophical experience.* Charles Scribner's Sons.

Glenberg, A. M. (2008). Embodiment for education. In P. Calvo & A. Gomila (Eds.), *Handbook of cognitive science* (pp. 355–372). Elsevier. https://doi.org/10.1016/B978-0-08-046616-3.00018-9

Glenberg, A. M., & Robertson, D. A. (1999). Indexical understanding of instructions. *Discourse Processes, 28*(1), 1–26. https://doi.org/10.1080/01638539909545067

Goffman, E. (1956). *The presentation of self in everyday life.* University of Edinburgh.

Goldin-Meadow, S., & Beilock, S. L. (2010). Action's influence on thought: The case of gesture. *Perspectives on Psychological Science, 5*(6), 664–674. https://doi.org/10.1177/1745691610388764

Goldin-Meadow, S., Cook, S. W., & Mitchell, Z. A. (2009). Gesturing gives children new ideas about math. *Psychological Science, 20*(3), 267–272. https://doi.org/10.1111/j.1467-9280.2009.02297.x

Goldin-Meadow, S., Nusbaum, H., Kelly, S. D., & Wagner, S. (2001). Explaining math: Gesturing lightens the load. *Psychological Science, 12*(6), 516–522. https://doi.org/10.1111/1467-9280.00395

Goldin-Meadow, S., & Sandhofer, C. M. (1999). Gestures convey substantive information about a child's thoughts to ordinary listeners. *Developmental Science, 2*(1), 67–74.

Goldin-Meadow, S., & Singer, M. A. (2003). From children's hands to adults' ears: Gesture's role in the learning process. *Developmental Psychology, 39*(3), 509–520. https://doi.org/10.1037/0012-1649.39.3.509

Goldin-Meadow, S., & Wagner, S. M. (2005). How our hands help us learn. *Trends in Cognitive Sciences, 9*(5), 234–241. https://doi.org/10.1016/j.tics.2005.03.006

Goldstone, R. L., Landy, D., & Son, J. Y. (2008). A well grounded education: The role of perception in science and mathematics. *Symbols, Embodiment, and Meaning,* 327–355.

Gómez, L. E., & Glenberg, A. M. (2022). Embodied classroom activities for vocabulary acquisition. In S. L. Macrine & J. M. B. Fugate (Eds.), *Movement matters: How embodied cognition informs teaching and learning* (pp. 77–90). MIT Press.

González, J., Barros-Loscertales, A., Pulvermüller, F., Meseguer, V., Sanjuán, A., Belloch, V., & Ávila, C. (2006). Reading cinnamon activates olfactory brain regions. *NeuroImage, 32*(2), 906–912. https://doi.org/10.1016/j.neuroimage.2006.03.037

Graham, B. M., Denson, T. F., Barnett, J., Calderwood, C., & Grisham, J. R. (2018). Sex hormones are associated with rumination and interact with emotion regulation strategy choice to predict negative affect in women following a sad mood induction. *Frontiers in Psychology, 9*. https://www.frontiersin.org/articles/10.3389/fpsyg.2018.00937

Gray Carlson, D. (2007). *A commentary to Hegel's science of logic*. Palgrave Macmillan.

Harari, Y. N. (2014). *Sapiens: A brief history of humankind*. Penguin Random House.

Harris, F. (2011). A source for Freire's philosophy of human nature and its educational implications. *Encounters in Theory and History of Education, 12*, 19–36. https://doi.org/10.24908/eoe-ese-rse.v12i0.2364

Hasenkamp, W., & Barsalou, L. (2012). Effects of meditation Experience on functional connectivity of distributed brain networks. *Frontiers in Human Neuroscience, 6*. https://www.frontiersin.org/articles/10.3389/fnhum.2012.00038

Hauk, O., Johnsrude, I., & Pulvermüller, F. (2004). Somatotopic representation of action words in human motor and premotor cortex. *Neuron, 41*(2), 301–307.

Havas, D. A., Glenberg, A. M., & Rinck, M. (2007). Emotion simulation during language comprehension. *Psychonomic Bulletin & Review, 14*(3), 436–441. https://doi.org/10.3758/BF03194085

Hayes, S. C., Strosahl, K. D., & Wilson, K. G. (1999). *Acceptance and commitment therapy*. Guilford press.

Henriques, G. (2011). *A new unified theory of psychology*. Springer.

Hildebrand, D. (2021, Winter). John Dewey. In E. N. Zalta (Ed.), *The Stanford Encyclopedia of philosophy*. https://plato.stanford.edu/archives/win2021/entries/dewey/

Hobbes, T. (1651). Chapter XIII, Section 9. In *Hobbes's leviathan*.

Horgan, T., & Tienson, J. (1989). Representations without rules. *Philosophical Topics, 17*(1), 147–174.

Horton, M., & Freire, P. (1990). *We make the road by walking: Conversations on education and social change*. Temple University Press.

Hostetter, A. B. (2011). When do gestures communicate? A meta-analysis. *Psychological Bulletin, 137*(2), 297–315. https://doi.org/10.1037/a0022128

Hurley, S. (2001). Perception and action: Alternative views. *Synthese, 129*(1), 3–40.

Hutto, D. D., & Myin, E. (2012). *Radicalizing enactivism: Basic minds without content*. MIT press.

Iverson, J. M., & Goldin-Meadow, S. (1998). Why people gesture when they speak. *Nature, 396*(6708), 228–228.

James, K. H. (2010). Sensori-motor experience leads to changes in visual processing in the developing brain. *Developmental Science, 13*(2), 279–288.

James, K. H. (2022). The embodiment of letter perception: The importance of hand-writing in early childhood. In S. L. Macrine & J. M. B. Fugate (Eds.), *Movement matters: How embodied cognition informs teaching and learning* (pp. 55–76). MIT Press.

James, K. H., & Engelhardt, L. (2012). The effects of handwriting experience on functional brain development in pre-literate children. *Trends in Neuroscience and Education, 1*(1), 32–42.

James, K. H., & Gauthier, I. (2006). Letter processing automatically recruits a sensory–motor brain network. *Neuropsychologia, 44*(14), 2937–2949. https://doi.org/10.1016/j.neuropsychologia.2006.06.026

Jansz, J. (2000). Masculine identity and restrictive emotionality. *Gender and Emotion: Social Psychological Perspectives*, 166–186.

Jennings, P. A., Doyle, S., Oh, Y., Rasheed, D., Frank, J. L., & Brown, J. L. (2019). Long-term impacts of the CARE program on teachers' self-reported social and emotional competence and well-being. *Journal of School Psychology, 76*, 186–202. https://doi.org/10.1016/j.jsp.2019.07.009

Kabat-Zinn, J. (2009). *Wherever you go, there you are: Mindfulness meditation in everyday life*. Hachette.

Kana, R. K., Blum, E. R., Ladden, S. L., & Ver Hoef, L. W. (2012). "How to do things with Words": Role of motor cortex in semantic representation of action words. *Neuropsychologia, 50*(14), 3403–3409.

Kang, S., Hallman, G. L., Son, L. K., & Black, J. B. (2013). The different benefits from different gestures in understanding a concept. *Journal of Science Education and Technology, 22*(6), 825–837. https://doi.org/10.1007/s10956-012-9433-5

Kang, S., & Tversky, B. (2016). From hands to minds: Gestures promote understanding. *Cognitive Research: Principles and Implications, 1*(1), 4. https://doi.org/10.1186/s41235-016-0004-9

Kaptelinin, V. (2014). *Affordances and design*. The Interaction Design Foundation. https://www.interaction-design.org/literature/book/the-encyclopedia-of-human-computer-interaction-2nd-ed/affordances

Keenan, J. P., McCutcheon, B., Freund, S., Gallup, G. G., Sanders, G., & Pascual-Leone, A. (1999). Left hand advantage in a self-face recognition task. *Neuropsychologia, 37*(12), 1421–1425. https://doi.org/10.1016/S0028-3932(99)00025-1

Kelly, G. P., & Altbach, P. G. (1984). Introduction: The four faces of colonialism. *Education and the Colonial Experience*, 1–5.

Kelly, S. D., Özyürek, A., & Maris, E. (2010). Two sides of the same coin: Speech and gesture mutually interact to enhance comprehension. *Psychological Science, 21*(2), 260–267. https://doi.org/10.1177/0956797609357327

Keng, S.-L., Smoski, M. J., & Robins, C. J. (2011). Effects of mindfulness on psychological health: A review of empirical studies. *Clinical Psychology Review, 31*(6), 1041–1056. https://doi.org/10.1016/j.cpr.2011.04.006

Kessell, A. M., & Tversky, B. (2005). Gestures for thinking and explaining. *Proceedings of the Annual Meeting of the Cognitive Science Society, 27.*

Khan, M. S. L., & Réhman, S. ur. (2015). Embodied head gesture and distance education. *Procedia Manufacturing, 3,* 2034–2041. https://doi.org/10.1016/j.promfg.2015.07.251

Killingsworth, M. A., & Gilbert, D. T. (2010). A wandering mind is an unhappy mind. *Science, 330*(6006), 932–932. https://doi.org/10.1126/science.1192439

Kirsh, D., & Maglio, P. (1994). On distinguishing epistemic from pragmatic action. *Cognitive Science, 18*(4), 513–549.

Kleinberger, R. (Rébecca H. M. F.). (2014). *Singing about singing: Using the voice as a tool for self-reflection* [Thesis, Massachusetts Institute of Technology]. https://dspace.mit.edu/handle/1721.1/95607

Kohler, E., Keysers, C., Umilta, M. A., Fogassi, L., Gallese, V., & Rizzolatti, G. (2002). Hearing sounds, understanding actions: Action representation in mirror neurons. *Science, 297*(5582), 846–848.

Kosslyn, S. M. (1980). *Image and mind.* Harvard University Press.

Kring, A. M., & Gordon, A. H. (1998). Sex differences in emotion: Expression, experience, and physiology. *Journal of Personality and Social Psychology, 74,* 686–703. https://doi.org/10.1037/0022-3514.74.3.686

Krishnamurti, J. (1953). *Education and the significance of life.* Harper San Francisco.

Krishnamurti, J. (1954). *The first and last freedom.* Random House.

Krishnamurti, J. (1963). *Life ahead: On learning and the search for meaning.* New World Library.

Krishnamurti, J. (1969). *Freedom from the Known.* Random House.

Krishnamurti, J. (1970). *Think on these things* (D. Rajagopal, Ed.). Harper & Row.

Krishnamurti, J. (1973). *The awakening of intelligence.* Penguin Random House.

Krishnamurti, J. (1985). *The way of intelligence.*

Krüger, M., & Hermsdörfer, J. (2019). Target uncertainty during motor decision-making: The time course of movement variability reveals the effect of different sources of uncertainty on the control of reaching movements. *Frontiers in Psychology, 10,* 41.

Kumar, A. (2013). *Curriculum as meditative inquiry.* Palgrave Macmillan US.

Kurt, S. (2021, Fall). *Descartes' theory of ideas* (E. N. Zalta, Ed.). https://plato.stanford.edu/archives/fall2021/entries/descartes-ideas/

Lakoff, G., & Johnson, M. (1980). *Metaphors we live by.* University of Chicago press.

Lakoff, G., & Johnson, M. (1999). *Philosophy in the flesh: The embodied mind and its challenge to Western thought.* Basic Books.

Lakoff, G., & Núñez, R. E. (2000). *Where mathematics comes from: How the embodied mind brings mathematics into being.* Basic Books.

Lamont, C. (1961). New light on Dewey's common faith. *Journal of Philosophy, 58*(1), 21–28. https://doi.org/10.2307/2023566

Laurillard, D. (1993). *Rethinking university teaching: A conversational framework for the effective use of learning technologies*. Routledge.

Leitan, N. D., & Chaffey, L. (2014). Embodied cognition and its applications: A brief review. *Sensoria: A Journal of Mind, Brain & Culture, 10*(1), 3–10.

Lenski, R. E. (2000). Evolution: Fact and theory. *ActionBioScience*. https://ncse.ngo/evolution-fact-and-theory

Li, J. X., & James, K. H. (2016). Handwriting generates variable visual output to facilitate symbol learning. *Journal of Experimental Psychology: General, 145*(3), 298.

Longcamp, M., Anton, J.-L., Roth, M., & Velay, J.-L. (2003). Visual presentation of single letters activates a premotor area involved in writing. *NeuroImage, 19*(4), 1492–1500. https://doi.org/10.1016/S1053-8119(03)00088-0

Luberto, C. M., Shinday, N., Song, R., Philpotts, L. L., Park, E. R., Fricchione, G. L., & Yeh, G. Y. (2018). A systematic review and meta-analysis of the effects of meditation on empathy, compassion, and prosocial behaviors. *Mindfulness, 9*(3), 708–724. https://doi.org/10.1007/s12671-017-0841-8

Luders, E., Phillips, O. R., Clark, K., Kurth, F., Toga, A. W., & Narr, K. L. (2012). Bridging the hemispheres in meditation: Thicker callosal regions and enhanced fractional anisotropy (FA) in long-term practitioners. *NeuroImage, 61*(1), 181–187. https://doi.org/10.1016/j.neuroimage.2012.02.026

Lueke, A., & Gibson, B. (2015). Mindfulness meditation reduces implicit age and race bias: The role of reduced automaticity of responding. *Social Psychological and Personality Science, 6*(3), 284–291. https://doi.org/10.1177/1948550614559651

Lutz, A., Slagter, H. A., Dunne, J. D., & Davidson, R. J. (2008). Attention regulation and monitoring in meditation. *Trends in Cognitive Sciences, 12*(4), 163–169. https://doi.org/10.1016/j.tics.2008.01.005

Lux, V., Non, A. L., Pexman, P. M., Stadler, W., Weber, L. A., & Krüger, M. (2021). A developmental framework for embodiment research: The next step toward integrating concepts and methods. *Frontiers in Systems Neuroscience, 70.*

Macedonia, M. (2019). Embodied learning: Why at school the mind needs the body. *Frontiers in Psychology, 2098.*

Macedonia, M., & Knösche, T. R. (2011). Body in mind: How gestures empower foreign language learning. *Mind, Brain, and Education, 5*(4), 196–211. https://doi.org/10.1111/j.1751-228X.2011.01129.x

Macrine, S. L., & Fugate, J. M. B. (2021). Translating embodied cognition for embodied learning in the classroom. *Frontiers in Education, 6.* https://www.frontiersin.org/articles/10.3389/feduc.2021.712626

Macrine, S. L., & Fugate, J. M. B. (2022). *Movement matters: How embodied cognition informs teaching and learning.* MIT Press.

Magalhães, S., Nunes, T., Soeiro, I., Rodrigues, R., Coelho, A., Pinheiro, M., Castro, S. L., Leal, T., & Limpo, T. (2022). A pilot study testing the effectiveness of a mindfulness-based program for Portuguese school children. *Mindfulness*, *13*(11), 2751–2764. https://doi.org/10.1007/s12671-022-01991-8

Markie, P., & Folescu, M. (2021, Winter). *Rationalism vs. Empiricism* (E. N. Zalta & U. Nodelman, Eds.). https://plato.stanford.edu/archives/spr2023/entries/rationalism-empiricism/

Martin, T., & Schwartz, D. L. (2005). Physically distributed learning: Adapting and reinterpreting physical environments in the development of fraction concepts. *Cognitive Science*, *29*(4), 587–625.

McCafferty, S. G., & Rosborough, A. (2014). Gesture as a private form of communication during lessons in an esl-designated elementary classroom: A sociocultural perspective. *TESOL Journal*, *5*(2), 225–246. https://doi.org/10.1002/tesj.104

McClelland, J., Dahlberg, K., & Plihal, J. (2002). Learning in the Ivory tower: Students' embodied experience. *College Teaching*, *50*(1), 4–8. https://doi.org/10.1080/87567550209595863

McGilchrist, I. (2009). *The master and his emissary: The divided brain and the making of the Western world* (2nd ed.). Yale University Press.

Mcleod, S. (2024, July 16). Nature vs. Nurture in psychology. *Simply Psychology*. https://www.simplypsychology.org/naturevsnurture.html

McNeill, D. (2005). *Gesture and thought*. University of Chicago press.

Mendelson, T., Greenberg, M. T., Dariotis, J. K., Gould, L. F., Rhoades, B. L., & Leaf, P. J. (2010). Feasibility and preliminary outcomes of a school-based mindfulness intervention for urban youth. *Journal of Abnormal Child Psychology*, *38*(7), 985–994. https://doi.org/10.1007/s10802-010-9418-x

Merleau-Ponty, M. (1962). *Phenomenology of Perception* (2nd ed.). Routledge.

Merriam, S. B., & Bierema, L. L. (2014). *Adult learning: Linking theory and practice*. Jossey-Bass.

Merriam, S. B., Caffarella, R. S., & Baumgartner, L. M. (2007). *Learning in adulthood: A comprehensive guide* (3rd ed.). John Wiley & Sons.

Merriam, S. B., & Kim, Y. S. (2008). Non-Western perspectives on learning and knowing. *New Directions for Adult and Continuing Education*, *2008*(119), 71–81. https://doi.org/10.1002/ace.307

Metz, S. M., Frank, J. L., Reibel, D., Cantrell, T., Sanders, R., & Broderick, P. C. (2013). The effectiveness of the Learning to BREATHE program on adolescent emotion regulation. *Research in Human Development*, *10*, 252–272. https://doi.org/10.1080/15427609.2013.818488

Naka, A., Lauwerys, J. A., Nakosteen, M. K., Marrou, H.-I., Anweiler, O., Bowen, J., Browning, R., Chambliss, J. J., Meyer, A. E., & Gelpi, E. (2022, August 23). Education. *Encyclopedia Britannica*. https://www.britannica.com/topic/education

Nakamura, H., Ito, Y., Honma, Y., Mori, T., & Kawaguchi, J. (2014). Cold-hearted or cool-headed: Physical coldness promotes utilitarian moral judgment. *Frontiers in Psychology*, *5*, 1086.

Napoli, M., Krech, P. R., & Holley, L. C. (2005). Mindfulness training for elementary school students: The attention academy. *Journal of Applied School Psychology*, *21*, 99–125. https://doi.org/10.1300/J370v21n01_05

Nathan, M. J. (2008). An embodied cognition perspective on symbols, gesture, and grounding instruction. *Symbols and Embodiment: Debates on Meaning and Cognition*, *18*, 375–396.

Nathan, M. J. (2022). *Foundations of embodied learning: A paradigm for education.* Routledge.

Nguyen, D. J., & Larson, J. B. (2015). Don't forget about the body: Exploring the curricular possibilities of embodied pedagogy. *Innovative Higher Education*, *40*(4), 331–344. https://doi.org/10.1007/s10755-015-9319-6

Nicholson, T., Williams, D., Carpenter, K., & Kallitsounaki, A. (2019). Interoception is impaired in children, but not adults, with autism spectrum disorder. *Journal of Autism and Developmental Disorders*, *49*(9), 3625–3637.

Noë, A., & Thompson, E. (2004). Are there neural correlates of consciousness? *Journal of Consciousness Studies*, *11*(1), 3–28.

Novack, M. A., Congdon, E. L., Hemani-Lopez, N., & Goldin-Meadow, S. (2014). From action to abstraction: Using the hands to learn math. *Psychological Science*, *25*(4), 903–910. https://doi.org/10.1177/0956797613518351

O'regan, J. K., & Noë, A. (2001). A sensorimotor account of vision and visual consciousness. *Behavioral and Brain Sciences*, *24*(5), 939–973.

Pagis, M. (2009). Embodied self-reflexivity. *Social Psychology Quarterly*, *72*(3), 265–283. https://doi.org/10.1177/019027250907200308

Prinz, J. J. (2014). *Beyond humann Nature: How culture and experience shape the human mind.* ww Norton & Company.

Proctor, C. P., Silverman, R. D., Harring, J. R., & Montecillo, C. (2012). The role of vocabulary depth in predicting reading comprehension among English monolingual and Spanish–English bilingual children in elementary school. *Reading and Writing*, *25*(7), 1635–1664. https://doi.org/10.1007/s11145-011-9336-5

Provençal, N., Arloth, J., Cattaneo, A., Anacker, C., Cattane, N., Wiechmann, T., Röh, S., Ködel, M., Klengel, T., & Czamara, D. (2020). Glucocorticoid exposure during hippocampal neurogenesis primes future stress response by inducing changes in DNA methylation. *Proceedings of the National Academy of Sciences*, *117*(38), 23280–23285.

Pulvermüller, F. (2005). Brain mechanisms linking language and action. *Nature Reviews Neuroscience*, *6*(7), 576–582.

Raes, F., Griffith, J. W., Van der Gucht, K., & Williams, J. M. G. (2014). School-based prevention and reduction of depression in adolescents: A cluster-randomized controlled trial of a mindfulness group program. *Mindfulness*, *5*, 477–486. https://doi.org/10.1007/s12671-013-0202-1

Ramsey, G. (2023). *Human nature*. Cambridge: Cambridge University Press.

Rao, M. P. (2014). Concept and meaning of education. In A. K. Srivastava (Ed.), *Basics in education*. National Council of Educational Research and Training.

Reiss, J., & Sprenger, J. (Winter, 2020). Scientific objectivity. In E. N. Zalta (Ed.), *The Stanford Encyclopedia of philosophy*. Metaphysics Research Lab, Stanford University. https://plato.stanford.edu/archives/win2020/entries/scientific-objectivity/

Richard, E., Tijou, A., Richard, P., & Ferrier, J.-L. (2006). Multi-modal virtual environments for education with haptic and olfactory feedback. *Virtual Reality*, *10*(3), 207–225. https://doi.org/10.1007/s10055-006-0040-8

Richerson, P. J., & Boyd, R. (2008). *Not by genes alone: How culture transformed human evolution*. University of Chicago press.

Ridley, M. (2003). *Nature via nurture: Genes, experience, and what makes us human* (Vol. 19). HarperCollins.

Risko, E. F., & Gilbert, S. J. (2016). Cognitive offloading. *Trends in Cognitive Sciences*, *20*(9), 676–688. https://doi.org/10.1016/j.tics.2016.07.002

Roazzi, M., Nyhof, M., & Johnson, C. (2013). Mind, soul and spirit: Conceptions of immaterial identity in different cultures. *International Journal for the Psychology of Religion*, *23*(1), 75–86.

Robinson, H. (2020, Fall). Dualism. In E. N. Zalta (Ed.), *The Stanford Encyclopedia of philosophy*. Metaphysics Research Lab, Stanford University. https://plato.stanford.edu/archives/fall2020/entries/dualism/

Roeser, R. W., Schonert-Reichl, K. A., Jha, A., Cullen, M., Wallace, L., Wilensky, R., Oberle, E., Thomson, K., Taylor, C., & Harrison, J. (2013). Mindfulness training and reductions in teacher stress and burnout: Results from two randomized, waitlist-control field trials. *Journal of Educational Psychology*, *105*, 787–804. https://doi.org/10.1037/a0032093

Rosenberg, E. L., Zanesco, A. P., King, B. G., Aichele, S. R., Jacobs, T. L., Bridwell, D. A., MacLean, K. A., Shaver, P. R., Ferrer, E., Sahdra, B. K., Lavy, S., Wallace, B. A., & Saron, C. D. (2015). Intensive meditation training influences emotional responses to suffering. *Emotion (Washington, D.C.)*, *15*(6), 775–790. https://doi.org/10.1037/emo0000080

Roth, W.-M. (2001). Gestures: Their role in teaching and learning. *Review of Educational Research*, *71*(3), 365–392. https://doi.org/10.3102/00346543071003365

Rueschemeyer, S.-A., Glenberg, A., Kaschak, M., Mueller, K., & Friederici, A. (2010). Top-down and bottom-up contributions to understanding sentences describing objects in motion. *Frontiers in Psychology, 1*. https://www.frontiersin.org/articles/10.3389/fpsyg.2010.00183

Sah, P., Fanselow, M., Quirk, G. J., Hattie, J., Mattingley, J., & Tokuhama-Espinosa, T. (2018). The nature and nurture of education. *Npj Science of Learning, 3*(1), Article 1. https://doi.org/10.1038/s41539-018-0023-z

Sanger, K. L., & Dorjee, D. (2016). Mindfulness training with adolescents enhances metacognition and the inhibition of irrelevant stimuli: Evidence from event-related brain potentials. *Trends in Neuroscience and Education, 5*(1), 1–11. https://doi.org/10.1016/j.tine.2016.01.001

Sato, M., Cattaneo, L., Rizzolatti, G., & Gallese, V. (2007). Numbers within our hands: Modulation of corticospinal excitability of hand muscles during numerical judgment. *Journal of Cognitive Neuroscience, 19*(4), 684–693. https://doi.org/10.1162/jocn.2007.19.4.684

Schnall, S., Haidt, J., Clore, G. L., & Jordan, A. H. (2008). Disgust as embodied moral judgment. *Personality and Social Psychology Bulletin, 34*(8), 1096–1109.

Schonert-Reichl, K. A., Oberle, E., Lawlor, M. S., Abbott, D., Thomson, K., Oberlander, T. F., & Diamond, A. (2015). Enhancing cognitive and social–emotional development through a simple-to-administer mindfulness-based school program for elementary school children: A randomized controlled trial. *Developmental Psychology, 51*(1), 52–66. https://doi.org/10.1037/a0038454

Schugurensky, D. (2011). *Paulo Freire* (Vol. 16). Bloomsbury Publishing.

Searle, J. R. (1980). Minds, brains, and programs. *Behavioral and Brain Sciences, 3*(3), 417–424.

Semple, R. J., Lee, J., Rosa, D., & Miller, L. F. (2010). A randomized trial of mindfulness-based cognitive therapy for children: Promoting mindful attention to enhance social-emotional resiliency in children. *Journal of Child and Family Studies, 19*, 218–229. https://doi.org/10.1007/s10826-009-9301-y

Shapiro, L. (2007). The embodied cognition research programme. *Philosophy Compass, 2*(2), 338–346.

Shapiro, L. (2011). *Embodied cognition: New problems of philosophy* (1st ed.). Routledge.

Shapiro, L. (2019). *Embodied cognition: New problems of philosophy* (2nd ed.). Routledge.

Shapiro, L., & Spaulding, S. (2021, Winter). Embodied cognition. In E. N. Zalta (ed.), *The Stanford Encyclopedia of philosophy*. https://plato.stanford.edu/archives/win2021/entries/embodied-cognition/

Shapiro, L., & Stolz, S. A. (2019). Embodied cognition and its significance for education. *Theory and Research in Education, 17*(1), 19–39. https://doi.org/10.1177/1477878518822149

Sharma, C. (2000). *A critical survey of Indian philosophy*. Motilal Banarsidass.

Shipp, A. J., & Aeon, B. (2019). Temporal focus: Thinking about the past, present, and future. *Current Opinion in Psychology, 26*, 37–43.

Sibinga, E. M. S., Webb, L., Ghazarian, S. R., & Ellen, J. M. (2016). School-based mindfulness instruction: An RCT. *Pediatrics, 137*(1). https://doi.org/10.1542/peds.2015-2532

Singer, M. A., & Goldin-Meadow, S. (2005). Children learn when their teacher's gestures and speech differ. *Psychological Science, 16*(2), 85–89. https://doi.org/10.1111/j.0956-7976.2005.00786.x

Smith, D. W. (2018, Summer). Phenomenology. In *The Stanford Encyclopedia of philosophy.* https://plato.stanford.edu/cgi-bin/encyclopedia/archinfo.cgi?entry=phenomenology

Smith, L. B. (2006). Movement matters: The contributions of Esther Thelen. *Biological Theory, 1*(1), 87–89.

Soylu, F., Lester, Jr., F. K., & Newman, S. D. (2018). You can count on your fingers: The role of fingers in early mathematical development. *Journal of Numerical Cognition, 4*(1), 107–135. https://doi.org/10.5964/jnc.v4i1.85

Spivey, M. (2008). *The continuity of mind.* Oxford University Press.

Sterelny, K. (2010). Minds: Extended or scaffolded? *Phenomenology and the Cognitive Sciences, 9*(4), 465–481.

Stevenson, L., Haberman, D. L., Wright, P. M., & Witt, C. (2018). *Thirteen theories of human nature* (7th ed.). Oxford University Press.

Stewart, K. L., Ahrens, A. H., & Gunthert, K. C. (2018). Relating to self and other: Mindfulness predicts compassionate and self-image relationship goals. *Mindfulness, 9*(1), 176–186. https://doi.org/10.1007/s12671-017-0760-8

Stoljar, D. (2023, Summer). Physicalism. In E. N. Zalta & U. Nodelman (Eds.), *The Stanford Encyclopedia of philosophy.* https://plato.stanford.edu/archives/sum2023/entries/physicalism/

Stolz, S. A. (2015). Embodied learning. *Educational Philosophy and Theory, 47*(5), 474–487. https://doi.org/10.1080/00131857.2013.879694

Sugiura, M., Kawashima, R., Nakamura, K., Okada, K., Kato, §, Takashi, Nakamura, §, Akinori, Hatano, §, Kentaro, Itoh, §, Kengo, Kojima, S., & Fukuda, H. (2000). Passive and active recognition of one's own face. *NeuroImage, 11*(1), 36–48. https://doi.org/10.1006/nimg.1999.0519

Tang, Y.-Y., Lu, Q., Geng, X., Stein, E., Yang, Y., & Posner, M. (2010). Short-term meditation induces white matter changes in the anterior cingulate. *Proceedings of the National Academy of Sciences of the United States of America, 107*(35). https://doi.org/10.1073/pnas.1011043107

Thagard, P. (2023, Spring). Cognitive science. In E. N. Zalta & U. Nodelman (Eds.), *The Stanford Encyclopedia of philosophy.* Metaphysics Research Lab, Stanford University. https://plato.stanford.edu/archives/spr2023/entries/cognitive-science/

Thapan, M. (2014). *Ethnographies of schooling in contemporary India.* SAGE Publications.

Thelen, E. (1995). Time-scale dynamics and the development of an embodied cognition. *Mind as motion: Explorations in the dynamics of cognition,* 69–100.

Thelen, E., Corbetta, D., Kamm, K., Spencer, J. P., Schneider, K., & Zernicke, R. F. (1993). The transition to reaching: Mapping intention and intrinsic dynamics. *Child Development, 64*(4), 1058–1098.

Thelen, E., & Smith, L. B. (1996). *A dynamic systems approach to the development of cognition and action.* MIT press.

Toadvine, T. (2019, Spring). Maurice Merleau-Ponty. In *The Stanford Encyclopedia of philosophy.* https://plato.stanford.edu/cgi-bin/encyclopedia/archinfo.cgi?entry=merleau-ponty

Towner, W. S. (2005). Clones of God: Genesis 1:26–28 and the image of God in the Hebrew Bible. *Interpretation: A Journal of Bible and Theology, 59*(4), 341–356. https://doi.org/10.1177/002096430505900402

Tran, C., Smith, B., & Buschkuehl, M. (2017). Support of mathematical thinking through embodied cognition: Nondigital and digital approaches. *Cognitive Research: Principles and Implications, 2*(1), 16. https://doi.org/10.1186/s41235-017-0053-8

Uzgalis, W. (2022, Fall). *John Locke* (E. N. Zalta & U. Nodelman, Eds.). https://plato.stanford.edu/archives/fall2022/entries/locke/

Van Gelder, T. (1995). What might cognition be, if not computation? *The Journal of Philosophy, 92*(7), 345–381.

Van Gordon, W., Shonin, E., & Richardson, M. (2018). Mindfulness and nature. *Mindfulness, 9*(5), 1655–1658. https://doi.org/10.1007/s12671-018-0883-6

Varela, F. J., Rosch, E., & Thompson, E. (1991). *The embodied mind.* MIT Press.

Vega, M., Glenberg, A., & Graesser, A. (2008). An embodied cognition perspective on symbols, gesture, and grounding instruction. In *Symbols and EmbodimentDebates on meaning and cognition.* Oxford University Press. https://doi.org/10.1093/acprof:oso/9780199217274.001.0001

Vinci-Booher, S. A., & James, K. H. (2016). Neural substrates of sensorimotor processes: Letter writing and letter perception. *Journal of Neurophysiology, 115*(1), 1–4.

Viswanathan, G. (1988). Currying favor: The politics of British educational and cultural policy in India, 1813-1854. *Social Text, 19/20*, 85–104. https://doi.org/10.2307/466180

Walsh, R. (1999). *Essential spirituality: The 7 central practices to awaken heart and mind.* Wiley.

Watson, B. (2007). *The analects of Confucius.* Columbia University Press.

Watson, J. D., & Crick, F. H. (1953). Molecular structure of nucleic acids: A structure for deoxyribose nucleic acid. *Nature, 171*(4356), 737–738.

Watts, R. (2009). Education, empire and social change in nineteenth century England. *Paedagogica Historica, 45*(6), 773–786. https://doi.org/10.1080/00309230903407519

Whitehurst, G. J., & Lonigan, C. J. (1998). Child development and emergent literacy. *Child Development, 69*(3), 848–872. https://doi.org/10.1111/j.1467-8624.1998.tb06247.x

Wilson, A., & Golonka, S. (2013). Embodied cognition is not what you think it is. *Frontiers in Psychology, 4.* https://www.frontiersin.org/articles/10.3389/fpsyg.2013.00058

Wilson, E. O. (2004). *On human nature: With a new preface*. Harvard University Press.

Wilson, E. O. (2013). On human nature. In S. M. Downes & E. Machery (Eds.), *Arguing about human nature: Contemporary debates* (pp. 7–23). Routledge.

Wilson, M. (2002). Six views of embodied cognition. *Psychonomic Bulletin & Review, 9*(4), 625–636.

Wilson, M. (2008). How did we get from there to here? An evolutionary perspective on embodied cognition. In *Handbook of Cognitive Science* (pp. 373–393). Elsevier.

Wilson, R. A., & Foglia, L. (2011, Fall). Embodied cognition. In *The Stanford Encyclopedia of Philosophy*. https://plato.stanford.edu/archives/fall2011/entries/embodied-cognition/

Wilson, R., & Foglia, L. (2017). Embodied cognition. *Stanford Encyclopedia of philosophy*.

Xu, M., Purdon, C., Seli, P., & Smilek, D. (2017). Mindfulness and mind wandering: The protective effects of brief meditation in anxious individuals. *Consciousness and Cognition, 51*, 157–165. https://doi.org/10.1016/j.concog.2017.03.009

Young, S. (2016). What is mindfulness? A contemplative perspective. In K. A. Schonert-Reichl & R. W. Roeser (Eds.), *Handbook of mindfulness in education: Integrating theory and research into practice* (pp. 29–45). Springer. https://doi.org/10.1007/978-1-4939-3506-2_3

Zarate, K., Maggin, D. M., & Passmore, A. (2019). Meta-analysis of mindfulness training on teacher well-being. *Psychology in the Schools, 56*(10), 1700–1715. https://doi.org/10.1002/pits.22308

Zosh, J. N., Hopkins, E. J., Jensen, H., Liu, C., Neale, D., Hirsh-Pasek, K., Solis, S. L., & Whitebread, D. (2017). *Learning through play: A review of the evidence*. LEGO Fonden Billund.

Index

Printed in the United States
by Baker & Taylor Publisher Services